Geek Chic: Smart Women in Popular Culture

edited by
Sherrie A. Inness

palgrave
macmillan

GEEK CHIC

First published in 2007 by
PALGRAVE MACMILLAN™
175 Fifth Avenue, New York, N.Y. 10010 and
Houndmills, Basingstoke, Hampshire, England RG21 6XS
Companies and representatives throughout the world.

PALGRAVE MACMILLAN is the global academic imprint of the Palgrave Macmillan division of St. Martin's Press, LLC and of Palgrave Macmillan Ltd. Macmillan® is a registered trademark in the United States, United Kingdom and other countries. Palgrave is a registered trademark in the European Union and other countries.

ISBN-13: 978–1–4039–7902–5 hardcover
ISBN-10: 1–4039–7902–2 hardcover
ISBN-13: 978–1–4039–7903–2 paperback
ISBN-10: 1–4039–7903–0 paperback

Library of Congress Cataloging-in-Publication Data

Geek chic : smart women in popular culture / edited by Sherrie A. Inness
    p. cm.
  Includes bibliographical references and index.
  Contents: Who remembers Sabrina? Intelligence, gender, and the media—Beauty and the geek: changing gender stereotypes on . . . —Lab coats and lipstick: smart women reshape science—"You can see things that other people can't"—"Pretty smart": subversive intelligence . . . —Super slacker girls—Back to the future—Dangerous minds—Raising the bar—Savvy women, boy's school politics, and the west wing—Heckling Hillary.
    ISBN 1–4039–7902–2 (alk. paper)
    ISBN 1–4039–7903–0 (pbk. : alk. paper)
     1. Women in popular culture—United States. 2. Gifted women.
  3. Women in mass media. 4. Mass media—United States. 5. Intellect—Social aspects—United States. I. Inness, Sherrie A.

HQ1421.G43 2007
302.23082'0973   2006051029

A catalogue record for this book is available from the British Library.

Design by Newgen Imaging Systems (P) Ltd., Chennai, India.

First edition: May 2007

10 9 8 7 6 5 4 3 2 1

Printed in the United States of America.

Geek Chic: Smart Women in Popular Culture

Southampton
SOLENT
University

MOUNTBATTEN LIBRARY
Tel: 023 8031 9249

Please return this book no later than the date stamped.
Loans may usually be renewed - in person, by phone,
or via the web OPAC. Failure to renew or return on time
may result in an accumulation of penalty points.

For Alycia Moulton

Contents

List of Figures

Acknowledgments

This anthology has benefited from the input of friends and colleagues. I would like to thank the people who have read drafts of the entire book or chapters before its completion, including Kristin J. O'Hara and Whitney Womack. I wish to thank everyone at the press who helped make this book possible, including Amanda Johnson Moon, Rick Delaney, and Erica Warren.

I also appreciate my friends' support. Irene Gammel, Di Maddison, Janice Molloy, Gillian O'Driscoll, and Wendy Partridge deserve my gratitude. My Miami University colleagues, including Mark Christian, Elizabeth Claussen, Norma Evans, Kelli Johnson, John Krafft, Diana Royer, Carol Shulman, Connie Webb, and Whitney Womack provided invaluable support and encouragement during the process of writing this book. Finally, I wish to thank Alycia Moulton, whose kindness and compassion continue to inspire.

INTRODUCTION

Who Remembers Sabrina? Intelligence, Gender, and the Media

Sherrie A. Inness

Flashing her million-watt smile and tossing her famous blonde mane, Jill Munroe (Farrah Fawcett) chased down villains each week on the 1970s television show *Charlie's Angels*. Blonde and beautiful, Jill epitomized what was considered appealing in a woman. Her poster was plastered in millions of prepubescent boys' bedrooms or lockers, and millions of girls and women wanted to look exactly like her, mimicking her hair and clothing. But the other Angels never achieved the same stature as sex symbols. The most brilliant Angel was Sabrina Duncan (Kate Jackson), who was attractive and well dressed but lacked Jill's stunning California beach-girl looks. Sabrina wore practical pantsuits, while Jill wore barely there dresses or bikinis. Whom did women want to resemble? Jill. She was depicted as sexier than her more sensible friends, and countless women tried to emulate her. Who cared if she lacked Sabrina's brilliance?

In the original *Scooby-Doo, Where Are You!* (1969–1976), a gang of teenagers solved comic mysteries. The team included two females, Daphne Blake and Velma, and two males, Shaggy and Freddy. Daphne was tall, blonde-haired, and attractive; Velma was short, dark-haired, and plain. Somehow, even though clearly Daphne's intellectual superior, Velma always seemed to be fumbling around for her lost glasses. She was not the one to emulate, and the cartoon implied that any woman or girl would wish to be Daphne, who went off finding adventures with the handsome Freddy, while Velma was stuck with Shaggy and Scooby-Doo, whose comedy overshadowed Velma's talents. Whether portraying Jill and Sabrina or Daphne and Velma, the television programs made it clear who was sexually appealing. What female viewer wanted to be a brainiac like Sabrina or Velma? No one. Jill and Daphne had countless companions, too. American popular culture cannot seem to get enough of stereotypical "dumb blondes," and, for generations, the mass media have featured scores. "Dumb" women were typically blonde, but sometimes they were ditzy brunettes or redheads. What most defined these women was that they were beautiful and "dumb." No matter how brilliant Sabrina, Velma, or their sisters were, they were shown as lacking the sexual allure of their "airhead" female cohorts.

Whether in the media or real life, why are "brainy" women frequently depicted negatively compared with less intelligent ones? One reason is that mainstream American society has a deeply rooted fear of brilliant women. According to the common cultural stereotype, women are not supposed to be too smart and, in particular, are not supposed to be as intelligent as their husbands or boyfriends. To attract a mate, a smart woman is expected to appear less intelligent than she really is. Why do brilliant women make U.S. society ill at ease? We do not share the same fear about highly intelligent men. Especially since the computer revolution, men are supposed to be smart, and it makes them more alluring, not less. Our society does not have the same expectation that a man should worry that he might appear smarter than his date, so he should act like a dumb blonde.

In recent decades, a greater number of brilliant women than in earlier years have appeared in U.S. popular culture. In cartoons, Daria, Lisa Simpson, the Powerpuff Girls, and other stars have shown that it is "cool" to be brilliant. Similarly, in prime-time dramas, a number of shows feature brilliant women characters, including Ainsley Hayes on *The West Wing* and the scientist Fred on *Angel*, who is more intelligent than anyone else, including the men. As more brilliant women appear, it is no longer assumed that the most intelligent person on a television show or film is "naturally" male. What cultural events have influenced this shift? How do brilliant women challenge and change gender stereotypes, while also, sometimes simultaneously, reaffirming and per-petuating them? *Geek Chic: Smart Women in Popular Culture* explores these questions. As we shall find, popular media provide a fertile environment for challenging the stereotype that the most intelligent people are men. At the same time, however, the media also affirm that a brilliant woman should be slender and beautiful, showing that women can break some gender stereotypes, but not all.

"Not the brightest pixels in the plasma TV": Dumb Blondes

Before turning to brilliant women, it is helpful to discuss dumb blondes. They have a long history of starring in the popular media, including television shows and films. The early stars included Jean Harlow, Marilyn Monroe, and Carol Channing, the last of whom remarked in 1955, "I didn't have to be bright. . . . All I had to do was be blonde."[1] These women and others were depicted as sex symbols, not rocket scientists. Who cared how low your IQ was if you looked like Marilyn? She downplayed her intelligence because U.S. society in the 1950s had an insatiable desire for dumb blondes. The media sent a clear message to women that it was more important to be beautiful and blonde than brainy.

Even today in the new millennium after second-wave feminism, dumb blondes remain popular. Journalist Alec Foege writes in "The Return of the Dumb Blonde" (2004): "Pop culture seems to be dominated by blonde young women whose concerns, at least onscreen, are amazingly shallow. . . . In an age of international terrorist threats and global warming, the giggly 'dumb blonde' stereotype is the cultural equivalent of comfort food, a frothy, empty-calorie pleasure that harks back to an earlier, less intimidating era."[2] Dumb blondes, however, play a more complex role than being merely "comfort food." Although it is increasingly less acceptable to depict African Americans or other ethnic and racial groups as less intelligent than whites, it is still acceptable to depict blondes as dumb. Writing for the *Village Voice* in 2005, Michael Musto describes one reason that they continue to be popular: "With the communications explosion bringing savvy to every household, you can't necessarily feel smarter than the person next to you, but you can enjoy intellectual superiority to a bevy of [blonde] bimbos."[3] Even Daphne could have figured out that the vast majority of dumb blondes in the popular media are female, helping to perpetuate the stereotype that blondes are less intelligent than brunettes or redheads, a myth that refuses to die. In *Vanity Fair* in 2004, Martha Barnette writes, "The 'dumb blonde' stereotype is still as stubborn as a red-wine stain on a white silk jacket."[4] She mentions one study undertaken by Dr. Druann Heckert, an assistant professor of sociology researching stereotypes of women. She discovered that a common stereotype of blondes is that "they're not the brightest pixels in the plasma TV."[5] Heckert found that this stereotype remains potent, and women with long blonde hair are especially stereotyped as dumb.

It is not only blondes who are ridiculed; *all* women wrestle with the stereotype that women are less intelligent than men. This cultural stereotype goes back to the founding of the United States (and much earlier), when women were not given the right to vote because they were assumed to lack the intelligence of men, a stereotype pervaded every level of society. When men pursued higher education, women were restricted because it was assumed that they lacked the intellectual ability. It was such a ubiquitous assumption that scientists in the nineteenth century studied the reasons for the gap. Victorian scientists "argued that women's brains were too small to be fully human. On the intelligence scale, researchers recommended classifying human females with apes."[6]

The stereotype that women are not the intellectual equals of men lingers. One of the most notorious examples of this stereotype occurred in 2005 when the president of Harvard University, Lawrence H. Summers, spoke at the NBER Conference on Diversifying the Science and Engineering Workforce. He mentioned that women were rarely found in engineering jobs, suggesting that boys and girls have "taste differences." He gave an example from his own life: "My experience with my two-and-a-half-year-old twin daughters who were not given dolls and who were given trucks, and found themselves saying to each other, 'Look, daddy truck is carrying the baby truck,' tells me something."[7] Socialization and discrimination, according to Summers, are relatively small factors in the reasons that women do not hold more high-powered jobs in academic science or math.[8] Little seems to have changed since Victorian times. The president's speech set off an uproar as female scientists, including ones at Harvard, refuted his claims that they lacked the intelligence to succeed in science and engineering.[9] The furor resulted in his resignation in 2006. Perhaps that does demonstrate a change from the Victorian period, when his words would not have been questioned. But his speech shows that the stereotype that women are less intelligent than men continues to thrive at all levels of society.

Summers overlooked the social forces that shape women. Girls learn early that society holds negative attitudes toward smart girls and judges them more harshly than smart boys. In 1992, the Miami University educational psychologist Richard Luftig observed, "Gifted girls are seen as relatively humorless, very competitive, not cooperative. . . . Because girls tend to take things . . . seriously, [this] alienates them from peers."[10] The negative social reaction to brilliant girls teaches them that it is not acceptable to be intelligent, and they should hide their academic ability in search of social success.

It is not only brilliant girls who are stigmatized but boys as well, especially "nerds," the ones at the bottom of the social hierarchy in most U.S. schools. In a study of school social groups in public middle schools, researcher John H. Bishop described the bottom as composed of "freaks, Goths, losers, druggies, and nerds. . . . Being a nerd is like having a communicable disease."[11] Gradually, the stereotype of the nerd or geek is changing, especially since "nerd" now is equated with a pathway to economic fame and fortune, such as that followed by Bill Gates, Steve Jobs, and other geeks.[12] No matter how much the status of the nerd has changed in recent decades, being a nerd is a social identity that shuts out many girls. As the social critic Ron Eglash observes, "Female exclusion from the male domain of technology is mediated by the opposition between nerd sexual formations . . . and female youth gender formations, which emphasize strong sociality."[13] He continues, the word "nerd" and "its routes to science and technology access are still guarded by the unmarked signifiers of whiteness and male gender."[14] At an early age, girls and young women are taught that they cannot be real "nerds." Although many females rebel against this sexist stereotype, they must struggle against a culture that doubts their intellectual acumen.

Beyond Baywatch: *Smart Women in the Popular Media*

In a mass culture that remains ambivalent about women's intelligence, the manner in which women are portrayed in popular culture influences and shapes how society views intelligence. The media are only one force that shapes these ideas, but they are tremendously powerful, especially in shaping gender norms. For example, Pamela Anderson on the old television show *Baywatch* was depicted as a curvaceous "babe," with limited intelligence, not a molecular biologist with a PhD from Stanford University. It is so incongruous to think about her as a research scientist who just sidelines as a lifeguard when not working at her UCLA laboratory that our reaction is to laugh. Why do we find it impossible to imagine her as a scientist? The prime reason is that she is depicted as a sexy, dumb "babe" who cares more about improving her tan than earning a Nobel Prize. Most media consumers are cagey enough to recognize that her world is make-believe; however, she helps to support the stereotype that women are stupid, a myth that continues to linger in our cultural subconscious.

In a similar fashion, brilliant female characters also help shape viewers' ideas about intelligence. For example, Lisa Simpson of *The Simpsons* is one of the most influential smart female characters on television, but she is not depicted entirely positively, being too studious and serious when compared with her brother Bart. Another animated character, Daria, starred on a five-season MTV series (1997–2002). Always clad in the same "green blazer, short skirt, boots, and oversize eyeglasses," she was the "voice of the intelligent, the sane, the unpopular."[15] But she struggled to cope with parents, school, and her younger sister, Quinn, who never had a problem finding a new boyfriend. Like Lisa and Daria, Willow Rosenberg on *Buffy the Vampire Slayer* (1997–2003) was studious and intelligent, but she was not depicted as positively as Buffy, the show's beautiful lead. In all these shows, the most intelligent characters are depicted as outsiders.

In the popular media, smart women are often shown as aberrations. For example, in her examination of the female graduate student in the television shows *Party of Five*, *E.R.*, and *Beverly Hills, 90210*, cultural critic Michele Byers argues that the female graduate student is "an outsider looking in" to a community to which she can never fully belong.[16] Her outsider status is reinforced because she is often eventually forced out of the show. Byers writes, "The female academic remains . . . grotesque/ negatively constructed/abnormal for her ability to penetrate male academic space."[17] The female graduate student is an oddity in the world of television.

If brilliant women are not portrayed as outsiders, they vanish entirely from other popular media texts or are depicted less commonly than their male counterparts. For example, Candace White and Katherine N. Kinnick studied the depiction of women who use computers in television commercials.[18] Focusing on 351 commercials that aired in 1998, White and Kinnick found that female computer users were more likely to be depicted as clerical workers and not as skilled computer professionals. White and Kinnick wrote, "Women are significantly more likely than men to be shown in non-professional occupations, particularly that of secretary or telemarketer. Even though these women may be shown as quite proficient, there is a tremendous difference between being proficient in entering data on a keyboard and in being proficient in the advanced applications of a computer programmer or consultant."[19] Such images pervade commercials, television shows, and myriad other media texts, conveying the message that women are less intellectually capable of handling science, math, and computer science.

Such cultural stereotypes continue to resonate in U.S. society, so it is crucial to explore how intelligent women are depicted in the mass media. The first two chapters focus on the worlds of computer science and applied science, arenas where women have been stereotyped as lacking men's intelligence. In the popular media, computer scientists and scientists are commonly men, although this stereotype is gradually changing. In chapter 1, Karin E. Westman writes about how American society has long equated "geek" with males and masculinity, while "beauty" has been equated with females and femininity. This division has shaped U.S. culture and molded the technological revolution in ways that offer power and influence to men, but not to women. Westman suggests that the assumption that women, including beautiful ones, cannot be as brilliant geeks as men is being challenged. Studying real life, the Internet, and the popular television show *Gilmore Girls*, she demonstrates that "geek" is no longer exclusively male. Brilliant female geeks who run their own computer companies or are computer scientists show that women are geeks, too. In addition, *Gilmore Girls* creates a world where female geeks thrive. Both virtual worlds like Girl Geeks and television shows like *Gilmore Girls* suggest that attractive women can be geeks, fighting the stereotype that all beautiful women are dumb.

Whereas Westman focuses on computer science, Lorna Jowett turns to science. Both in real life and in the media, scientists have been predominantly men, perpetuating a myth that women are not capable of rigorous scientific thought. This ideology, Jowett suggests, has shaped science education and vocation in the United States and created a realm where males still hold more positions than women. It is important to include women scientists in media texts so that society recognizes that women are scientists, too. After examining women scientists in science fiction, Jowett focuses on a television show, *Angel* (1999–2004), that challenges the notion that only men can be scientists. The show features Fred, a scientist and "nerd." She is the most brilliant person on the show and was a physics graduate student before she was transported through a portal into an alternate world. She makes even her former graduate school professors uneasy because of her brilliance, which they cannot match, and plays a revolutionary role, since her appearance throws into question the cultural stereotype that women cannot be top scientists. Jowett, however, suggests that the program "tones down" Fred's revolutionary character by depicting her romantic trials and tribulations and showing her playing a caretaking role to others. Both tactics are used to emphasize that she, or any other woman, must not stray too far from traditional feminine roles based on romance and nurturance.

The next three chapters move from the world of science to girls' popular culture. To understand the lessons about intelligence that the media convey, one must study the vast universe of works that are targeted at preteen and teenage girls. This media exposure is especially important because it forms some of the earliest socializing lessons that girls receive about how to "be" a girl, including powerfully gender- stereotyped lessons about intelligence. Remember the infamous talking Barbie in the 1990s that said, "Math is hard?" Although being intelligent is sometimes secondary to getting a "hot" date for the prom in the world of girls' popular culture, some important characters challenge this assumption. Among the most influential was Daria, the bespectacled animated character who was the star of her own series. Cindy Conaway suggests that Daria was especially important because she wore glasses, which few girls in the popular media ever did before. Conaway explores the history of glasses-wearing and women and shows that the stereotype that a woman wearing glasses is unattractive and needs to "be made over" has existed for generations, but also that it has changed. In *Gidget* and *The Brady Bunch*, the intelligent girl abandoned her glasses; in *Daria*, the title character keeps her glasses.

Like Conaway, Rebecca C. Hains focuses on television programs that challenge stereotypes about brilliance being undesirable for girls. Writing about *The Powerpuff Girls*, *Totally Spies*, and Disney's *Kim Possible*, Hains explores the reasons that the first show was popular when it first came out and argues that to understand its success, one has to turn to the early 1990s, when many writers and commentators began to focus on teen girls and why they were not achieving their true potential. How were girls to be saved? The girl power movement was one answer, since it offered girls the empowering message that they mattered. The other two shows followed in the footsteps of *The Powerpuff Girls*. The three programs offer unusual heroes who are always depicted as more brilliant than anyone else, including boys and men. The girls use what Hains refers to as "subversive niceness" to make their intelligence less threatening to societal norms. By being kind and nice to others—enemies and authority figures alike—the heroes have a chance to use their brilliance and shape society for the better.

The next chapter also focuses on girls' culture and how it molds gender roles. Michele Paule analyzes super slacker girls, who, despite their intellectual potential, drop out of society, whether that means not attending college or pursuing jobs that do not reflect the young women's true ability. She suggests that the popularity of such characters results from a world where opportunities for success are increasingly not as available to young women as they were to their mothers and fathers. Paule analyzes three television shows: *Dead Like Me*, *Wonderfalls*, and *Joan of Arcadia*. Each of these features a brilliant woman—Georgia, Jaye, and Joan—who drops out of society. Georgia (George) drops out of college, and when talking to a temporary agency to find a job, she is randomly struck dead by a space station's toilet-seat hurtling from orbit. The show tracks her life after death. Jaye graduates from college but then drops off the traditional career path, finding a job at a gift store in Niagara Falls. Joan Girardi is in high school, and her life changes dramatically when her family moves to a new town. She is forced to rethink what it means to be successful, especially when God begins to speak to her. Paule argues that dropping out offers power to the women so they may maintain their individuality, creativity, and quirky brilliance. She questions, however, how successful dropping out is for any super slacker girl, whether in popular culture or in real life.

But what happens when brilliant girls mature and become adults? The following chapters explore three possible paths, focusing on witches, professors, and lawyers. Linda Baughman, Allison Burr-Miller, and Linda Manning analyze the television show *Bewitched*, which, they suggest, still haunts modern popular culture. The image of the brilliant witch, often more brilliant than mere mortals, reoccurs in U.S. society because she offers women a way to rebel against society's gender limitations. Baughman, Burr-Miller, and Manning argue that the *Bewitched* series, even today, reveals a great deal about the mainstream fascination with brilliant women, including witches.

Leigh H. Edwards moves from witches to professors. In two shows, *Jack and Bobby* (2004) and *The Education of Max Bickford* (2001–2002), she examines female brilliance. Although both focus on women academic stars, the programs do not depict them in a completely positive fashion. They succeed brilliantly at school, but they do not succeed at home. Grace McCallister is a successful, gifted professor at Plains State University, but she is often shown as a controlling mother when it comes to raising her teenage boys. Although she is revealed to be the mother of the future president, Grace is shown to be too intellectual to be a mother. A similar woman, Andrea Haskell, appears in *The Education of Max Bickford*. A gifted American Studies professor who holds a distinguished endowed chair, she confronts problems and setbacks in her personal life. For Grace and Andrea, success in academe does not transmit to success at home. Edwards suggests that both television shows reflect a society that is still unsure whether women can truly have it all, both at home and at the workplace.

Moving from academics to law, Sharon Sutherland and Sarah Swan explore the changing depiction of women lawyers on television dramas, including *L.A. Law*, *Ally McBeal*, *Sex and the City*, and *Judging Amy*. Since the legal profession has been male-dominated for centuries, it has long resisted female lawyers. However, starting in the 1970s and up to the present, a greater number of women have become lawyers. This reality is reflected on television, where a plethora of shows feature brilliant women lawyers. Sutherland and Swan argue that the programs serve a positive function by showing that women can be as brilliant legal minds as men, but limits exist.

For example, most television women lawyers are beautiful, slender, and white, suggesting that while women can be brilliant, they still need to adhere to traditional stereotypes of female beauty.

The last two chapters focus on politics, another venue, like law, where women challenge the gender status quo. Beth Berila writes about the sexism and racism that brilliant women face in the political world, especially when they move into positions of power. She discusses *The West Wing*, an award-winning show that draws millions of viewers and, potentially, can change or influence how people view real politics, including the women in it. Thus, Berila argues, knowing how brilliant women are depicted on the show is crucial to understanding how real women negotiate power and authority in politics and suffer persecution when they challenge the established male-centered social order. In the final chapter, Jeannie Banks Thomas also examines women in politics, social focusing on how Hillary Clinton is depicted in jokes, on both late-night television programs and the Internet. Although she is a brilliant politician, a very different image of her emerges in jokes that ridicule her intelligence and disparage her feminism. The jokes focus on her as a dumb blonde, a witch, and a child hater, a portrayal that is dramatically at odds with her real life. Thomas argues that jokes reveal that our culture remains uneasy about having a brilliant woman in a position of tremendous power, so she is attacked through jokes that focus on her gender.

Because media images are closely related to social reality, the authors in *Geek Chic* do more than focus on the media as isolated from reality. Instead, each writer explores historical and cultural changes that influence and shape the media. Whether Karin E. Westman analyzes the history of women in computer science, Sharon Sutherland and Sarah Swan explore the rise of women in the legal profession, or Beth Berila examines women in high positions in the White House, the writers focus on the challenges that face brilliant women every day, especially when they challenge traditional bastions of male power. The authors show that media images make a difference beyond the television or movie screen.

Regardless of what changes for women, the dumb blonde stereotype lingers and influences real women's lives, whether at Harvard or beyond its lofty gates. The stereotype that women are not as intelligent as men remains widespread, especially in science, mathematics, engineering, computer science, and other similar fields. As Summers's comments highlight, U.S. society has a persuasive myth that women lack men's intelligence, a myth that pervades everywhere, from the nursery school to the boardroom. Since this stereotype endures, it is crucial to study how intelligent women are portrayed in the media. The idea that a brilliant scientist or computer hacker must be a man has undergone a change, and over recent decades an increasing number of women have appeared in such roles. Brilliant women, however, still appear less frequently than men, and when they do, their intelligence is frequently toned down to make it more palatable to mainstream society. For example, they might be depicted as more concerned about romance than their careers in science or law, or they might give up their jobs in order to raise families; thus, the audience is reassured that no matter how brilliant women might become, they have not forgotten about their traditional gender roles.

Notes

1. Quoted in Karen Thomas, "She's Having a Blonde Moment," *USA Today*, 28 October 2003, 2D. For additional work on the dumb blonde stereotype, see D. Greenwood and L. M. Isbell, "Ambivalent Sexism and the Dumb Blonde: Men's and Women's Reactions to Sexist Jokes," *Psychology of Women Quarterly* 26.4 (2002): 341–351; and Rebecca Tyrrel, "I'm Not a Dumb Blonde, I'm an Angry One," *Daily Telegraph*, 12 February 2006, 26.
2. Alec Foege, "The Return of the Dumb Blonde," *Brandweek*, 1 March 2004, 22.
3. Michael Musto, "The Death of the Dumb Blonde," *Village Voice*, 15 November 2005, 26.
4. Martha Barnette, "Think Blondes Have More Fun?" *Vanity Fair*, October 2004, 278.
5. Quoted in Barnette, 279.
6. Deborah Blum, "When Are You Guys Going to Get It?" *Los Angeles Times*, 13 February 2005, M1.
7. Lawrence H. Summers, "Remark at NBER Conference on Diversifying the Science and Engineering Workforce," Office of the Harvard President, 10 April 2005. http://www. president.harvard.ed/ speeches/2005/nber.html.
8. After his speech, someone in the audience asked, "What about the rest of the world? . . . France [has] very high powered women in science in top positions." He replied, "I don't know too much about it."
9. Reactions to Lawrence H. Summers and his comments include Piper Fogg, "Harvard's President Wonders Aloud about Women in Science and Math," *Chronicle of Higher Education*, 28 January 2005, A12; Amanda Ripley et. al., "Who Says a Woman Can't Be Einstein?" *Time*, 7 March 2005, 50; and Jay Tolson, Vicky Hallett, and Alex Kingsbury, "Hard Lessons," *U.S. News and World Report*, 7 March 2005, 30.
10. Quoted in "Why Kids Don't Like Very Smart Girls," *USA Today Magazine*, January 1992, 5.
11. John. H. Bishop et al., "Why We Harass Nerds and Freaks: A Formal Theory of Student Culture and Norms," *Journal of School Health* 74.7 (2004): 237.
12. For an article that focuses on geek as fashionable and trendy, see Lev Grossman, "The Geek Shall Inherit the Earth," *Time*, 3 October 2005, 14. For works that focus on girl geeks, see Jaqueline Lalley, "Beyond the Valley of the Geeks," *Bitch Magazine*, Fall 2005, 42–47; and "Ruth Kelly Aims to Prove that Girls Can Be Geeks, too," *Education* 183 (June 2005), 3.
13. Ron Eglash, "Race, Sex, and Nerds: From Black Geeks to Asian-American Hipsters," *Social Text* 20.2 (2002): 58.
14. Eglash, 60.
15. Anita Gate, "Still the Sane if Not Successful Voice, Daria Bows Out," *New York Times*, 26 January 2002, 7.
16. Michele Byers, "Constructing Divas in the Academy: Why the Female Graduate Student Emerges in Prime-Time Television Culture," *Higher Education Perspectives* 1 (1996–1997): 112.
17. Byers, 112.
18. Candace White and Katherine N. Kinnick, "One Click Forward and Two Clicks Back: Portrayal of Women Using Computers in Television Commercials," *Women's Studies in Communication* 23.3 (2000): 410. Works on the changing images of women and girls in the popular media include Theresa Carilli and Jane Campbell, eds., *Women and the Media: Diverse Perspectives* (Lanham: University Press of America, 2005); Susan J. Douglas, *Where the Girls Are: Growing Up Female with the Mass Media* (New York: Times Books, 1994); and Lara Naaman, "Age of Uninnocence," *Alice Magazine*, May 2000: 64.
19. White and Kinnick, 409.

CHAPTER 1

Beauty and the Geek: Changing Gender Stereotypes on the *Gilmore Girls*

Karin E. Westman

"I guess what I'm trying to say is that I'd rather be a geek than a girl. But I hate having to make that choice," comments Annalee Newitz.[1] Her words reflect a society that has traditionally assumed that geeks are male, with the result that a female geek betrays society's gendered expectations. Though this paradigm persists, female geeks have flourished in the popular media, especially during the past decade. To succeed, however, these women must often carry a passport for public acceptance: the passport of beauty. To be recognized and accepted as intellectually brilliant frequently depends on a physical brilliance, a beauty underwritten by cultural norms of Western aesthetics. While female geeks can sometimes achieve public acclaim without this passport of beauty, brilliant women in the media's spotlight must be beautiful if they are to be valued for their intelligence.

Why must women choose between being a "geek" and being a "girl," as Newitz suggests? To answer this question, I begin with a brief history of female geeks since the 1980s; the first section, "Division of Labor," highlights the persistent separation of "beauty" and "geek" in the public sphere. By analyzing cultural trends and images of the geek during these decades, we can better understand how "geek" is a role available only to men. The next section, "Diminishing Divides," shows the beauty passport in action: how being a "girl" can offer cover for being a "geek" and can help women secure access to predominately male enclaves of information technology (IT). Though beauty is a double-edged sword, displays of conventional femininity can allow female geeks to exercise their intelligence and gain recognition for it, as long as the image of their beauty does not occlude their intelligence. I conclude by looking to some locations in popular culture where "beauty" and "geek" are no longer mutually exclusive terms—a place where, as the section title announces, "Geek is Beautiful."

In the world of Web sites like GirlGeeks.org and the television world of shows like the *Gilmore Girls*, female intellectual brilliance is socially valued and varied, as viewers experience multiple and recurring images of smart women in a variety of ages, occupations, and body types. As we enter the twenty-first century, popular television, as well as the free-access Web, can offer a space where both women and men can be geeks.

Division of Labor

The *Oxford English Dictionary* offers no indication that "geek" is a gendered term, a history of the word that Newitz and many others would question. From the word's first recorded use in 1957, the *OED* asserts that a geek is "an overly diligent, unsociable student" or "any unsociable person obsessively devoted to a particular pursuit," often someone who is also, since 1984, "extremely devoted to and knowledgeable about computers or related technology."[2] However, an alternative history emerges at *Wikipedia*, the highly democratic online encyclopedia that invites readers to submit additions and corrections to its text. Its entry for "geek" provides a gendered definition that is more in tune with the word's popular use. The anonymous *Wikipedia* authors expand the *OED*'s definition to include the "strong misogynistic behaviors and attitudes" associated with the term, as well as the geek's "inability to accept any woman regardless of qualifications as the geek[']s equal or superior."[3] *Wikipedia* captures what the *OED* leaves out: "geek" has long been considered appropriate for a man, but not for a woman.

The masculine gendering of "geek" was hardly a foregone conclusion as the country experienced the technology boom of the 1950s. Indeed, during this decade companies actively recruited women for careers in technology, even drawing upon conventional gender roles in brochures "addressed to 'My Fair Ladies.' "[4] "Geek" acquired masculine associations thanks to a nexus of institutional forces and gendered expectations, all of which snowballed during the 1980s and 1990s. Women's presence in IT had been on the rise between 1950 and 1980 and reached a peak in the mid-1980s. In 1984, women earned "nearly 40 percent of computer science and computer engineering degrees,"[5] and by 1986, women represented 40 percent of those working in IT.[6] By 1999, however, the American Association of University Women reported that only 28 percent of women earned degrees in computer science and computer engineering,[7] and the number of women employed in IT jobs witnessed a corresponding drop to 29 percent.[8] Women who worked in IT during these decades attribute the decline to a rise in "geek culture" that had become, in the view of one female IT professional, "inherently anti-woman."[9] A number of scientific studies corroborate her personal experience. Researchers Andrea Tapia and Lynette Kvasny, for instance, report that "IT culture is described as largely white, male-dominated, anti-social, individualistic, competitive, all-encompassing and non-physical," a place where "expert" translates into "male . . . behaviors, attitudes, and values."[10] "Geek" had become associated not only with IT but also with being a man.

Jane Margolis and Allan Fisher offer a useful genealogy for this masculine "geek culture" and its institutionally broad root system in *Unlocking the Clubhouse: Women in Computing* (2002). In this study, Margolis and Fisher trace our gendered view of "geek" to an early 1980s icon, the hacker, and the women-free world he inhabits, a world captured by Steven Levy in his book *Hackers: Heroes of the Computer Revolution* (1984). Levy's study collected several legendary portraits of male geek culture, including the one provided by the MIT computer scientist Joseph Weizenbaum. Hackers, according to Weizenbaum, are

> bright young men of disheveled appearance, often with sunken glowing eyes, [who] can be seen at computer consoles, their arms tensed and waiting to fire their fingers, already posed to strike, at the buttons and keys on which their attention seems to be riveted as a gambler's on the rolling dice. . . . Their rumpled clothes, their unwashed and unshaven faces, and their uncombed hair all testify that they are oblivious to their bodies and to the world in which they move. These are the computer bums, compulsive programmers.[11]

Weizenbaum's language signals the masculine ideals embodied by the hacker: he is a Lone Ranger and a gambler on the IT frontier, ready to "strike" out—in battle, across the territory—with complete disregard for such feminine niceties as well-kept hair or social relationships. This masculine image permeated not only the workplace of the 1980s but also the classroom, where girls of various educational levels felt locked out of the "boys' clubhouse" of IT.[12] In junior high, as Jo Shuchat Sanders and Antonia Stone explain in their study *The Neuter Computer: Computers for Boys and Girls* (1986), "girls do a sort of mental and emotional arithmetic" and conclude that the balance is not in their favor: "The minus of accepting the invitation—entering what they perceive as a male domain and therefore throwing their sex-role development into confusion and running the risk of losing their friends—can easily outweigh the plus of learning a valuable and enjoyable new skill."[13] In 1987, Myra Sadker, David Sadker, and Charol Shakeshaft, on the basis of their research during the previous years, posited a similar scenario for teachers to consider: "Your high school advanced calculus class is almost all male. You encourage a gifted young woman to take the course. She says that the boys would tease her. Also, she doesn't want the other kids to think that she's a study geek."[14] This "geek mythology," in Margolis and Fisher's words, prevented girls from exploring IT and related fields, which, in turn, hindered women from entering the profession. By the late 1980s, "geek" occupied a decidedly masculine territory of American culture, and neither girls nor women felt welcome.

The 1990s offered little change to the masculine "geek mythology." If anything, the decade hardened cultural perceptions of a firm line between a masculine IT "geek" and a feminine other. In one 1995 study, the term "geek" prompted 98 percent of college-aged respondents to imagine a man, even though these same male and female respondents reported using the term "geek" to refer to a man or a woman. As Deborah James, the study's author, concludes, "[A]ctual use of [a term like geek], for both sexes, is more gender-impartial than these students' stereotypes of how the terms are used."[15] Change in cultural perception therefore lags behind change in behavior. In 1996, these gendered perceptions received nationwide support through the popular documentary *Triumph of the Nerds*, which aired on PBS stations around the country and in college classrooms. Offering proof of the IT high life in Silicon Valley, the video made much of the founding fathers of Apple and Microsoft. Conspicuously absent, however, were all but one of the 28 percent of IT professional women who still remained in Silicon Valley.[16] For a young woman thinking about a college major and a career in IT, "the video would have convinced her that neither she nor any other woman was appropriate for or welcome to the computing field."[17] If the ranks of college-aged and professional women in IT were diminishing in the mid-1990s, as studies showed, such media representations might well have hastened their departure.[18]

Even when those prospective female majors in computer science and engineering did stick around the college classroom, their identity as "geeks" superseded their identity as "girls." In Lisa Michaud's "The Guy's Guide to Geek Girls, V2.0" (drafted in 1995 and posted online since 1996), the humor emerges from the perceived rarity of the species: "Contrary to popular belief," Michaud writes, "the geek girl is not some mythical, impossible-to-find creature." Part of their allure, Michaud assures the geek guy, is that "unlike the cute things you've been chasing, geek girls learned a long time ago that physical attributes aren't as important as the person underneath." Michaud's emphasis falls upon the fact that "most geek girls have low-maintenance appearances in their regular, day-to-day lives," even if "they can be quite striking when the mood suits them."[19] For the geek girl, beauty is possible, but hardly an organizing principle of being. In Michaud's humorous user manual, the geek girl's (masculine) intelligence and tech skills, rather than her display of (feminine) beauty, make her desirable to the geek guy. Instead of pursuing the unattainable "cute things," the geek guy should recognize the masculine "geek" girl beside him. Geek girls in the 1990s, then, are less girl than geek.

These gendered perceptions of "geek" trickled down the educational line throughout the 1990s, as they did in the late 1980s. By the late 1990s, however, the news media began to take interest. CNN.com, for example, reported on "Valley of the Boys? Women Struggle to Find Niche in Male-Oriented Tech Culture" (2000). Along with information about women's departures from IT, CNN.com also reported the challenges facing the women who remained. Furthermore, the report placed those departures and challenges within a larger cultural context. To illustrate the widespread cultural assumptions about gender and IT, including physical appearance, the article provided two hand-drawn portraits by schoolchildren and reported that "when the Information Technology Association of America and *CIO Magazine* [for Chief Information Officers] asked students to draw their impressions of IT workers, the results were less-than-flattering images of male geeks" (see figure 1.1).[20] Sketched in profile, these decidedly male figures work in happy isolation, with only their computers for company. As these drawings make clear, perceptions of IT are inextricably linked to images of masculinity, particularly "geek" masculinity, even at the turn of the twenty-first century. The figures' intimacy with their computers—that lone-hacker image—recurs in a study of middle- and high-school girls by the American Association of University Women (2000). Its Commission found that girls have a "can do, but don't want to" view of IT. Rather than hearing concerns about fear of computers, "the Commission heard girls critiquing the culture of the field."[21] Outfitted with glasses and pocket-protectors, heads and bodies turned toward their PCs and away from the viewer, these hand-drawn male geeks are the gendered face of IT and represent the masculine "culture of the field."

A few years into the new century, such gendered perceptions of "geek" are holding fast. "The last thing a fourteen-year-old girl wants to be associated with is a geek with broken glasses and a pocket-protector," declared Joan Korenman, director of the Center for Women and Information Technology, in 2001, adding, "They see it as a

Figure 1.1 School children draw IT workers. Courtesy of ITAA and CIO Magazine.

threat to their femininity."[22] As if to play upon the tension and titillation of this illicit pairing between "beauty" and "geek," the boyish actor-turned-producer Ashton Kutcher, fresh from his successful MTV reality television show *Punk'd*, launched a new reality show, *Beauty and the Geek*, on the youthful WB network for its 2005 summer season. "New Reality Show Matches Wits with Twits, Hotties with Notties," announced the network on 4 May 2005, in anticipation of the show's debut, thus declaring it to be "part social experiment, part competition, and all heart—Beauty and the Geek is what happens when good looks meet good grades." The seven women ("academically impaired") are matched with seven men ("brilliant but socially challenged") and, in pairs, they compete in challenges: "A spelling bee for the girls, massage lessons for the guys, and an introduction to actual rocket science when the girls compete to see who can build a working rocket." Though men and women are "practically a different species," the network admits, one lucky pair nonetheless "could walk away gifted and gorgeous," sharing the $250,000 prize. Kutcher's own pitch suggests less parity in the results: "We gave seven guys a fantasy and seven girls a reality check," he reported, adding, "Ultimately, that's what 'Beauty and the Geek' is."[23] The gendered rhetoric of the network and the show's producer is striking: not only is "geek" completely severed from "beauty," but there is more value to being the "brilliant" male geek who gets a "fantasy" fulfilled than to being the "academically impaired" female beauty who receives a "reality check" about her intelligence and the value of her beauty. The show's premise polarizes the two terms of its title, and the hype further emphasizes the split.

Regardless of—or perhaps because of—this split, the ratings for *Beauty and the Geek* went through the roof. "An instant ratings winner" for its time slot with the coveted 18- to 34-year-old demographic, the show also drew a sizable number of viewers from the 12–17 and 35–49 demographics, especially women.[24] In response, the WB network requested a second season of *Beauty and the Geek*, which aired in 2006 with two additional episodes; a third season has aired in 2007. The success of *Beauty and the Geek* demonstrates how men and women still accept the cultural stereotypes underwriting geek identity since the 1980s: intelligence is for men, and beauty is for women. In its premise and ratings, *Beauty and the Geek* shows the persistent gendered divide in popular culture between "beauty" and "geek."

Diminishing Divides

While the general trend in popular culture has been to establish a border, a *cordon sanitaire*, between masculine "geek" and feminine "beauty," a number of brilliant women have breached the masculine geek line by emphasizing, rather than diminishing, their beauty. This feminine beauty allows them to "pass," to be accepted by both the geek subculture and popular culture, as they display those physical attributes associated with female beauty in contemporary Western culture: a classical aesthetic of balance and proportion; Caucasian features; well-defined breasts; and young, white skin.[25] For geek guys, such women should offer the best of both worlds. If the geek guys desire beautiful women—those "cute things," as Michaud describes in "The Guy's Guide to Geek Girls"—and geek guys desire geeks like themselves, then beautiful women with brilliant minds should offer the complete fantasy in one package. However, masculine distrust of feminine brilliance complicates such an easy equation, both in geek culture and in popular culture more generally. Beauty passport in hand, brilliant and beautiful women gain recognition and acceptance in popular culture because their beauty contains their brilliance, signaling their adherence to conventions of femininity even if they use masculine smarts. Beauty becomes a Trojan horse into the otherwise masculine realms of prestige and power.

Including women such as Kim Polese, Rachel Muir, and Ellen Spertus, many women in IT have paired beauty and brains and have become spokeswomen for computer science. They can begin to claim both identities—"geek" and "beauty"— for their own. However, the beauty passport is an ambivalent, if ultimately useful, tool toward building a more permanent alliance between beauty and geek in popular culture. Feminist theorists have long questioned whether the advantages of beauty's power outweigh its debilitating effects on the women who deploy its outward signs, from Mary Wollstonecraft in *A Vindication of the Rights of Woman* (1792) to Naomi Wolf in *The Beauty Myth* (1991). More recently, Kathy Davis (*Reshaping the Female Body*, 1995), Mary Russo (*The Female Grotesque: Risk, Excess, Modernity*, 1995), Sander Gilman (*Making the Body Beautiful*, 1999), Elaine Scarry (*On Beauty and Being Just*, 2000), and Deborah Caslav Covino (*Amending the Abject Body*, 2004) have continued this line of inquiry by noting the ambivalent power attendant on beauty in Western culture.[26] We find further evidence to support their concerns as we watch brilliant and beautiful women like Kim Polese wield beauty's double-edged sword.

Polese's experience with the popular media as a "poster child of the new high-tech economy" in the mid- to late 1990s[27] provides a cautionary tale of beauty's role in a brilliant woman's career and demonstrates how beauty can benefit and compromise her acceptance as a female geek. Polese, who earned a BS in biophysics from the University of California, Berkeley, and studied computer science at the University of Washington, Seattle,[28] first appeared on the media radar in 1995 when she served as the product manager at Sun Microsystems for a new program, Java, which bears the name she created. A year later, Polese and three colleagues left Sun for a new start-up, Marimba, which became a highly successful software company. It was during her tenure at Marimba that Polese had "her bizarre tumble with the media."[29]

Polese's success in a booming field—and her status as a young, beautiful, and single woman—landed her a number of magazine features, from industry magazines such as *Red Herring* to popular magazines such as the high-fashion *Vogue* and the news magazine *Time*, which "anointed" her "the 'It Girl.' "[30] These features lauded her accomplishments as they lingered over her beauty in glamorous photos. Polese was displayed as a wondrous anomaly: not only an incredibly successful businesswoman, but also a beautiful geek. A story in *Fortune* from 1 March 1999, however, criticized her for creating a "glamour queen" image to sell the company's product and for turning herself into "a geek sex symbol who's more famous than her company," according to the story's author.[31] The beauty that had assisted Polese's acceptance in the popular media now jeopardized her status as a businesswoman.

The article in *Fortune* became a flashpoint for the women in the IT industry and prompted further media attention as well as media analysis. In support of Polese, other high-profile women expressed frustration at the double standard implied by *Fortune*'s angle. "Had an attractive man used his good looks to pump up the valuation of a company—as Larry Ellison and Steve Jobs do—they would not have been under this kind of media backlash," claimed Sylvia Paul, adding that "it smacks of hostility toward women who have made it in a field once reserved for men alone, and the more attractive the female, the stronger the hostility."[32] "The most egregious aspect of the *Fortune* feature," according to Janelle Brown, who reported on the story and its aftershocks for *Salon.com*, "wasn't the article's text but its accompanying art":

> While the author criticized Polese for posing for "glamorous close-up [photos] with her face softly lit and airbrushed, eyes beaming up at the camera," *Fortune* decorated the article with a series of its own glamorous close-up photos of Polese, dolled-up and beaming at the camera. Apparently, *Fortune* wanted to criticize a woman for using her sex appeal and capitalize on that sex appeal at the same time—to have its cheesecake and knock it, too.[33]

The photo opening the *Fortune* article (snapped by the renowned photographer Bonnie Schiffman) illustrates Brown's point: with her half-closed eyes, exposed neck, prominent lips, flowing hair, polished skin, and direct gaze at the viewer, Polese beckons to the observer. Photographed apart from the products and company that depend on her brains, she can offer only beauty in this head-shot image, just as *Fortune* proclaims.

Polese's experience with the media is an extreme example of what other high-profile women professionals in IT experience regularly. Like Polese, Katrina Garnett suffered bad press after her controversial decision to "[pose] for Richard Avedon in a sexy black dress for an ad touting her company"; in popular media accounts and industry lore, her display of beauty and sexuality runs a close second in fame to Polese's glamour shots.[34] High-profile women must also negotiate frequent requests for the "female executive interview," where the media pictorially frames their professional accomplishments within traditional female roles: "They want to talk to your husband, take a picture of you in your home," describes Ellen Handcock, a veteran of several high-profile jobs at National Semiconductor, IBM, and Apple.[35] "One thing you notice," adds Heidi Roizen, "is that when you're interviewed or profiled, you are almost always physically described."[36] Often, the beautiful body overwhelms the brains, shifting the balance to the point that we might ask, as reporter Diane Feen does, "Why is it that whenever a woman rises to the top in the high-tech world, stories in the non-tech media imply that her sexuality must have had something to do with it?"[37] The goal, many women agree, is to maintain as much control as possible over one's media image. Polese's recent appearance in the media suggests that she is gaining such control: when interviewed recently at her new company, SpikeSource, she "resists all photo shots of her alone— insisting that work colleagues be included."[38] Deliberately placed within the context of her business skill, Polese's beauty now complements rather than trumps her brilliance.

Two other women, Rachel Muir and Ellen Spertus, offer further examples of female geeks who use public perceptions of beauty to their professional advantage— in their case, the somewhat tongue-in-cheek "Sexiest Geek Alive" award, a contest that ran from 2000 until 2003. While the award ostensibly "emphasizes brains over beauty,"[39] it sought to recognize, according to its founder Steven Phenix, the "emerging coolness" associated with geeks.[40] Phenix's choice of adjective for the award, "sexiest," reflects his initial goal: to redefine cultural perceptions of male geeks in particular, encouraging associations of action, passion, and consummation in place of simply an ideal physical appearance. Though he created the contest for men, the award had 18,000 entries in its first year,[41] about half of which were from women.[42] Such numbers indicate that female geeks, like their male counterparts, wished to alter perceptions of geek identity, and they had to disrupt yet another all-male enclave to do so.

Whereas Polese's beauty threatened to undermine her brilliance, in entering the "Sexiest Geek Alive" contest, Muir and Spertus had the advantage of self-deprecating humor on their side to mitigate any threat they might pose: though there were elimination rounds and the chance at a prize, the award was all in good fun, a light-hearted gesture that might catch the media's human-interest eye. However, "Sexiest Geek" began to assume a less ironic, less frivolous status for some contestants such as Muir, given the power the word "sexiest" has in popular culture. For Muir, founder of the nonprofit organization GirlStart, the adjective "sexiest" represented an opportunity to reimagine "geek" for a new generation of girls and align it with an image of beauty and its attendant sexual power. Muir's decision to enter the 2000 contest developed from her work for GirlStart, which since 1997 seeks to "empower girls to excel in math, science, and technology."[43] Eager to "show young women that being smart can be sexy," Muir hoped to alter their views of technology by supporting the event: "It's about [helping] girls realize that intelligence is sexy and knowledge is power,"

Muir explained to *Wired News*. She added, "Being a powerful geek is almost like being a celebrity. It's totally hip to be a geek, and I want to show girls that they can be geeky and sexy, too."[44] As the face of GirlStart, Muir combines beauty and brilliance, but her stint as a contestant for "Sexiest Geek Alive" was less about her own beauty and more about the power of PR (see figure 1.2). Quoted in media reports about the award, Muir was able to leverage popular media time and attention for her own nonprofit organization and bring two opposing terms—"sexiest" and "geek"—closer in the public imagination.

Figure 1.2 Rachel Muir, founder of Girl Start. Photograph by Christopher Caselli.

Figure 1.3 Professor Ellen Spertus, Sexiest Geek in 2001. © Lauren J. Bricker, 2001.

Muir's interest in using the "Sexiest Geek Alive" award to shift public perception of female geeks in popular culture is of a piece with Ellen Spertus's goals. Though not a media-appointed beauty, Professor Spertus is best known in the popular press for winning the "Sexist Geek Alive" award in 2001, an honor that she has parlayed into increased recognition for women in her field and increased applications from young women to study computer science with her at Mills College. Sporting the "rare appellation MIT-Cubed (bachelor's, master's, and doctorate in computer science)"[45] as well as "a PVC corset with a printed-circuit board pattern and a black slit skirt, which allowed [her] to holster a slide rule" on her leg,[46] Spertus entered the contest to raise the awareness of women in IT, and her efforts were successful (see figure 1.3).

Not only has her award yielded her mention in more than fifty articles (at least twenty-nine articles nationally and at least twenty-two internationally),[47] but directly following the award, "her website was getting 10,000 hits a day," which in turn "translated to several hundred applications for admission to Mills."[48] "There's been a real increase in the number of students who want to study computer science, and particularly who want to study with Ellen," remarked Janet L. Holmgren, the president of Mills College, in 2002.[49] Spertus's concerns about the number of women in IT began long before she submitted her name for the contest: as a graduate student at MIT, she wrote a paper titled "Why Are There So Few Female Computer Scientists?" (1993), in which she argues that the hypermasculine hacker culture deters women who may believe that "sacrificing everything to computers might not be something that a psychologically healthy human being does."[50] Her working definition of "geek" on her Web site reiterates her desire to redefine and re-gender the term. "Geeks are intelligent, enthusiastic people full of curiosity and passion," she writes, people who like to interact with other people even more than with computers: "If geeks didn't want to communicate with each other, they wouldn't have created the Internet."[51] By linking feminine qualities of communication and passion with conventionally masculine "geek" qualities of intelligence, by making young women feel welcome in the field of computer science, Spertus advocates a new cultural perception of "geek" that diminishes the distance between "beauty" and "geek."

There are certainly dangers inherent in deploying a term like "sexiest" alongside "geek," if one wishes to claim a space for women within masculine geek culture. As likely to be co-opted as Polese's glamour shots, the term "sexiest" has the potential to undermine attempts to alter public perception that women are all "beauty" and no "geek," rather than active and beautiful agents in an intellectual world. The "Girls of Geekdom 2006" wall calendar, created by the "*über* geek" David B. Grelck of WDBG Productions,[52] would be a case in point. Closer to *Beauty and the Geek* than the "Sexiest Geek Alive," the calendar's soft-core porn of "beautiful sexy girls"[53] plays upon the titillating novelty of seeing smart and sexy in the same package. Its Web site claims that the calendar seeks to remind everyone that "geeks are everywhere, they're sexy too and they've been neglected for FAR TOO LONG!" but the result may well be a heterosexual fantasy for the male gaze rather than a call to political action. The "Geek Gorgeous 2006" wall calendar suffers from similar complicity. Produced by Lilac Mohr, a senior Java developer, the calendar exists to "show the world that there are plenty of beautiful, intelligent, interesting women in the fields of computing and engineering."[54] Mohr claims that she created the calendar to "dissolve the 'computer nerd' stereotype," and she even plans to funnel profits from sales into a college scholarship for girls interested in computer science, but the women's images trump their technical expertise.[55] Regardless of whether the women themselves perceived their participation as "a form of empowerment and just something fun," perception is in the gendered eye of the beholder.[56] These female geeks may have just "wanted to show off their sexy sides," as Mohr explains, but what will most viewers remember: sex or tech?[57]

It is indeed, as Mohr states in her calendar's defense, a "difficult task to create a product that breaks stereotypes yet has market potential in a society driven by physical appearance," but it is not impossible.[58] The efforts of Kim Polese, Rachel Muir, and Ellen Spertus yoke "beauty" and "geek," "sexiest" and "geek," with the goal of institutional change. Their use of the beauty passport allows them to "pass," and, once inside the masculine geek border, they can be free agents for change.

Geek is Beautiful

Geek may have become officially chic by 1991, according to the *OED*, but by 2000, geek was still far from officially beautiful, as the previous two sections have shown. "Geek chic" became a fashion trend for college-aged students and celebrities, prompting a run on thick black-rimmed glasses for men and women alike, yet women still struggled to enter, let alone redefine, a "geek culture" that often excluded them. Two virtual spaces emerged around 2000, though, that offered hope for uniting "beauty" and "geek": virtual online communities dedicated to women in IT, and the virtual community of Stars Hollow, Connecticut, on the television series *Gilmore Girls*. In these locales, geek is beautiful.

The turn of the twenty-first century saw a rapid rise in online communities for women, especially women in IT. Thanks to the tireless efforts of Anita Borg (1943–2003), founder of the Institute for Women and Technology, female geeks have had at least one virtual space of their own for nearly three decades. As early as 1987, Borg began an online e-mail community called Systers, "one of the oldest electronic networks for women in computer science,"[59] which is still going strong with over 3,000 members.[60] Such virtual communities have created professional networking and mentoring spaces for women of all ages and all IT interests, whether those communities are small (such as LinuxChix.org and Debian Women) or large (such as GirlGeeks.org and the Center for Women and Information Technology). These online communities have also contributed to shifts in popular opinion, particularly when the online community reaches from virtual to material space. GirlGeeks.org exemplifies this potential. Founded in 1998 by Kristine Hanna and Peter Crosby "as a documentary film project about women's past, present, and future impact on computing," GirlGeeks.org "originally included a question mark—GirlGeeks?— because the filmmakers wanted to explore the stereotype of the word 'geek,' meeting women who considered 'geekiness' to be an insult and others that considered it a badge of honor." Their research showed that they should "drop the question mark": more women valued the name "geek" than questioned it.[61]

After their informational Web site received numerous hits and became the hub of their research efforts, Hanna and Crosby developed a content-rich site for women's professional development in IT.[62] In 1999, for instance, backed by commercial funding, the Web site "served as many as 50,000 unique visitors a month," as well as hosting "live GirlGeek events at Comdex in Las Vegas and Chicago," each with over 1,500 people in attendance.[63] Such live events not only extended the virtual community into material space but also garnered attention in the popular press. By broadening the reach and public recognition of GirlGeeks, Hanna and Crosby had further opportunities to tell the story of their site and to communicate its mission to the media: "We wanted to show that you can be a beautiful, sophisticated and very savvy geek," announced Hanna for a BBC news story in 2000.[64] The Web site itself fore-grounds the number of women working in various IT fields by featuring a "Girl Geek of the Week" and archiving past winners. Their interviews and biographical profiles show aspiring girl geeks how women have embraced this role and forged new perceptions about women in technology, thereby offering inspiration as well as prac-tical advice for education and employment. Along with a host of sites dedicated to providing a supportive and informative environment for women on the Web, GirlGeeks.org is unabashedly female and feminine, from content to Web design, and shows that geek can be beautiful.

Online sites like GirlGeeks.org reach self-identified female geeks who are seeking information and support about IT, but network television commands a bigger and broader audience. The virtual world of Stars Hollow—the setting for the hour-long family series *Gilmore Girls*—unites "beauty" and "geek," imagining a space where brilliant women are not only beautiful, but their beauty and intelligence make them the heart of the community rather than its outsiders. Unlike other contemporary shows that have been claimed by geeks or recognized for their high-geek content, such as *The X-Files* and *Buffy the Vampire Slayer*, *Gilmore Girls* "is the only geek show on TV that doesn't revolve around geek things (superheroes, space travel, demon hunting, vampires, witches, etc.)," writes the reviewer David Grelck, adding, "I think that this fact gives it something that most geek shows don't have. Mainstream credibility."[65] A contributing factor, according to some critics, is the show's realism: "The characters live in an actual world—our world—and not some TV bubble, no matter how fanciful their storybook town in Connecticut can sometimes get," writes Diane Werts for *Newsday*.[66] The "geekiness" of *Gilmore Girls*, therefore, resides not in its connection to the world of IT, but in its attention to intellectual wordplay and to a combination of arcane and current cultural references, all within a realistic setting.

Reviewers consistently praise Amy Sherman-Palladino's hour-long comedy-drama as intelligent, witty, brainy, and smart. This unusual selection of adjectives marks not only the show's eccentricity within the family-friendly genre but also its progressive vision of gender. *Gilmore Girls* debuted on the WB network in 2000 as the eccentric relative of family-friendly television, shunning the didactic morals of *Seventh Heaven* as well as the teen-centered angst of *Dawson's Creek*. To describe the series' appeal, reviewers have turned and returned to appropriately atypical comparisons: the domestic realism of *Roseanne*[67] and *Malcolm in the Middle*,[68] the quirky humor of *Northern Exposure*,[69] the fast-paced dialogue of *The West Wing*,[70] and, reaching beyond the frame of the small screen, the screwball comedies of the 1930s.[71] "So wickedly intricate, so wildly intelligent," in the words of reviewer Gail Pennington,[72] the series' scripts revel in the "simple pleasures of language"[73] and encyclopedic knowledge of the world. All of its characters exemplify, in varying degrees, the obsessive devotion to knowledge associated with the geek, but the characters are also extremely sociable and witty. In this combination, they represent only one part of the conventional "geek" image—intelligence—and dispose of the other parts of the definition: the masculine and the unsociable. Regardless of its nontech and non-sci-fi focus, then, viewers and the popular media embrace *Gilmore Girls* as a "geek" show and praise it for its "geek" qualities. As a result, the show offers a new definition of "geek," one that embodies intelligence, community, and people of both sexes.

In the world of the *Gilmore Girls*, women are brilliant, education is cool, and intelligence is a team sport. Brimming with wide-ranging cultural references delivered with conversational élan, *Gilmore Girls* exceeds the industry standard not only for script length (eighty pages instead of the usual fifty-five) but also for female intelligence, offering multiple and recurring images of smart women in a variety of ages and occupations.[74] Lorelai (Lauren Graham) and Rory (Alexis Bledel), the mother-daughter friends of the title, forge the emotional core of the show, and their complementary brilliance is often the center of our attention and amusement. We certainly view them as beautiful according to our cultural expectations, given their flawless fair skin, glossy brown locks, and well-toned bodies. During the show, however, the camera directs our attention to their rapid-fire exchanges rather than their features—a carefully crafted approach, according to Sherman-Palladino. "These television shows that have fourteen shots of somebody looking at each other with the wind blowing through their hair drive me crazy," she tells the interviewer Virginia Heffernan: "Who's got that kind of time? We got that the girl was pretty when she walked in the door."[75] Instead of Lorelai and Rory with their hair in the wind, we get "banter," exchanges "consistently peppered with obscure references, often to decades-old pop culture"[76] and to cultural events contemporaneous to the show's initial broadcast. References to literature (Beckett's *Waiting for Godot*, Dickens's *Oliver Twist*), popular culture (Gomer Pyle), recent American history (Oliver North and Fawn Hall), European history (Guy Fawkes Day, Napoleon and Elba), celebrity culture (Madonna and Demi Moore's embrace of the Kabbalah), feminist activism (Gloria Allred, president of the Women's Equal Rights Legal Defense and Education Fund), and current events (the Valerie Plame leak) are scattered liberally throughout the scripts and often appear without contextual clues—as a viewer, you either get the reference or you don't. These references pose a "puzzle" for the show's audience, according to Lauren Graham,[77] and the audience's pleasure resides in sharing the characters' knowledge or in sharing the characters' pleasure in their exchange. Either way, the series signals that geek intelligence is no longer exclusively gendered male.

Gilmore Girls features not only female geeks but also young female geeks. While we might expect Lorelai, as a mother in her early thirties, to display a quick wit peppered with puns and pop culture references, the teenaged Rory's inclusion in these conversations and the social context for her brilliance defy industry stereotypes of "beautiful" girls in popular culture. Rory's difference is purposeful, since Sherman-Palladino "created the character to fill a vacuum in TV's representation of teenaged girls."[78] Rory's unashamed love of books and her passion for learning are not the consequence of a failed beauty (as they might be in more conventional narratives of teenage life) but simply who she is: beauty and brains coexist within her character. As the reviewer Kim Linekin remarks, "[Rory's] interest in school is not just a character trait—it's the backbone of the entire series," and concludes that *Gilmore Girls* is "refreshing" because "Rory's intelligence is a given."[79] Linekin rightly claims that Rory is "no geek" in the conventional sense of the term: she is hardly male, antisocial, and unattractive. Instead, through Rory's character, Sherman-Palladino redefines "geek" as beautiful and brilliant.

What allows Rory's intelligence to be a "given," in Linekin's terms, and allows *Gilmore Girls* to so thoroughly redefine "geek" to include beautiful and brilliant women, is the geek community surrounding Rory and her mother. Lorelai's and Rory's intelligence is not an anomaly within the series; it is simply the most prominent example of a quality shared by others. Female geeks abound at Chilton, Rory's private school, where we meet characters such as the overachieving and tunnel-visioned Paris Geller as well as the two more social, lighter-weight intellects of Madeline and Louise, who nonetheless get good grades and plan to attend select four-year colleges. The townspeople of Stars Hollow are equally interested demonstrating their intellects. "A sort of geek Greek chorus," in the words of the reviewer Robert Bianco,[80] this motley crew takes pleasure in language and cultural allusions even when Rory and Lorelai are offstage. In one episode, struggling to find the best name for a newly discovered town heroine who gave herself to a British general in order to assist the Revolutionary troops, the town's reenactors (who include the town's minister and mayor) run through a range of possibilities: "Streetwalker," "concubine," "scarlet woman" ("Too Nathaniel

Hawthorne," one reenactor replies), "harlot," "woman of accommodating morals," "bit of stuff" ("Too Monty Python," another replies).[81] The play of references across the conversation, combined with the goal of the conversation itself, is of a piece with Lorelai's and Rory's attempts to make sense of their world through the language and matter of culture, both high and low. Everyone in Stars Hollow, it appears, is obsessed with language and cultural references.

Whether organizing experience through popular music, as Rory's friend Lane does, or through phrases for loose women, as the reenactors do, the "geek chorus" of *Gilmore Girls* contributes to the often humorous, almost always clever tone of the series. "All the principals on 'Gilmore Girls' sound alike," complains the reviewer Alessandra Stanley in the *New York Times*,[82] but that consistency of tone is part of Sherman-Palladino's point, I think, as she creates a realistic setting where intelligence shines from not just one or two characters, but all. Lorelai and Rory perform their geeky brilliance for each other, but the performance often includes the other characters in their conversational jaunts through history and pop culture. Unlike other family-friendly shows of the late 1990s and the first decade of the twenty-first century, the landscape of *Gilmore Girls* is populated by a number of smart women who are surrounded by a number of smart men. By not making an intelligent woman a singularity, *Gilmore Girls* illustrates an exceptional portrait of American social life in popular media: a culture of intelligence, built around the pleasures of language, broad cultural knowledge, and collaborative exchange. This inclusivity—of the viewer, of the other characters—fosters the community of the show, expanding the circle of brilliance to others rather than containing it.

The success of *Gilmore Girls* with a wide-ranging demographic—young girls, women 18–34, women over 34, and an increasing number of men—points to the social ramifications of Sherman-Palladino's redefinition of "geek" for the twenty-first century. Though she is glad that "young girls are watching, because they see a girl who loves her mother and reads Dorothy Parker," Sherman-Palladino is quite clear that *Gilmore Girls* is "more than just a show for little girls."[83] The classical beauty of Lorelai and Rory gives the show its most public face in publicity shots and promotional trailers, but Sherman-Palladino is quite interested in reminding viewers that women's brilliance can emerge from a variety of body types, aged to various years. The resulting show provides a constellation of brilliance not bound by only one definition of beauty or by one gender. Reviewers note how women and men of various ages enjoy the series,[84] as industry ratings confirm, and both women and men over thirty are quite willing to blog about their love for the show. As Sherman-Palladino remarked in an interview, "Audiences are as smart as you will allow them to be."[85] Her viewers suggest that they live up to Sherman-Palladino's vision of her audience: like her characters, her audience values a brilliance not limited by the conventions of gender, a world of female and male geeks.

Female Geekdom for the Twenty-First Century

Sherman-Palladino's approach in *Gilmore Girls* is certainly atypical in the current media environment populated by the next installments of *Beauty and the Geek* and the "Girls of Geekdom" wall calendar. In the cultural imagination, "geek" still suggests, first and foremost, a reclusive and socially awkward male immersed in the minutia of computing rather than an intellectual and beautiful woman. Such cultural perceptions are hardly surprising, given the continued prominence of men in IT. In May 2005, the U.S. Department of Labor released its report on "Women in the Labor Force: A Databook," and the statistics looked all too familiar: in 2004, women held only 27 percent of jobs in computer programming and 13 percent of jobs in computer hardware engineering.[86] The National Science Foundation cites similar numbers for the fields of science and engineering, where women represent "only approximately 25% of the science and engineering workforce at large, and less than 21% of science and engineering faculty in 4-year colleges and universities."[87] Studies funded by the National Science Foundation on women's continued absence from IT repeat the reason we have heard for several decades: "the perception of it as being 'geeky.' "[88] For many women and men and girls and boys, "geek" remains decidedly male and masculine, off-limits to those who are female and feminine. Those girls and women who do breach the geek line are likely to find themselves in an untenable gendered position, caught between being a woman and being a geek. Furthermore, professional livelihood is at stake, and so is gender identity. Absent from science and engineering, women lose the personal and financial rewards that accompany such opportunities.

For now, the challenge remains. Still frustrated with having to make the choice between being a geek and being a girl, Annalee Newitz, along with coeditor Charlie Anders, asked women to submit personal essays for a new collection, *She's Such a Geek* (2006). "This anthology will celebrate women who have flourished in the male-dominated realms of technical and cultural arcane," according to Newitz and Anders, and it "aims to bust stereotypes of what it means to be a geek, as well as what it means to be female."[89] Newitz and Anders's anthology posits female geeks not as anomaly but as given, worthy of recognition and celebration. It also signals another phase for the female geek in contemporary American culture, one that relies less upon visual images of conventional feminine beauty as a counterbalance to geeky brains.

The success of geek-friendly communities for women—whether those communities are textual, virtual, or real—does suggest that it is possible to redefine "geek" for women's everyday lives. Beauty's role in this endeavor will always be a double-edged sword, both helping and hindering women's reception into the "clubhouse" of male geekdom. Images of female beauty can easily overshadow female brilliance, as the photographs of Kim Polese in *Fortune* and the "Girls of Geekdom 2006" demonstrate. However, if women can craft the right balance between "beauty" and "geek," "sexy" and "geek"—whether by means of humor, irony, or another strategy—the results can alter public perception as well as the next set of statistics from the National Science Foundation. By challenging and changing the maleness and masculinity of the geek identity, women may yet realize and be recognized for their brilliance in the century ahead.

Notes

1. Annalee Newitz, "Techsploitation: Women Like Me," *Metroactive*, 6 April 2000, http://www.metroactive.com/papers/metro/04.06.2000/work-0014.html (accessed 22 October 2005).

2. "Geek," *The Oxford English Dictionary*, 2005, http://dictionary.oed.com/ (accessed 22 October 2005).

3. "Geek," *Wikipedia, 2005*, http://en.wikpedia.org/wiki/Geek (accessed 22 October 2005). The entry for "Nerd" mentions that both terms have been "traditionally used to describe men and boys."

4. Quoted in Nancy Ramsey and Pamela McCorduck, "Where Are the Women in Information Technology? Preliminary Report of Literature Search and Interviews," (Boulder: University of Colorado, 2005), 15, http://www.anitaborg.org/ncwit/wherearethe_women.pdf (accessed 22 October 2005).

5. "Valley of the Boys? Women Struggle to Find Niche in Male-Oriented Tech Culture," *CNN.com*, 5 August 2000, http://archives.cnn.com/2000/TECH/computing/08/03/it.women/index.html (accessed 22 October 2005).

6. Ramsey and McCorduck, 4.

7. "Valley."

8. Ramsey and McCorduck, 4.

9. Ramsey and McCorduck, 15.

10. Quoted in Ramsey and McCorduck, 9.

11. Quoted in Jane Margolis and Allan Fisher, *Unlocking the Clubhouse: Women in Computing* (Cambridge: MIT Press, 2002), 66.

12. Margolis and Fisher, 3.

13. Jo Shuchat Sanders and Antonia Stone, *The Neuter Computer: Computers for Girls and Boys* (New York: Neal-Schuman, 1986), 14.

14. Myra Sadker, David Sadker, and Charol Shakeshaft, "Sex, Sexism, and the Preparation of Educators," *Peabody Journal of Education* 64 (1987): 222, *JSTOR*, http://www.jstor.org (accessed 22 October 2005).

15. Deborah James, "Gender-Linked Derogatory Terms and Their Use by Women and Men," *American Speech* 73 (1998): 400, 412, *JSTOR*, http://www.jstor.org (accessed 25 October 2005).

16. Ramsey and McCorduck, 4.

17. Anita Borg, "What Draws Young Women to and Keeps Women in Computing?" Institute for Women and Technology, n.d., http://www.annalysnyas.org/cgi/reprint/869/1/102.pdf (accessed 26 October 2005).

18. "Valley"; Ramsey and McCorduck, 4.

19. Lisa Michaud, "The Guy's Guide to Geek Girls V2.0," Pathways: Women in Computer Science, 1995, http://cs.wheatonma.edu/pathways/humor/GuidetoGeekGirls.html (accessed 22 October 2005).

20. "Valley."

21. Margolis and Fisher, 73.

22. "Women Are Geeky People, Too," *Wired News*, 1 May 2001, http://www.wired.com/news/women/0,1540,43393,00.html (accessed 22 October 2005).

23. "New Reality Show Matches Wits with Twits, Hotties with Notties," *WB*, 4 May 2005; "Beauty and the Geek—News, Recaps, Gossip, Photos, Commentary," *Reality TV Calendar*, 2005, http://www.realitytvcalendar.com/shows/beauty-geek.html (accessed 23 October 2005).

24. " 'Beauty and the Geek' Back by Popular Demand," *WB*, 21 June 2005, *The Futon Critic*, http://www.thefutoncritic.com (accessed 23 October 2005).

25. Deborah Caslav Covino, *Amending the Abject Body: Aesthetic Makeovers in Medicine and Popular Culture* (Albany: State University of New York Press, 2004), 46–50, 109.

26. For a cogent review of the two dominant schools of thought on feminism and beauty, as well as the role that Foucault's theories play in both, see Covino, 6–13.

27. Matt Marshall, "A 'Geek Girl' Sees Doors Opening Again," *Silicon Valley.Com*, 14 March 2005, http://www.siliconvalley.com/mld/siliconvalley/11132522.htm (accessed 23 October 2005).

28. Diane Feen, "Non-Tech Media Fail to Give Women Their Due," *O'Dwyer's PR Services Report*, November 1999, *Lexis-Nexis*, http://web.lexis-nexis.com/universe (accessed 30 October 2005).

29. Marshall, "A 'Geek Girl.' "

30. Marshall, "A 'Geek Girl.' "

31. Quoted in Janelle Brown, "Beauty and the Geeks," *Salon.com*, 11 March 1999, http://archive.salon.com/21st/feature/1999/03/cov_11feature.html (accessed 23 October 2005).

32. Quoted in Brown, "Beauty and the Geeks."

33. Brown, "Beauty and the Geeks."

34. Feen, "Non-Tech Media."

35. Brown, "Beauty and the Geeks."

36. Quoted in Brown, "Beauty and the Geeks."

37. Feen, "Non-Tech Media."

38. Marshall, "A 'Geek Girl.' "

39. "Woman Crowned 'Sexiest Geek Alive,' " *CBC News*, 21 June 2001, http://cbc.ca/ (accessed 22 October 2005).

40. Brad King, "In Search of the Sexiest Geek," *Wired News*, 17 April 2001, http://www.wired.com/news/culture/0,1284,43091,00.html (accessed 23 October 2005).

41. "Sexiest Geek Declared," *BBC News*, 21 June 2001, http://news.bbc.co.uk/1/hi/sci/tech/140333.stm (accessed 23 October 2005).

42. King, "In Search."

43. "About Us," *GirlStart*, 2005, http://www.girlstart.org (accessed 23 October 2005).

44. Quoted in Joyce Slaton, "Grrrl Geeks Are Sexy, Too," *Wired News*, 11 February 2000, http://www.wired.com/news/culture/0,1284,34237,00.html (accessed 23 October 2005).

45. Sam Whitting, "The Bay Area's Brain Trust," *San Francisco Chronicle*, 1 September 2002, http://sfgate.com/ (accessed 23 October 2005).

46. Ellen Spertus, "Ellen Spertus," n.d., http://people.mills.edu/spertus/Geek (accessed 23 October 2005).

47. Ellen Spertus, "Articles about Ellen Spertus and SGA 2K+1," n.d., http://people.mills.edu/spertus/Geek /articles.html (accessed 23 October 2005).

48. Whitting, "The Bay Area's."

49. Quoted in Whitting, "The Bay Area's."

50. Quoted in Margolis and Fisher, 72–73.

51. Spertus, "Ellen Spertus."

52. Chris Jordan, "It's Chic to Be Geek!" *Home News Tribune*, 2 July 2005, *Detroit News*, http://www.detnews.com/2005/screens/0507/06/ent-234753.htm (accessed 23 October 2005).

53. "The Girls of Geekdom—They're Smart! They're Sexy—They're Geeks!" *Girls of Geekdom*, http://wwww.girlsofgeekdom.com (accessed 22 October 2005).

54. Lilac Mohr, "The Producer," *GeekGorgeous.com*, 2005, http:// www.geekgorgeous.com/producer.htm (accessed 20 November 2005).

55. Mohr, "The Producer."

56. Lilac Mohr, "Response," *GeekGorgeous.com*, 2005, http://www.geekgorgeous.com/response.htm (accessed 20 November 2005).

57. Mohr, "Response."

58. Mohr, "Response."

59. Lakshmi Chaudhry, "Building the Digital Sisterhood," *Wired News* 15 February 2000, http://www.wired.com/news/culture/0,1284,34175,00.html (accessed 23 October 2005).

60. "The Google 2006 Anita Borg Scholarship," *Google*, 2005, http:// www.google.com/ anitaborg (accessed 23 October 2005).

61. "About GirlGeeks: History of GirlGeeks Empowering Women," *GirlGeeks.org*, n.d., http://www.girlgeeks.org/about/history.shtml (accessed 22 October 2005).

62. "About GirlGeeks."

63. "About GirlGeeks."

64. "It's Chic to Be Geek," *BBC News*, 17 November 2005, http://news.bbc.co.uk/1/hi/ business/1027754.stm (accessed 22 October 2005).

65. David B. Grelck, "Gilmore Girls, 'Written in the Stars,'" *Entertainment Geekly*, 5 October 2004, http://entertainment-geekly.com/web/general/oct2004/gilmoregirls5.3 (accessed 23 October 2005).

66. Diane Werts, "The World according to 'Gilmore,'" *Newsday*, 8 February 2005, *Lexis-Nexis*, http://web.lexis-nexis.com/universe (accessed 7 August 2005).

67. Werts, "The World according to 'Gilmore.'"

68. Caryn James, "Home Sweet Home, but Not Saccharine," *New York Times*, 25 February 2001, *Lexis-Nexis*, http://web.lexis-nexis.com/universe (accessed 4 August 2005).

69. Jill Vejnoska, "Quirkiness, Depth Make a Hit," *Atlanta Journal-Constitution*, 8 February 2005, *Lexis-Nexis*, http://web.lexis-nexis.com/universe (accessed 7 August 2005).

70. Molly Willow, "'Girls' Power," *Columbus Dispatch*, 15 February 2005, *Lexis-Nexis*, http://web.lexis-nexis.com/universe (accessed 7 August 2005).

71. Dave Walker, "Girls Grown Up," *Times-Picayune* (New Orleans), 22 February 2005, *Lexis-Nexis*, http://web.lexis-nexis.com/universe (accessed 7 August 2005); Vejnoska, "Quirkiness, Depth Make a Hit."

72. Gail Pennington, "It's Fun Starting Over with the 'Gilmore Girls,'" *St. Louis Post-Dispatch*, 4 May 2004, *Lexis-Nexis*, http://web.lexis-nexis.com/universe (accessed 4 August 2005).

73. Robert Bianco, "'Gilmore Girls' Finale Is Worth Your While," *USA Today*, 10 May 2001, *Lexis-Nexis*, http://web.lexis-nexis.com/universe (accessed 4 August 2005).

74. Walt Belcher, "The Woman Behind the 'Girls,'" *Tampa Tribune*, 8 October 2002, *Lexis-Nexis*, http://web.lexis-nexis.com/universe (accessed 4 August 2005).

75. Virginia Heffernan, "Job Title: The Gilmore Noodge," *New York Times*, 23 January 2005, *Lexis-Nexis*, http://web.lexis-nexis.com/universe (accessed 7 August 2005).

76. Willow, "'Girls' Power."

77. Quoted in "Welcome to the 'Gilmore Girls,'" "Special Features," *Gilmore Girls: The Complete First Season*, Warner's Home Video, 2004.

78. Quoted in Samantha Bornemann, "Wouldn't It Be Nice?" *Pop Matters*, 13 September 2005, http://www.popmatters.com/tv/review/g/gilmore-girls-050913.shtml (accessed 23 October 2005).

79. Kim Linekin, "Single Smart Female," *Box Populi*, 15 July 2004, http:/www.eye.net/eye/ issue/issue_07.15.04/film/boxpopuli.html (accessed 23 October 2005).

80. Robert Bianco, "'Girls' Must Compete, But They're Up to It," *USA Today*, 9 October 2001, *Lexis-Nexis*, http://web.lexis-nexis.com/universe (accessed 26 October 2005).

81. Amy Sherman-Palladino, "Women of Questionable Morals," *The Gilmore Girls*, 2004.

82. Alessandra Stanley, "A President-to-Be and His Rosebud," *New York Times*, 10 September 2004, *Lexis-Nexis*, http://web.lexis-nexis.com/universe (accessed 26 October 2005).

83. Quoted in Belcher, "The Woman Behind the 'Girls.'"

84. Pennington, "It's Fun."

85. Quoted in Pennington, "It's Fun."

86. Elaine Cho and Kathleen P. Utgoff, "Women in the Labor Force: A Databook," *Bureau of Labor Statistics*, May 2005, http://www.bls.gov/cps/wlf-databook-2005.pdf (accessed 25 November 2005).

87. "ADVANCE: Increasing the Participation and Advancement of Women in Academic Science and Engineering Careers," *National Science Foundation*, 2005, http://www.nsf.gov/pubs/2005/nsf05584/nsf05584.htm (accessed 25 November 2005).

88. Marianne Kolbasuk McGee, "IT's Gender Gap," *InformationWeek*, 21 November 2005, http://www.informationweek.com/story/showArticle.jhtml?articleID=174301061 (accessed 25 November 2005).

89. "Call for subs: She's Such a Geek," *Lorem Ipsum*, 15 November 2005, http://www.kith.org/journals/jed/2005/11/15/3245.html (accessed 20 November 2005).

CHAPTER 2

Lab Coats and Lipstick: Smart Women Reshape Science on Television

Lorna Jowett

Lab coats and lipstick—why not? Does science need reshaping? And if so, how can television help to do it?

All representations of science on television or in other popular media explore our relationship as humans with science and technology, which are key aspects of our twenty-first century world. Popular culture representations like these negotiate or maintain particular discourses or ways of making sense of the world.[1] Thus, depictions of women scientists can influence or shape ideas about gender and science. Representations of male scientists do the same. However, the discourse of science has traditionally been constructed as masculine. Female scientists challenge this stereotype in subversive ways. This chapter examines how real and fictional women scientists struggle against the traditional gendering of science as masculine and how they potentially reshape science. But television representations of women scientists face particular challenges in reshaping science to a more female or even feminist agenda.

In modern times, the pairing of women and science is still contentious. In January 2005, the president of Harvard caused great controversy when he publicly implied that women are innately or genetically less able in science and mathematics and thus linked gender and science in what many considered an inappropriate and indeed discredited way. Scholar Jane Donawerth begins a discussion of women and science in science fiction by suggesting why such opinions persist: "Our culture defines science as a masculine endeavor."[2] This way of defining science is changing, but more slowly than we might hope.

Following the second wave of feminism in the 1960s and 1970s, the conventions of science came under scrutiny by feminist scholars, who began to reevaluate it as part of our patriarchal society and recognize it as a gendered institution. Some scholars note "the prevalence of sexual metaphor within scientific discourses" and how such "metaphor serves symbolically to equate women with nature as that which is known, as opposed to that which is capable of knowing."[3] Identifying the scientist as male effectively excludes women from scientific knowledge. Notions of science dating back to the seventeenth century figured science itself as masculine, as a knowledge "designed to unclothe, penetrate, dominate and conquer a female nature, variously portrayed as virgin, Venus, unruly whore, and bountiful mother."[4] Such constructions firmly embed gendered and sexualized notions of science, and nature, into the discourse of science, and these notions have persisted in reality and in fiction. Comparing a biography of the molecular biologist Rosalind Franklin with Isaac Asimov's stories about the roboticist Susan Calvin, scholar Robin Roberts argues that historically in "real life or fiction, the female scientist is depicted as unnatural, and science is presented as the realm of men."[5] Because of this history, a female scientist may still be perceived as not belonging in the world of science.

This chapter addresses intersections between the experience of female scientists, scholarship on gendered science, and popular representations of women in science. Such depictions are not new: women scientists have appeared in fiction, especially science fiction, for many years. Their representation may vary according to the agenda (or possibly the gender) of their creator, and a scientist is presented as female sometimes almost entirely for novelty, although not always. Female scientist characters have provided an opportunity for popular fiction to address gender issues head-on, whether to perpetuate traditional versions of the discourses of gender and science (as Asimov's Susan Calvin seems to do, for instance) or to explore ways of reshaping science to include women.

I focus on the character Fred, an especially brilliant woman scientist who stars on the television show *Angel* (the spin-off from *Buffy the Vampire Slayer*).[6] Such depictions now draw on popular feminism as well as female scientists' real experience. At times, the apparent feminism of Fred's representation seems to mask a more traditional view of gender. The show suggests that women have a different approach to scientific inquiry than men, which allows for the valorization of characteristics most often associated with women, but the notion of difference can reinforce binary constructions of gender and traditional femininity. This chapter examines how being a woman genders intellectual characters like Fred. The gendered body complicates the representations of female scientists, especially where those representations cross into action, science fiction, and horror because these rely on particular discourses and conventions. Real women scientists struggle in their everyday work against the notion of science as male; fictional women scientists in popular culture struggle, too.

Jobs for the Boys?

An increasing number of women are working as scientists. The total with degrees in science or engineering and the total employed in these areas across the United States has risen since 1977 (the total employed had more than doubled by 1999).[7] Yet research suggests that these women may not have the same opportunity to develop their careers as men have had in similar positions. While 91 percent of female scientists in the United States would still choose a career in science if they had to start over, 77 percent believe it is harder for women to succeed in science.[8] Researchers in the United States identify four key obstacles to women succeeding as proficiently as their male counterparts in science and technology occupations. These are pipeline (training and encouragement to climb the ladder), climate hostile to women, unconscious bias against women in science, and balancing family and work (family responsibilities are still largely shouldered by women).[9] Thus, while now a greater number of women are employed in science and technology, the historical gendering of science continues to cause problems in the workplace. Writing of her own movement toward a feminist reenvisioning of science, Evelyn Fox Keller suggests, "Perhaps the most important barrier to success for women in science derived from the pervasive belief in the intrinsic masculinity of scientific thought."[10]

This "pervasive belief" in science as male also affects popular representations of scientists, as do other stereotypes. In an analysis of female scientists in film as role models, Jocelyn Steinke notes several recurring characterizations, categorizing these as "professional and realistic; mad and maniacal; clumsy and absentminded; nerdy and antisocial."[11] These characterizations are recognizable to most from film and television representations of male as well as female scientists. (There is a larger issue here about the representation of science in popular culture.) Steinke obviously values the "professional and realistic" characterization over the others, assuming that it makes for a more positive role model. More stereotypical scientists would be "nerdy and antisocial," and this is how *Angel* presents Fred initially; indeed she is a self-confessed "standard issue science nerd" ("Unleashed") throughout her three seasons on the show. Steinke might view this representation as negative, but Fred's nerdy characteristics are part of her show's geek ethic, which often makes heroes out of unlikely people.

We know that Fred is a science nerd largely because she talks like one. A physics graduate student, she was sucked through an interdimensional portal into an alternate world, named Pylea, where humans are enslaved. Five years later, when Angel meets her in Pylea, she seems to be slightly crazy (understandably so), but resourceful and smart. In "There's No Place Like Plrtz Glrb," he recognizes some of the words she is writing on the wall of her cave hideout as similar to those that opened the portal to Pylea. "They're not words," she tells him. "They're consonant representations of mathematical transfiguration formula." This is familiar television technobabble (like the "dilithium crystals" or "Heisenberg compensators" of *Star Trek*[12]), and it establishes Fred as an expert. Angel later introduces her to the team, saying, "She knows a lot about the portals." Her response—"Not a lot. It's a trionic speechcraft formulation; modification has to alter the dynamic reality sphere. Lutzbalm predicted it at Zurich in '89, [but they] laughed him off the stage"—establishes her style of expert technobabble *and* nerdy babble.

Fred talks about complex scientific processes and theories as though people can understand them. She observes, "I'm getting electromagnetic readings consistent with spiritual entities, but there's no ectoplasm matrix" ("Just Rewards"). She is even able to switch from one expert (masculine?) language to another, as when she gets her point about top physicists across to Gunn by comparing them with baseball players in "Supersymmetry." However, although Fred often talks about "masculine" science, Janine R. Harrison points out that her "communication styles are feminine. She speaks with a sweet Southern drawl using a recursive (female) rather than linear (male) speech pattern."[13] Her language establishes Fred as a woman, and characterizing her in this way draws attention to the possible split between "male" science and female scientist.

The show develops this tension in other ways, too. Fred's experiences reflect problems that real women scientists face in the workplace, given what recent research has revealed about hostile climates and unconscious bias. This is highlighted in "Supersymmetry," which explores the consequences of her "getting back into physics" by implicitly exposing the power relations of the scientific academy as gendered.[14] Here she reveals an old ambition: "I used to dream I'd discover some revolutionary concept and—it's silly. . . . I guess I just wanted all those people I look up to—I wanted them to see me too." This positions the pre-Pylea Fred as hopeful and ambitious, leaving home to "learn every damn thing they know up there and then figure out some stuff they don't" ("A Hole in the World"). But it also reveals a perception of her own low status in the academy: "all those people" she used to "look up to" are, implicitly, male.

The episode hinges around Fred's reunion with her old mentor, Professor Seidel, and the revelation that *he* sent her to Pylea. A series of Seidel's graduate students have disappeared but one, Laurie, is still there and teaches some of Seidel's classes. Fred recognizes Laurie: "You were the T.A. for high energy physics." Laurie replies wryly, "Still am. Not all of us are geniuses." Fred eventually tells Seidel, "It's kinda funny thinking how threatened you were by me back when I was a grad student. That's why you sent me and the others away, isn't it? You couldn't handle the competition. . . . That's why Laurie's still around. She's not smart enough to overshadow you, is she? Not like me." Seidel is cast as the jealous male mentor, unwilling to be overtaken by a brilliant young woman like Fred, while Laurie is the safely contained female scientist, a junior working for a male boss.

While the scientific academy, like other traditional institutions, might limit opportunities for women, Fred and Cordelia seem to operate within a more egalitarian system at Angel Investigations. This has consequences for how, as women, they can develop their own power and agency. Harrison describes Angel Investigations as having an "androgynous management style, one employing a balance of masculine and feminine qualities," and suggests that under Cordelia's influence, it adopts "feminine management concepts of communication and cooperation, which create 'family.' " Fred and Cordelia might benefit from a different working environment, but they have their own problems with gender. These stem partially from the notion of gender difference that Harrison employs here, as I explain later.[15]

After the move from Angel Investigations in season five, Fred is awarded a position commensurate with her brilliance when she becomes head of the science division at Wolfram & Hart. Arriving for her first day in "Conviction," she asks Wesley, "Have you seen my lab? It's giganimous and I'm in charge. I don't even understand half of what they're doing. There's this machine, six feet tall that makes this noise—woompah, woompah!" Here her cheerful admission of ignorance and nonstandard articulation undercut any status derived from being "in charge." This rejection of status could even be read as another traditionally feminine characteristic. While Fred's new role as professional scientist is visually coded by the lab coat she often wears during this season, she is rarely shown directing her team of scientists and is more usually seen working alone or with Knox, or reporting progress to other regular characters. In this way the show has her holding a high-status scientific post, but tends to avoid showing her actively directing the department—a clear contrast to the way Angel assumes the role of CEO and asserts the patriarchal authority that comes with it.

While not having a lab in earlier seasons might undermine Fred's credentials as a scientist, having her working on science outside the lab up to season five allows the show to figure science differently. This kind of science is not the kind that needs a lab, a sequestered environment apart from other people. Donawerth notes that in feminist science fiction the "placing of science in the homes of these people is important symbolically for the authors: the place of science indicates communal responsibility for its outcomes."[16] Similarly, Fred's science practice is located for the most part within Team Angel's "home," and it is part of a cooperative project, indicating that it could be read a more feminist version of science. I explore this notion of feminist science further in the next section.

Shifting to a version of science based in the home could alleviate the more usual division between career and domestic concerns, something that causes problems for professional female scientists. One of the biggest problems facing real female scientists is balancing career and family.[17] The focus on romance in most popular forms helps avoid this major obstacle, since protagonists tend to be single. In her survey, Steinke notes, "Most of the female scientists and engineers were single, and if they were married or later married in the films, most did not have children. Few films presented depictions of female scientists and engineer primary characters as working mothers."[18] This is generally true for television, too, and perpetuates the notion that scientists are "married to the job." While this kind of devotion has traditionally been an option for male professionals, it is not as readily available to women. "The responsibilities for family caretaking continue to fall disproportionately on women," states Jo Handelsman, writing about recent research on women scientists' experience in the academy.[19]

Even romance is increasingly presented as a problem for women in popular culture, begging the question about "having it all," if not confronting it. Steinke notes that most female scientist or engineer characters in films "were rarely shown compromising their professional positions for romance." Yet romance remains "a dominant theme" in the films that Steinke evaluates and in television and other pop culture representations, too.[20] Arguably romance is more of a problem for female protagonists when they take on traditionally masculine roles or attributes. The more recent female scientists in popular television science fiction are shown to have problems balancing romance and career, though Jadzia Dax does marry Worf in *Star Trek: Deep Space Nine* (only to die in the finale of the same season).

Fred's position vis-à-vis romance is typically both interesting and somewhat contradictory. On a practical level, keeping romance at work with characters such as Gunn and Wesley allows for two things: first, it means that romance and work need not clash but can exist simultaneously; second, it maintains the narrative and tension within the core cast of characters. This is an effective strategy for serial forms that allows the shows to raise the problem of romance for professional women, including scientists, and to use it for narrative effect, but does not force them to resolve it.

Fred's relationship with Gunn succeeded for some time largely because he displayed less anxiety about female independence than did the other men. The end comes, however, when he tries to stop her from taking vengeance on Seidel. As if by chance, Fred's return to institutional science *does* cause a problem for her personal relationships.

Thus, *Angel* presents Fred as a brilliant scientist and shows that choosing science as a profession is neither easy nor straightforward for women, given its traditional construction as male. Additionally, the show indicates how female practitioners might reshape the male field of science, as we shall discover.

A Woman's Touch: Toward a Feminist Science

Before being sent to Pylea, Fred was embarking on a career in theoretical physics. In her work on the development of science, Keller notes "the growing authority of physics, and physicists," and calls physics "the most powerful agent of change to come out of the entire corpus of scientific knowledge."[21] That Fred is a physicist, then, is significant. In choosing physics, she picks a definitively hard science, more traditionally masculine than other branches and also one that seems the most powerful, the most dedicated to exploring and uncovering the secrets of our world. Keller describes her own attraction to theoretical physics: "I saw the promise of touching the world at its most innermost being, a touching made possible by the power of pure thought."[22] This is very close to Fred's desire for knowledge, and we are told in "Supersymmetry" that she "was going to be a history major" but was persuaded otherwise by Professor Seidel's physics class. (Despite her training as a physicist, Fred is involved in science that combines biology, chemistry, physics, and mathematics.) Keller also mentions the way theoretical science is juxtaposed with what is politely never called " 'impure'—is called instead 'applied science,' or often, more simply, technology or engineering."[23] The first departure from traditional science disciplines, then, is that Fred is an engineer as well as a theoretical physicist. Her scientific knowledge is applied in the world, as when she builds a spring-loaded battle-ax "designed for serious to fatal wounding, if not outright decapitation," just in case "you had to do battle with your arms cut off" ("Fredless").

Yet Fred upholds the traditional notion of science as a rational and logical (masculine) approach, particularly in contrast with male characters, who are frequently aligned with magic and the supernatural. This is not a new way of presenting female scientists on television, and in *The X-Files* the FBI agent and scientist Dana Scully is paired with Fox Mulder in a reversal of roles that plays on these binaries. In Linda Badley's description, "Scully, the skeptic, stands for the rational-empiricist worldview of male science; Mulder stands for non-rational, intuitive ways of knowing often designated as feminine and subversive." Badley suggests that creator Chris Carter "empowered" Scully "to an unusual degree, giving her the authority, the language, and the tools associated with male-dominated institutions, including medicine."[24] Like Scully, Fred can be seen as initially representing "masculine" science or rationality, compared with *Angel's* feminized, intuitive male characters.

The intellectuals Fred and Wesley are often compared in this way. Like Daniel Jackson in *Stargate SG-1*, Wesley functions as a kind of universal translator, working out demon languages and cultures. This work puts him in the traditionally feminine role of communicator and definitely within the soft sciences, though this role is offset by his transformation into James Bond-style action man and dark hero.[25] Conversely, Fred operates in the "masculine" field of physics, but this role is offset by giving her overtly "feminine" characteristics. Wesley's background and family history with the Watcher's Council make him part of and heir to a patriarchal tradition (even if he apparently rejects it), while, as a female scientist, Fred remains apart from as well as a part of her chosen field.

Badley argues that women scientist characters are often split, and that since Scully is "a career scientist (an imitation man) who is secondarily a woman, she is characterized as divided against her 'feminine' self."[26] As I have already pointed out in relation to speech and language, *Angel* does assign Fred both "masculine" and "feminine" traits. These are not as obviously conflicting as they appear to be in Scully. Fred seems unconcerned with traditional femininity, but the show assigns visibly "feminine" attributes to her in terms of body and appearance (see below). It also develops a more female approach to science through her character.

Despite her traditional science training, Fred is different from other male scientists. In *Angel*'s parent show, *Buffy*, (female) mysticism and magic was often valorized over (male) use of science and technology, especially technological weapons. Thus, a "bad" female scientist, such as Maggie Walsh in *Buffy*, relies on a traditional ("masculine") approach to science and works with the military, while "good" characters, such as Willow or Jenny Calendar, embrace both technology and magic. *Angel* seems to follow suit in an early episode, "Happy Anniversary," which presents a brilliant physics graduate student who nearly causes the world to end. Angel calls him a "little madman bent on destroying the universe" and later simply a "mad scientist." At the end of the episode, the student tells Angel, "I had *no* idea I was putting the whole world in danger," a clear indication that to him his physics theory might be feasibly put into practice, but he has not really considered the consequences of doing so. Keller has noted a similar dissociation of theory and application in the recent history of physics.[27] Likewise in "Conviction," the Wolfram & Hart scientist Knox maintains, "I just mix the potions," and the unfolding plot involves a biological weapon designed by the science division for a client. These male scientists show a disregard for what Donawerth identifies as the "relational" or "holistic" aspects of science imagined by women[28] or the implied responsibility that "a sense of inclusiveness and contextuality as cognitive frameworks and modes of perceiving and understanding the world" might afford.[29] When Fred challenges Knox's attitude in "Conviction," it signals that she does not view science as purely theoretical, as having no consequences outside the lab.

In fact, Fred largely abandons traditional science for demonology when she becomes part of Team Angel. Donawerth notes that science fiction written by women often involves "revised definitions and discourse of science, . . . a conception of human's relation to nature as partnership not domination, and an ideal of science as subjective, relational, holistic, and complex."[30] Fred's experience of interdimensional portals forces her to accept that the world is different than standard science suggests and leads to her breakthrough in string theory—an example of what Donawerth terms "subjective" science. Thus, Fred follows a route similar to that of Scully in *The X-Files*, since, as Lisa Parks notes, Scully's "repeated physical contact with monstrous objects . . . prompts her to incorporate 'nonscientific' knowledge into her practice."[31] Fred's pursuit of demonology as a science similarly challenges and revises the definition of what science is.

Furthermore, Fred's methods are not the traditional methods of male science. Science is often seen as pursuing objective truths about the world. Yet this is a social construction: Science practice must be affected by its practitioners and by their point of view and experience; indeed this is *why* it came to be thought of as a male province. The two are now apparently inextricably linked, as Ruth Bleier points out: "This objective, value-free stance is precisely what our culture claims to be *the* characteristic both of the male mind and science." Thus science is seen as a particular type of learning or exploration, as a particular approach to solving problems or observing phenomena. In Bleier's description, science "is the male intellect: the active, knowing subject; its relationship to nature—the passive object of knowledge, the untamed—is one of manipulation, control, and domination."[32] This notion of science as a mode of control and domination informs the presentation of previous scientists featured on *Angel* and *Buffy*, especially in "Happy Anniversary."

So if there were more women in science, would this approach remain the same? In what ways might women do science differently? Is there such a thing as feminist science? Bleier notes, "Women's relationships to knowledge, to objects of study and knowing, [are] more usually ones of mutuality rather than invasion or dominance." Keller's biography of the geneticist Barbara McClintock has been influential in finding ways to articulate a more female version of science. Keller reported that McClintock worked with "a feeling for the organism" rather than with a desire to control and dominate. This leads to the notion that science can be "not the power to manipulate, but empowerment—the kind of power that results from an understanding of the world around us, that simultaneously reflects and affirms our connection to that world." That is, a female approach to science might be one that situates science *in* the world, as opposed to standing apart *from* it—a science not necessarily tucked away in labs but acting in the community, like Fred's science for Team Angel.[33]

One example of Fred adopting a "female" approach to science happens in season three: when she is on the verge of returning to Texas with her parents, she works out the reason for a demon attack by connecting the chain of evidence (crystallizing demon blood, a decapitated Durslar demon, and bug demons). Her realization that the bug demons laid eggs in the Durslar demon's head and are simply trying to retrieve their young allows the team to avoid further conflict. When she works out the answer, she compares her own situation (reaffirming family ties) with that of the bug demons. She develops "a feeling for the organism," finding the solution by empathizing with, not isolating, what she observes and by situating it in context, in relation to its surroundings.

Yet this reshaping of science can itself be problematic since it is based on ideas of difference that potentially reinforce gender binaries. Linda Birke discusses how in the late nineteenth century the "notion of a special female nature, or even superiority, was particularly prevalent" and how it included "what women saw as their better qualities (such as nurturance or moral rectitude)."[34] Bonnie J. Dow identifies a growing interest in difference during the conservative 1980s, noting, " 'Woman's difference' became a hot topic in mainstream media . . . as books and articles appeared in a variety of arenas arguing for the recognition of women's special qualities."[35] The problem, as in the nineteenth century, is, "Although difference feminism may advocate the extension of women's qualities from the private sphere to the public sphere, it further naturalizes women's responsibilities in the private sphere."[36] It does not matter whether those espousing difference present it as natural or inherent (as in the nineteenth century) or as something learned (social). Simply suggesting that women have special or different qualities tends to reinforce those qualities *as* feminine. In popular culture representations, this is particularly the case, since these usually rely on generic and narrative conventions and recognizable types.

The way these conventions relate to gender can mean that, in some instances, it is even possible to interpret the same aspect of a character in contradictory ways. Fred's quest for knowledge, for example, is established as a driving force central to her identity as a scientist (i.e., a traditionally masculine trait). This characteristic infuses her eulogy, delivered by Wesley: "How things work, what makes them special. She was always searching for what other people couldn't see. She was just curious" ("Shells"). Yet, curiosity is arguably used here with feminine associations, bringing to mind Pandora's box. Fred's curiosity ultimately gets her killed, and Knox relies on it in his plan to resurrect Illyria.[37] This highlights the way Fred's representation as a scientist vacillates between masculine and feminine identifiers.

While Fred's precocious intellect did not initially seem matched with social maturity (after all, Steinke would probably categorize her as nerdy and antisocial), in season five, with Cordelia (the only other female member of Team Angel) gone, she exhibits previously hidden depths. When she is called to Angel's office in "Hellbound" for a discussion about going eight thousand dollars over her budget for the quarter, Fred fights back, suggesting that he is letting personal feelings get in the way of his job (a charge more usually leveled at women). To the suggestion that Spike is manipulating her, she replies, "I know he's been playing me. . . . I'm not some idiot school girl with a crush," and forcefully concludes that their purpose in coming to Wolfram & Hart should be about using its resources to do "what's right, remember?" Thus Fred not only overturns her apparent ivory-tower naïveté but also begins to take on Cordelia's role of conscience or moral centre, in a way that extrapolates her more ethical view of science. Harrison notes that even on the point of death Fred calls for a reevaluation of the team's mission.[38]

Despite her new role as head of the science division, Fred's representation shifts subtly from science and smarts to morality and heart—qualities often considered to be specifically female. After her death, Spike remarks to Illyria, "You may not think you're as powerful as you were, Highness, but looking like Fred, for some of us . . . it's the most devastating power you have" ("Power Play"), thus identifying her power as emotional rather than intellectual. That this transition to emotional power is most evident when Fred is visibly a professional scientist is part of what I perceive as the show's balancing act, countering male science with female emotion. Throughout *Angel*, any sense of Fred's scientific expertise as masculine is offset by more traditionally feminine qualities, especially in terms of her appearance and body.

Serious Girl Spectacles: Can Women Embody Science?

While it presents Fred as a brilliant scientist, *Angel* also consistently feminizes her, emphasizing her body and its appearance as much as her intellectual strength.

This section examines how popular forms, and especially the conventions of genre, can work against an attempt to subvert binary oppositions of gender. When science and the female come together in one character, certain issues arise, especially in genres that emphasize the body. Badley describes *The X-Files'* Scully as "the necessary Flesh to Mulder's (and Carter's) Word,"[39] reading her as an embodiment of "female" nature. Parks suggests that Scully's "feminized body becomes the site through which scientific, rational technological, and legal discourses are articulated and negotiated."[40] Similarly, Fred embodies many contradictions as a woman scientist, especially given traditional gendering of intellect, emotion, and action. Perhaps women *can* embody science, but, apparently, traditional notions of femininity must be embodied at the same time.

The persistent gendering of science as male means that the physical appearance of female scientists is a contentious issue, and popular culture representations have ranged from frumpy to sexy in an attempt to negotiate this uncertain ground. In today's postfeminist, postmodern climate, independent young women no longer need to prove their independence by rejecting traditionally feminine modes of dress and appearance. As part of her analysis of film representations, Steinke notes that movies "often emphasized the femininity of the featured female scientists and engineers, but they did not necessarily . . . urge conformity to traditional stereotypes of women."[41] However, given the way her character moves between masculine and feminine poles, Fred's girlish appearance and manner often seem designed to offset her "masculine" scientific mind, as is clear in Spike's lines from "Just Rewards": "The Hows, the What Ifs, that's your cup of tea. You figure things out *in that cute little noggin of yours*" (emphasis added).

Furthermore, when Spike remarks on Fred's "serious girl spectacles" in "Unleashed," the show self-consciously points to the tactic of presenting female scientists simply by putting spectacles on conventionally attractive female actors. Indeed, during her analysis of female scientists in film, Steinke notes, "Many of these roles were performed by young, popular, and glamorous Hollywood actresses."[42] The creators of *The X-Files* argued with the network about the casting of Gillian Anderson as Scully when the network wanted someone "taller, leggier, and bustier."[43] Joss Whedon has similar opinions about the casting of Willow in *Buffy*, as David Lavery explains: "Whedon wanted a truly ensemble cast exhibiting a wide range of looks and types; the network wanted a 'supermodel in horn rims' to play Willow."[44]

Fred is not quite a "supermodel in horn rims," and she does not always wear her spectacles. Yet, despite a change to her wardrobe in season five, she is feminized through her appearance, as well as through romance. Her clothes initially tend to be body-hugging but boyish T-shirts and jeans or miniskirts, with the occasional sundress, and Harrison describes this look as "girlish and wholesome."[45] Although she has a sexual relationship with Gunn, Fred's later liaison with Wesley is presented as more about "wholesome" romantic love than physical attraction. Wesley's long-standing crush on Fred often seems designed to say more about his character than hers, though it does make her the object of conventional romantic interest. As already indicated, unresolved romance can be a key narrative drive for serial television. In season five, it appears that they may finally achieve happiness, but Wesley gets together with Fred (in the final scene of "Smile Time"), only to have her die in his arms—the most problematic representation of her that the show offers ("A Hole in the World," the very next episode), and one that undercuts her presentation as a scientist.

Badley notes of *The X-Files* that sex "is deferred, shifted from skin shows to the interiors of the body, to the deep truths Scully both seeks and (increasingly) represents."[46] In a similar fashion, Fred's sexuality is rarely emphasized on screen. This might be evidence of her intellectual rather than physical nature, but Wesley, *Angel*'s other intellectual, has an explicitly sexual fling with Lilah. This is clearly part of Wesley's "dark side," and, in a similar fashion, downplaying Fred's sexuality works to construct her as moral and good; sexuality is displaced onto idealized romance, allowing Fred to symbolize (female) virtue. Wesley's constant romantic longing for her is in direct contrast to his intensely physical relationship with Lilah, and, together with the way in which Lilah is presented as, at best, amoral, it serves to enhance the opposition of bad sexuality versus good romance.[47] Fred becomes a kind of ideal female figure to Wesley, and then to other male characters, as she increasingly represents the mission or heart of Team Angel, rather than science or intellect.

As part of this idealization, her traditionally feminine characteristics, such as emotion or physical weakness (as opposed to intellectual strength), are reinforced. While Fred's mind may be capable of excelling in science, her feminized body has limited success in another typically male field: action. In her analysis of women scientists in film, Steinke counts more primary characters in action-adventure movies than in any other genre.[48] The increasing visibility of female action heroes in popular culture has been well documented, and this element of action brings yet another facet to the characterization of female scientists. Arguably, the female characters on *Angel* get less action than the male characters, but unlike Wesley, whose bookish character undergoes a gradual transformation into the stubble-jawed action man of later seasons, Fred is established early on as practical and resourceful. She survives in Pylea, developing practical skills by necessity and in the field. As she later tells Professor Seidel, "Five years of pain and suffering in a hell dimension will make a girl capable of a lot of things" ("Supersymmetry")—though this can also be seen as an acceptable excuse for her action abilities.

Thus the flashback of Fred leaving her Texas home for Los Angeles in "A Hole in the World" shows a character whom viewers have never actually known. Apparently adhering to the stereotype of the nerdy scientist, she tells her mother, "I'll be careful. I'll even be dull, boring, cross my heart," but the scene cuts to present-day Fred in the sewers fighting monsters with a flamethrower. This is the Fred we know, the one who tells Angel that she dumped bodies over a cliff in "There's No Place Like Plrtz Glrb" and who is competent enough to demonstrate hi-tech weaponry to an arms dealer in "Lineage."

Yet in "The Magic Bullet," she admits to Angel, "I've been so alone and scared. I'm not like you, not a champion." To be called a champion seems to require supernatural strength, such as Angel's vampirism, or Cordelia's transformation into a half-demon. *Angel* presents ordinary people as well as superheroes fighting the good fight, and while neither Wesley nor Gunn has any superpowers, both have trained to fight demons and vampires. As a result, emphasis is placed on their physical prowess (in Wesley's case, on its development). It is ironic that Amy Acker, who plays Fred, commented early on about her character, "I think she'll get to fight a lot. I've studied combat, and I think that's part of why they wanted me."[49] Fred does get to fight physically as well as intellectually, but Acker's combat skills are not fully exploited until the advent of Illyria.

Fred's relation to action is further complicated in *Angel* by her recurrent positioning as the damsel in distress, the tried-and-tested fem-jep (woman-in-jeopardy) scenario (a complaint also made about Scully's role in *The X-Files*). Taking on the traditionally male role of scientist does not mean that Fred avoids other stereotypical female roles. On the contrary, while her rescue from Pylea is less straightforward than it might seem, the presentation of her difficulty in adjusting back to Los Angeles life tends to emphasize instability and vulnerability rather than survival instincts. Her first words to Angel in "Through the Looking Glass," "Handsome man, saved me from the monsters," cast a long shadow and position Fred in particular gendered ways. (While she consistently refers to Angel saving her, no character ever points out that she saved him, too.)

Fred subsequently acknowledges that waiting to be rescued is not a viable strategy ("Fredless"), and thereafter, she struggles to become more independent. As she matures, she begins to complain about the way her male coworkers cast her in a passive role. When the operation with the arms dealer goes wrong in "Lineage" and Wesley uses two guns, John Woo style, she comments wryly, "Yes, thank you, Wesley, I'd love a gun." Later in the same episode, after Wesley feels guilty that she was wounded, she asks, "Do you realize how patronizing that sounds? *Protecting* me?" Even close to death, Fred insists, "I am not the damsel in distress, I am not some case" ("A Hole in the World").

The crux of this somewhat paradoxical representation is the male characters' perceptions, especially Angel's. In "Lineage" he takes Wesley to task for putting Fred in danger. His words, "We found her bleeding to death on the ground," call into play the other women in his past—Buffy, Darla, Cordelia, even Lilah (compare Mulder's angst over his lost sister in *The X-Files*). Despite Angel's predilection for independent women, so strong is his perception of female as victim that his comments cause Wesley to change *his* notion of what happened. When Knox reveals that he engineered Illyria's return and thus Fred's death, he tells Gunn, "I don't just care about Fred, I practically worship it." He explains, "I chose Fred because I love her" ("A Hole in the World"). In this way, he constructs Fred as an idealized figure, literally intending to worship her as a god when he resurrects Illyria. As a "baddie" responsible for the death of a regular character, Knox is condemned for doing this, but most male characters share his idealization.

Fred articulates the tendency to align femininity and goodness in "Supersymmetry": "Angel and Gunn want me to be all sweetness and light. Cute little Fred, she'll turn the other cheek like a good girl." It even ends her relationship with Gunn. While she sees vengeance as something that will empower her, Gunn sees it as manipulating her: "Don't let him do this to you." Yet by killing Seidel himself in order to prevent Fred from carrying the responsibility for his murder (protecting her moral purity), Gunn removes her agency, and their relationship soon peters out. *Angel* works to present Fred as a brilliant scientist with practical skills, and her position as damsel requiring protection is a visible construction of her male coworkers rather than a position upheld by the show.

One reason key characters insist on seeing her as a "girl" who needs shielding from the big, bad world may be that her body is both gendered and idealized in terms of size. Susan Bordo has noted that slenderness is overdetermined "as a contemporary ideal of specifically *female* attractiveness."[50] Fred is so slender that Lilah calls her "the Texas twig" ("Apocalypse, Nowish"), but in a culture of dieting and eating disorders, the show is careful to point out that she has a healthy appetite.[51] There are various possible readings of this slenderness. Bordo observes that "the degree to which slenderness carries connotations of fragility, defenselessness, and lack of power over against a decisive male occupation of social space is dramatically represented;"[52] in many cultural images and in almost every episode of *Angel* the smaller, slender bodies of female characters are juxtaposed with the much larger, bulkier bodies of male ones (something *Buffy* often worked against). Paired with Fred's nature as an intellectual, it is easy to read this as indicating a physical weakness that requires (male) protection. Thus for her, as with Scully, being a female scientist "does not free her from gendered embodiment; instead she becomes hyper-embodied in forms that reinstate femininity."[53] Her physical size and costuming contribute to this "hyper-embodiment" of (weak) femininity, in direct contrast to her presentation as a powerful, technology-wielding scientist.

But, as Bordo observes, slenderness can also be read as a form of power.[54] She notes that as far back as the 1920s, being slim was seen by some women as "not so much the containment of female desire, as its liberation from a domestic, reproductive destiny,"[55] a rejection of traditional feminine roles, in other words, and one that could be read as in keeping with Fred's pursuit of science. Intellectual Fred apparently remains in control of her body, right up to the point that it is taken over by a supernatural force. The ancient god-king Illyria infects her and literally erupts from within to take over her body. This transformation is interesting in terms of body image, and both Bronwen Calvert and Stacey Abbott point out that Illyria is ambiguously gendered: It is always referred to as a god or a god-king, and it is not clear whether its previous form was gendered.[56]

In addition, Calvert notes that Fred's death continues a theme related specifically to *Angel*'s female characters and their bodies, that of "infection and pregnancy."[57] Many female scientists in popular culture undergo some form of possession or bodily control from alien forces, from Jadzia's generally positive relationship with the Dax symbiont (*Star Trek: Deep Space Nine*) to Jean Grey's ambivalent encounter with the Phoenix force (*X-Men* comics), to Fred's death when Illyria takes over. Horror film commentators have often noted the feminizing effect of reproduction and possession, and Angel himself is sometimes in this position. In "Soul Purpose," Fred is the scientific observer to his passive object of study, for example. Yet as Matt Hills and Rebecca Williams note, this is a comedic scene, undercutting or limiting the sense of Angel as feminized victim.[58] The invasion of Cordelia's and then Fred's bodies by alien entities, on the other hand, puts them much more unambiguously in the position of victim.

Women in science have traditionally been defined as objects of study by male scientists, and what happens to Scully, Fred, and other contemporary female scientist characters makes them objects of control and study *as well as* scientific subjects, observers, and seekers of knowledge. They cannot simply embody science, but they have to embody traditional femininity, too. Scully's "masculine" rationality does not prevent her from taking on the typical female role: Parks suggests that the "placement of alien matter within Scully's body constructs her monstrosity through both reproduction and possession" and notes how she "brings science and nature together."[59] Fred's transformation into Illyria (like Cordelia's pregnancy with Jasmine) is both reproduction and possession, and it focuses on the female body as out of control, rather than as embodying the rational control of science. Notably, because of her idealization, Fred's transformation is much less sexualized than Cordelia's and, in keeping with her scientist character, it is medicalized. This offers a striking counterpoint to the sentimental Victorian aspects that Abbott notes in Fred's death scene.[60] She is first sequestered in some kind of hospital room, then she collapses in her own science lab; both scenes show the female body confined, or at least surrounded, by "masculine" science and technology (as similar scenes presented Scully in *The X-Files*). However, her extended death scene finishes in the domestic sphere (also a testament to her "down home" Southern image), complete with stuffed toy rabbit and grieving lover. Both presentations shift the emphasis from active and intellectual qualities to feminized passivity.

Although the manner of her death might undercut Fred's presentation as an outstanding female scientist, it cannot completely erase the positive impression built up over three seasons. Furthermore, the show again deflects the more traditional constructions of gender onto other characters. It is Wesley, Angel, Gunn, Spike, and Lorne, not necessarily the viewer, who seem inclined to remember Fred as another dead woman whom they failed to save. The montage showing her male colleagues coming to terms with her death actually reinforces her as an explorer when it flashes back to her leaving Texas in pursuit of a scientific career ("Shells"). The song "A Place Called Home," which plays over this montage, could, rather than invoking the typically feminine domestic, indicate that as a woman scientist she needs an alternative home, a place to develop her version of science without encountering the hostility found in other, more traditional environments. Fred finds this alternative home with Team Angel. As a valued colleague she achieves a high-status professional role and continues to reshape science until her death.

Successful Experiments?

The increasing number of real women working in science, coupled with feminist challenges to its historical construction, have undoubtedly affected representations of women scientists on television, though these remain limited to some extent by the constraints of the popular (especially romance) and of generic conventions (action, science fiction, horror). These constraints often seem to mitigate any attempt to destabilize gender and other binaries; in the case of female scientists, the limits could work against a completely successful reshaping of male science.

While *Angel* presents Fred as an intellectual scientist and the most brilliant character on the show, it does not altogether abandon gendered science since it stresses Fred's traditional female virtues. The moral purpose of Team Angel and Fred's role in recalling that mission add to her increasingly emphasized position as idealized female or moral guardian as well as brilliant but nerdy scientist. Because *Angel* deals explicitly with morality, this aspect of Fred's representation may be more obvious and more developed than in other female scientist characters, but since other television female scientists tend to work within "good" or utopian organizations (often with a peace-keeping or law-and-order function), this positions them as upholding morality.

Although Fred shares key aspects with other female scientists in television, *Angel* attempts to negotiate difficult territory by owning up to, even highlighting, some of the problems in bringing women and science together. Intellect, career, appearance, and relationships are all explored. Yet the obstacles facing real women in science tend to be merely acknowledged rather than resolved, and the embodiment of female scientist characters like Fred often contradicts their construction as objective, technology-using, scientific explorers. The tensions here demonstrate the difficulties of making a brilliant woman scientist character fit into a popular television show, with prerequi-sites that include romance and action. As experienced viewers, however, we know that a prime-time network television show can only go so far in producing challenging new versions of gender.

Angel manages to present its brilliant female scientist relatively successfully in the face of these limitations, because it plays stereotypes and conventions against one another. It draws on a mixture of genres, and where these brush up against one another is often where gender roles come under most scrutiny. As a female scientist, Fred is a hybrid of traditionally masculine and feminine qualities, and the contradictions that arise from this fact help make her an engaging character. In effect, *Angel* negotiates science and gender by employing both traditional and contemporary ideas about them. Yet the show does not endorse one particular view, and more traditional notions about women and science tend to be assigned to other characters, demon-strating how deeply rooted assumptions about these can be, but not closing down alternatives.

Both real and fictional female scientists continue to struggle against ingrained ideas about what women are and what science is. Reshaping traditional notions of male science is part of the project of feminist science. The first step in that project was to recognize the ways in which science has been constructed in gendered terms, to recognize male science as a social discourse. Fred and other similar characters demon-strate this and go some way toward reshaping science by being brilliant women who hold key positions in their respective teams, and who are much more than just "imitation men" or "supermodels in horn rims." She clearly indicates what the limitations of popular representations currently are; indeed, *Angel* self-consciously plays with vari-ous stereotypes to highlight these limitations. Characters like Fred break new ground for those coming after, and I look forward to seeing how future female scientists on television wear their lab coats and lipstick.

Notes

1. Some have claimed that science fiction's direct engagement with science as a discourse makes it a unique genre. See Justine Larbalestier, *The Battle of the Sexes in Science Fiction* (Middletown, CT: Wesleyan University Press, 2002), 8; and Brian Attebery, *Decoding Gender in Science Fiction* (New York and London: Routledge, 2002), 1.
2. Jane Donawerth, *Frankenstein's Daughters: Women Writing Science Fiction* (New York: Syracuse University Press, 1997), 1.

3. Marina Benjamin, ed., *Science and Sensibility: Gender and Scientific Enquiry, 1780–1945* (Cambridge, MA: Blackwell, 1991), 3.
4. Benjamin, 3.
5. Robin Roberts, "The Woman Scientist in *Star Trek: Voyager*," in *Future Females, The Next Generation*, ed. Marleen Barr (Lanham, MD: Rowman & Littlefield, 2000), 280.
6. *Angel*, created by Joss Whedon and David Greenwalt, Mutant Enemy Inc./Kuzui Enterprises/Sandollar Television/20th Century Fox Television/David Greenwalt Productions, 1999–2004.
7. "The Changing Representation of Women in Science and Engineering," Association for Women in Science, 13 September 2005, http://awis.org/statistics/ Rep_of_Women_in_ S&E.pdf.
8. "The Bayer Facts of Science Education IV—By Gender, 1998," Association for Women in Science, 13 September 2005, http://www.awis.org/resource/statistics/Bayer_Facts.html. (Accessed 13 September 2005).
9. "Women 'Take Back Seat' in Science," *BBC News*, 20 August 2005, http:// news.bbc.co.uk/go/pr/fr/-/2/hi/science/nature/4163248.stm (Accessed 13 September 2005).
10. Evelyn Fox Keller, *Secrets of Life, Secrets of Death: Essays on Language, Gender and Science* (New York: Routledge, 1992), 23.
11. Jocelyn Steinke, "Cultural Representations of Gender and Science: Portrayals of Female Scientists and Engineers in Popular Film," *Science Communication* 27.1 (2005): 42.
12. The Heisenberg compensator is an in-joke, of course, playing on the fact that the transporter works in contravention of Heisenberg's Uncertainty Principle.
13. Janine R. Harrison, "Gender Politics in *Angel*: Traditional vs. Non-Traditional Corporate Climates," in *Reading Angel: The TV Spin-off with a Soul*, ed. Stacey Abbott (London: I. B. Tauris, 2005), 129. Fred also speaks in a high register, making her sound girlish; Illyria, played by the same actor, speaks very differently (thanks to Bronwen Calvert for pointing this out).
14. The episode is written by two women, Elizabeth Craft and Sarah Fain.
15. Harrison, 118, 120, 125–126.
16. Donawerth, 29.
17. See "Women 'Take Back Seat,'" and Alison Schneider, "Female Scientists Turn Their Backs on Jobs at Research Universities," *Chronicle of Higher Education*, 18 August 2000, http://chronicle.com/free/v46/i50/50a01201.htm (Accessed 13 September 2005).
18. Steinke, 54.
19. Quoted in "Women 'Take Back Seat.'"
20. Both Steinke, 53.
21. Keller, 42, 76.
22. Keller, 78.
23. Keller, 78.
24. Linda Badley, "Scully Hits the Glass Ceiling: Postmodernism, Postfeminism, Posthumanism, and *The X-Files*," in *Fantasy Girls: Gender in the New Universe of Science Fiction and Fantasy Television*, ed. Elyce Rae Helford (Lanham, MD: Rowman & Littlefield, 2000), 63, 61.
25. In a departure from this representation, "Provider" mentions Wesley's "web articles on DNA fusion comparisons in Tri-ped demon populations" as proof of his intellect. However, in this episode Fred is judged more intelligent by the Nahdrah. Wesley is the only member of Team Angel who can "translate" or understand Fred's science, as demonstrated in "Supersymmetry." Yet he is also increasingly associated with magic, another aspect that potentially feminizes him (thanks to Stacey Abbott for this last observation).
26. Badley, 68.

27. Keller, 84, discusses the atomic bomb in particular.

28. Donawerth, 26.

29. Ruth Bleier, *Science and Gender: A Critique of Biology and Its Theories on Women* (New York: Pergamon Press, 1984), 201.

30. Donawerth, 26.

31. Lisa Parks, "Special Agent or Monstrosity? Finding the Feminine in *The X-Files*," in *"Deny All Knowledge": Reading The X-Files*, ed. David Lavery, Angela Hague, and Marla Cartwright (Syracuse, NY: Syracuse University Press, 1996), 125.

32. Bleier, 4, 196.

33. Bleier, 201; Keller, 32; Keller in Donawerth, 25.

34. Linda Birke, " 'Life' as We Have Known It: Feminism and the Biology of Gender," in Benjamin, *Science and Sensibility*, 251.

35. Bonnie J. Dow, *Prime-Time Feminism: Television, Media Culture, and the Women's Movement since 1970* (Philadelphia: University of Pennsylvania Press, 1996), 168.

36. Dow, 170.

37. Thanks to Stacey Abbott for this insight about Knox.

38. Harrison, 130.

39. Badley, 72.

40. Parks, 122.

41. Steinke, 53.

42. Steinke, 53. The youthfulness of such characters is also an issue, and, arguably, such young women would not have the experience or the training to be brilliant and respected scientists. *Angel* dodges the issue by implying that Fred is a genius.

43. Gillian Anderson in Sherrie A. Inness, *Tough Girls: Women Warriors and Wonder Women in Popular Culture* (Philadelphia: University of Pennsylvania Press, 1999), 96.

44. David Lavery, " 'Emotional Resonance and Rocket Launchers': Joss Whedon's Commentaries on the *Buffy the Vampire Slayer* DVDs and Television Creativity," *Slayage: The International Online Journal of Buffy Studies* 6 (2002): 15, http://www.slayage.tv/essays/slayage6/Lavery.htm (Accessed 17 January 2003).

45. Harrison, 129. Harrison notes that at Wolfram & Hart, Fred "wears mature apparel: blouses, skirts, heels and a lab coat." These ensembles simply reflect a different kind of femininity.

46. Badley, 80.

47. Good romance appears to win, although both female characters end up dead. The situation is, of course, rather more complex than this, since, like *Buffy*, *Angel* consistently challenges simplistic notions of morality.

48. Steinke, 39.

49. Amy Acker in Nancy Holder, Jeff Mariotte, and Maryelizabeth Hart, *Angel: The Casefiles* (New York: Pocket Books, 2002), 367.

50. Susan Bordo, "Reading the Slender Body," in *Body/Politics: Women and the Discourses of Science*, ed. Mary Jacobus, Evelyn Fox Keller, and Sally Shuttleworth (New York: Routledge, 1990), 101.

51. Even in Pylea, Fred mentions food as a key part of the world she has lost ("Tacos!"), and during her relationship with Gunn, he remarks that he loves watching her eat ("Couplet," see also "Double or Nothing"). In "Conviction," a team exploration of Wolfram & Hart's client files leads Fred to comment, "I think I've lost my appetite—which is kind of a first." In "Spin the Bottle," the show even suggests that slenderness is not always the most feminine body shape. Fred points out that the team (currently under the influence of a memory spell) do not look like the teenagers that they believe themselves to be, and

Cordelia notes that Fred has "filled out even more," leaving Fred to wistfully conclude that she "ain't gonna."

52. Bordo, 86.
53. Badley, 81.
54. Bordo, 90.
55. Bordo, 103.
56. Bronwen Calvert, "Monstrous Maternity: Motherhood as Demonic Possession in *Angel*" (paper presented at "Bring Your Own Subtext: Social Life, Human Experience and the Works of Joss Whedon" conference, Huddersfield, UK, June–July 2005), 9. Stacey Abbott, "Death Becomes Her: The Afterlife of *Angel*'s Women" (paper presented at "Bring Your Own Subtext: Social Life, Human Experience and the Works of Joss Whedon" conference, Huddersfield, UK, June–July 2005), 7. However, Illyria's "leather queen" outfit (as Spike calls it) feminizes her form and appearance, and Knox talks about seeing her "pressed between the pages of the forbidden texts," noting that his mother assumed he was looking at porn ("Shells").
57. Calvert, 9.
58. Matt Hills and Rebecca Williams, "*Angel*'s Monstrous Mothers and Vampires with Souls: Investigating the Abject in 'Television Horror,' " in *Reading Angel: The TV Spin-off with a Soul*, ed. Stacey Abbott (London: I. B. Tauris, 2005), 211.
59. Parks, 133.
60. Abbott, "Death Becomes Her," 6.

CHAPTER 3

"You Can See Things that Other People Can't": Changing Images of the Girl with Glasses, from *Gidget* to *Daria*

Cindy Conaway

Glasses function on television as a type of masquerade. More than most other aspects of costume design, they carry a freight that functions as symbolic shorthand for the entire character. In historic and contemporary mass media, glasses, especially on women, are an indicator of intelligence and the social limits that go with brilliance, and a barrier to sexual availability. Correspondingly, spectacles can serve as an indicator that the character sees more clearly than other characters, and this aspect of the pattern has become more visible in recent years. Fewer television characters wear glasses than their real-life counterparts would suggest they should, in part because most major characters on network television have the raw good looks and the body consciousness to be considered extremely attractive. And that means not wearing glasses.

If the role calls for glasses, it is generally because they are a cultural marker for defining a brilliant character. We seldom see anyone on television read, either for pleasure or for education, for any length of time, in large part because it is not fun or sexy to watch, yet glasses are shorthand to demonstrate that a character does these things. While it is not entirely unusual to see a character who is a doctor, scientist (mad or otherwise), academic, or author wearing glasses, it is remarkable when the character is a teen girl, because teen girls in particular are on the screen to be consumed by the audience. Even a brainy type must be a "hottie" underneath the shapeless clothes she will eventually trade in for those that are more form-fitting, and behind the glasses that will doubtless disappear, just before she gets a boyfriend.

Aside from signifying academic interest, glasses suggest a social cluelessness for these characters. The authors of *The Makeover in Movies* (2005) call them "signifiers of ugliness."[1] Glasses indicate that a female character is plain, flat-chested, uninterested in appearance, inexperienced in the world of romance, and lacking in the social skills that would allow her to recognize these facts and figure out how to become popular and attractive. In many cases, she meets a more conventionally attractive and popular friend who acts as midwife to her rebirth as a "knockout," which allows her, in turn, to become recognizable to the boy she has had her bespectacled eyes on who is often cute but considerably less bright than she. In many cases, her failure to understand that her glasses are holding her back is presented as a psychological problem that needs to be overcome before she can take her place as a "real girl" worthy of a real boy. The removal of her glasses may mean that she sees less clearly, but also that she appears in full relief for the first time.

Even when she returns to glasses, she has already been seen and is, therefore, taken more seriously by her peers and by the object of her affection. As Elizabeth A. Ford and Deborah C. Mitchell observe, "Only beautiful women are visible."[2] The archetypical brainy, bespectacled, nerdy teenage girl who sheds her awkwardness along with her glasses has been a staple of American media for decades. As the country moved from the *Father Knows Best* era in the 1950s through the women's lib generation to today's Third Wave feminism, the archetype itself has evolved, reflecting society's changes. More recently, we have seen the emergence of a new breed of brilliant glasses-wearing girls and women who use their glasses to see more clearly and comment more sharply on the world, and who are even allowed to have a kind of "cool."

Our culture seems to value genius, but on closer reflection, it is seen as frightening, particularly when it is applied to women. The glasses-wearing girl is portrayed as someone who cannot be intimidated into following the rules. This chapter traces the chronological changes that have occurred in society's attitudes to bespectacled girls and women and how the mass media particularly television have depicted them. The first section discusses the cultural history of glasses and how they have been conceived as relating to women's appearance and their intelligence. The next section traces the makeover story of the bespectacled teenage girl, starting with studious and plain glasses-wearing guest stars on shows like *Gidget* and *The Brady Bunch* who are made over by the main characters, and goes on to consider the changing role of the glasses-wearing girl over time and how she becomes a truly intelligent young woman who could find both love and academic success, but has to remove her glasses on the way, as on the television show *Life Goes On*. The final section discusses how more recent brilliant girls, like the glasses-wearing MTV character Daria, avoid being made over and remain happily outside the mainstream, able to see everyone else more clearly.

The Glasses Case

For women, the negative linking of glasses and appearance has been true since glasses were invented in the late 1200s in both northern Italy and China.[3] The use of glasses was originally considered vanity itself, but once their practical value was established, their use spread throughout Europe and, along with aiding the spread of scholarship, they became indicators of intelligence and of fashion. In 1679, one courtier visited

Spain and saw women wearing large glasses but noticed that "they made no use of them when they were really necessary—they only talked when they had them on. . . . It was done to make them look serious."[4] In most parts of Europe, however, women who needed glasses during the Renaissance would not wear them in public because of "vanity. One simply did not admit that one could not see unassisted in public. . . . Vision aids were designed to be pulled out and put away quickly, yet still maintain some semblance of style for the few minutes they were in use."[5] For this reason, women who wanted to be fashionable and to fit into the dominant society were more likely to use monocles or lorgnettes that they could put away than glasses that were constantly on the face. This practice continued through the eighteenth century. Even large lorgnettes were eventually considered vulgar, and by the end of the century they became so small they would be incorporated into other objects such as fans or perfume bottles. In the nineteenth century, fashionable women could still not afford to be seen wearing eyeglasses, and pince-nez were "never truly elegant when worn by women" but were "tolerated on informal occasions by fashionable ladies."[6]

Things did not change much in more modern times. Until the 1920s, glasses designers were still paying little attention to aesthetics. At about the same time that rimless glasses and those framed in tortoiseshell became all the rage, Dorothy Parker published her 1926 poem "News Item," which consisted only of the couplet "Men seldom make passes / At girls who wear glasses."[7] In the 1920s and 1930s, fashion designers took up the cause of making glasses attractive. Although the combination of fashion and glasses "led occasionally to extremes of eccentricity, it made possible the wearing of glasses . . . without embarrassment."[8] This may have been true in real life, but it did not extend to the mass media. Twenty-five years later, "Marilyn Monroe's character Pola Debevoise preferred walking into walls to being seen in glasses in the 1953 movie *How to Marry a Millionaire*."[9] Women who wanted to be seen as attractive by men had reasons for wanting to appear less serious and less brainy, and not wearing glasses was an easy way to start to accomplish this.

Glasses have always connoted brilliance, and brilliance has traditionally been, with few exceptions, associated with masculinity. Women who demonstrated their high intelligence, whether through taking high school offices, university spots, jobs, or awards that many thought should have gone to men, were suspect. Through much of the twentieth century, glasses were an indicator that girls might do just that, and teenage boys reacted by preferring girls without them. For many girls, wearing glasses was a stigma that seemed to ruin their lives. One girl who got her glasses at age twelve said that they "earned me an instant nerd label in the schoolyard and, later on, comments about how great I'd look without them."[10]

Up until the early 1960s, however, people with poor eyesight did not have much choice. They could wear glasses or be visually impaired. Although glass contact lenses had been invented in 1888 and plastic ones in the 1930s, both were uncomfortable for many users and could not be worn for long. However, by 1963 contact lenses became refined to the point that they were a viable alternative to glasses. For teenage girls, choosing to wear glasses became tantamount to a declaration that they did not care about their looks or social standing. It also meant that they were willing to be seen as brilliant, and hence they would give up their ability to attract boys. For many young women who did care about appearance and did not want to be automatically categorized as brainy, contact lenses were a godsend. They took away the dreaded "nerd" stigma.

While there were, doubtless, girls for whom the doffing of glasses revealed just how plain they really were, those with the raw materials could go from ugly duckling to beautiful swan with a trip to the eye doctor. But with the availability of contact lenses came a social weeding-out process. Girls who continued to wear their glasses could be considered socially deficient because they were not taking all the available steps to become as attractive as possible. If all it took was a few minor cosmetic changes for girls to become "hot," why did they not do it? If they did not trade their glasses in for contact lenses, they were likely not interested in their appearance and only worthy objects of desire for the boys lowest on the social totem pole—those bookish types who wore glasses themselves.

This attitude persists today and starts early. Children learn well before their teen years that the bespectacled are perfect objects of scorn. A study published in a 2005 issue of *Review of Optometry* notes: "Preadolescent children who wear glasses . . . are more than one-third more likely to be bullied than other kids. . . . Interestingly, the numbers were the same regardless of social class, gender or the child's visual impairment."[11] Brainy children, many of whom are bespectacled, are perceived as far less socially acceptable or popular than the non-glasses wearers in their schools. This has been, of course, borne out in the media's depiction of teenagers, especially teenage girls. Timothy Shary writes in "The Nerdly Girl and Her Beautiful Sister," which discusses teen movies about smart girl characters, that most movies "suggest to girls that intelligence is a burden more than an asset; more valuable assets . . . are fashion sense, physical beauty, agreeable attitude, and the attainment of a boyfriend."[12] Girls who attend movies and watch television are bombarded with the message that showing off one's brilliance is far less useful than being pretty and that glasses are far from attractive.

Along with glasses as a sure-fire man repellent, however, there is another thread in culture. Glasses on women have been seen as one of many obstacles to sexual availability, along with constrained hair or complicated clothes. Charles Taylor of the online journal *Salon* asks why even the best movies show glasses as a barrier to sex; as he discusses "the bookstore sequence in *The Big Sleep*, one of the sexiest scenes on film. Bogart's Philip Marlowe takes refuge from an afternoon rainstorm in a Los Angeles bookstore and offers a bottle of 'pretty good Rye' to the comely young thing manning the shop." After she closes the store, "Bogart tentatively asks her if she has to . . . and hesitates, indicating her glasses. Turning away, she removes them, lets down her hair and, when she turns back to him, is greeted with a friendly, lascivious '*Hell-lo*.' "[13] The image of the librarian or bookstore clerk with thick glasses and her hair restrained in a bun, letting down her hair for the right guy and becoming a raging nymphomaniac, is endemic in our culture. However, the idea of the prim librarian who becomes naughty implies that if she does not find a man to awaken her sexually she will end up like Donna Reed's Mary in the "alternative" scenario in *It's a Wonderful Life*: frumpy, lonely, and terrified. The message this dichotomy sends to the vision-impaired woman is that she must not wear glasses, but that if she does, they are simply another fashion accessory that can be used to lure a man with the promise of what lies behind them.

Even if she is actually brilliant, popular culture says, she is still just waiting for the right man to waken her from her boring life of the mind.

I've Created a Monster: Glasses Removal as Makeover

Throughout the television era, our culture's ideas about brilliant young women have been reinforced because of the medium's reliance on stereotypes. Owing to the generic similarity of many shows and the consistent messages that television gives about good behavior and bad, right and wrong, and appropriate and inappropriate ways to live, the medium acts not only as a mirror of our culture but also as an influence on it. Messages are constantly repeated until they seem natural. From television's first shows until quite recently, brilliant girls and women were either absent or were taught a lesson early on about minimizing their intelligence. This meant that any female glasses-wearing character was someone who needed to learn these lessons.

Teen television is especially didactic and sends lessons about the right and wrong ways to be a girl. The story of teenage girls on television has, since the earliest programs featuring them, and in many shows up to the present day, been primarily about popularity. Television has always dealt in stereotypes, so it teaches that there are a limited number of ways a girl can act. Viewers who watch shows featuring female teenage characters learn that those who act in appropriately girlish ways have fabulous friends and a cool bad boy to love them. In the 1960s and 1970s, roles for girl characters on television were even more limited than they are now, and there was a narrow view of appropriate girlhood that included not being too sexy or too smart. Traditionally, most television families, including the Cleavers of *Leave It to Beaver*, the Petries of *The Dick Van Dyke Show*, and the Taylors of *The Andy Griffith Show*, had sons. The few young female characters who *were* shown, such as Princess and Kitten of *Father Knows Best*, learned lessons when they tried to overshadow boys in traditionally male arenas like intelligence.

There was no way, in the mid-1960s, that a young woman who wore glasses could possibly be the central character in her own show, because the glasses-wearing stereotypes of the decade could not possibly be perky or feminine enough to meet viewers' expectations. A guest star on *Gidget* (ABC, 1965–1966), however, went through the now-standard transformation.[14] The show only lasted one season but has been in reruns frequently since then. Gidget, played by Sally Field, was not a brainy type herself. Ilana Nash observes that for white baby boomers, "Gidget was arguably the reigning exemplar of the all-American girl."[15] Susan Douglas describes her as "perky," with a sort of femininity that "bridged the polarities of sanctioned masculinity and femininity—it signaled 'assertiveness masquerading as cuteness.' "[16] Teen girls who did not act perky were gender transgressors who needed to be taught a lesson on proper female behavior. The notion of a brilliant girl was considered so intimidating for television viewers, or possibly just so unlikely, that the few such characters were "studious" rather than actively brilliant.

For example, the episode "Gidget's Foreign Policy" introduces a character who takes her schoolwork seriously. Inge (Brooke Bundy) is a Swedish exchange student and "a drudge who carries her own luggage, constantly volunteers to cook and clean, and spends the rest of her time studying."[17] Gidget makes Inge over. She teaches Inge to flirt, and in turn, Inge flirts with all of Gidget's male friends, including her boyfriend, and even her father. "Gidget," Douglas opines, "has created a monster."[18] Inge is taught a lesson by Gidget, who throws a dinner party, at which Gidget becomes self-effacing while Inge acts spoiled. She is taken to task by her own boyfriend, Gunnar, who wants her to act more like Gidget and actually spanks her.

A similar story takes place in a 1973 episode of *The Brady Bunch* that also concerns a bookish, but not necessarily brilliant, character. Even though Jan at one point gets glasses, the Brady girls would never be mistaken for the brainy bunch.[19] They are significantly more interested in popularity and romance than they are in reading, writing, math, or science. However, in the episode "My Fair Opponent," Marcia, the oldest Brady girl, helps a girl train for a competition to be hostess on Banquet Night.[20] Molly is a "wipeout" who hides behind giant cat's-eye glasses, wears an absolutely enormous dress, has her hair in an unfashionable ponytail, and can barely speak to the Brady boys. She demonstrates her interest in literature by crediting her best time at school to the "Readers and Writers Club." Marcia has her remove her glasses and exclaims, "You've got beautiful eyes!" This starts her on a journey of transformation. Molly, predictably, becomes a knockout and begins to rise in the ranks of popularity and power, to the point that she starts becoming more popular than Marcia. Of course, no one can be more popular than a Brady girl. Barry Williams, who played Greg on the show, comments on the episode in his memoir, saying that things "start to boil when Marcia attempts to stop the monster by beating it out for Banquet Night hostess. But when Molly swipes Marcia's brilliant campaign speech, she also swipes the election out from under her."[21] Since it is *The Brady Bunch*, Molly realizes her error and arranges for the girls to be cohostesses.

This is a typical Cinderella story on television shows featuring teenage girls. Gidget and Marcia act as fairy godmothers, and Inge and Molly both have their triumphs until the clock strikes twelve and they must face the consequences of their actions. The message of their stories is that while a girl should attempt to be pretty and popular, it is just as important to be nice. Assertiveness is frowned upon—one should get what one wants through womanly wiles. Braininess is something to be disguised. The glasses-wearing girl who goes for what she wants is "a monster" who needs to change, but only just enough.

A girl who wore glasses in the 1960s and the early 1970s had few role models in popular culture. The few glasses-wearing girls on television in the late 1970s and early 1980s were primarily "nerds" like Patty (Sarah Jessica Parker) from *Square Pegs*, who swore to become popular, but could not, and Lisa Loopner (Gilda Radner) in sketches on *Saturday Night Live*, whose only friend was the even dorkier Todd. Both Patty and Lisa were intelligent and musically talented, but this was overshadowed by their social deficiency. In the 1980s every show with teens had a resident girl book-worm, but, by this time, few wore glasses, and most of these shows had at least one episode that echoed the "monster" story of earlier television eras.

In 1989 there was a seismic shift. A glasses-wearing girl had an important role in the cast of a quality family drama. The show was *Life Goes On* (1989–1993), and it revolved around a family dealing with a son with Down's syndrome. While at first Corky (Chris Burke), the son, was the main character, more viewers were attracted to his sister, the brainy Becca (Kellie Martin). Becca did very well in school and struggled with teen embarrassments and her wish to be part of the popular crowd. In the early seasons of the show, her ability to become popular was hindered both by her brother and by her reputation as "a brain" and inability to measure up to the more conventionally attractive young women. She did not take these indignities without a fight, however. John Leonard of *New York Magazine* called Becca "a wonderful, bespectacled bundle of internal contradictions, of pubescent seething."[22] She fights for what she wants, whether it is respect or a boy, and uses her brilliance to try to get it.

Her glasses were an extremely important part of her makeup and were used by the show to trace her development from outcast to confident young woman. In the first season's opening credit sequence, we see the family in the morning getting ready for school and work. Becca is wearing her red-framed glasses and looks down at her chest and asks, "Where are you guys already?" When we meet her, she is shy, awkward, and unpopular. She pines for football player and Big Man On Campus Tyler Benchfield (Tommy Puett). Everyone knows that a girl who wears glasses cannot "get" him, but this series is different. In the closing episode of the first season, she attends a school dance without her glasses. At the dance, Tyler admits that he likes her and tries to kiss her. In the opening credit sequences of later seasons, we see the glasses on a wig head on Becca's dresser as she, apparently wearing contact lenses, bounds out the door to meet Tyler. Later she meets a different boyfriend, looking glamorous in sunglasses. The removal of Becca's glasses is as sure a sign of sexual maturity as are the "guys." She was a brilliant character who, nonetheless, became popular and attractive to boys.

Unlike earlier incarnations, smart girls could admire her and aspire to be like her, but she still was not an icon of "cool," and it did not mean that glasses-wearing girls had an all-new reputation. A year after *Life Goes On* premiered, *Beverly Hills, 90210* (Fox, 1990–2000) featured Andrea Zuckerman (Gabrielle Carteris), a brainy girl whom the "gang" never noticed until she appeared in a fashion show, sans glasses. The rich kids, however, accepted her only partially, and she never even got the object of her affection, Brandon Walsh (Jason Priestley). While Becca was a new kind of glasses-wearing character, her social success did not extend to the rest of popular culture, and Andrea's story was still a cautionary tale for girl viewers who liked to demonstrate their intelligence.

Visions of Daria

While brainy girls on television in the 1990s and today have had a much easier life than smart girls in earlier television incarnations, there is still a conception that any teenage girl who is engaged in intellectual pursuits is wasting time when she could be dating boys and making friends.[23] But in 1997 the time was right for a more nuanced depiction of a glasses-wearing girl who viewers could appreciate for her brilliance. The bespectacled Daria Morgendorffer (voiced by Tracey Grandstaff) is the high school heroine of MTV's animated series *Daria* (1997–2001). She is one of the few televised smart girls who does not conform to the traditional "remove glasses and instantly become beautiful and popular" story line. In contrast to most of those heroines, she resists the lessons that those around her try to teach her about beauty and appropriate girlhood, and is back to being her own iconoclastic self at the beginning of each episode. Her glasses are a big part of her character. Daria, like other fictional characters through history, uses her glasses purposefully as a mask that separates her from the rest of the world. She also uses them to see more clearly than anyone she knows.

Daria started life on MTV's earlier animated series *Beavis and Butthead* (1993–1997) as an occasionally occurring character who would be amused by the duo's infantile antics. Once on her own show, Daria, who wears a skirt, clunky boots, and big glasses in nearly every episode, is shown as smarter than her peers, teachers, and parents, and almost completely uninterested in popularity. She is content with one good friend, Jane, an artsy girl with a tough Goth look who similarly rejects the vapid image-obsessed society at Lawndale High. One writer calls Daria the teenage girl she wished she had been and describes her as "smart, bitter and animated, a blend of Dorothy Parker, Fran Lebowitz, and Janeane Garofalo, wearing Carrie Donovan's glasses."[24] Daria's command of wordplay, her immunity to societal standards, and yes, her big glasses, make her a real role model for both brilliant girls and brilliant women, who wish they had had as much courage of their convictions as Daria.

The episode "Through a Lens, Darkly" presents Daria's own view of her glasses. Mrs. Morgendorffer is teaching her to drive. With her thick glasses, Daria has poor peripheral vision and nearly hits a dog. Her mother encourages her to get contact lenses, but Daria thinks that her mother has ulterior motives and says, "You think if I get contacts I'll suddenly turn into the homecoming queen."[25] Contact lenses do not fit her persona. As a sardonic outsider, she is reluctant to substitute her spectacles for contacts. She expects that she will experience the sort of scenario she has seen on television and in the movies, in which the ugly duckling removes her glasses and becomes a beautiful swan. Most American girls have read *Seventeen* magazine, which "has been doling out makeover tips to teens for years, [reinforcing] the magic: one good haircut can turn a Plain Jane into a knockout."[26] The same is true for glasses. If her experience is anything like those in the articles in the magazine, suddenly she will become very popular. The cool kids of the school will want to be her friend, and a sexy bad boy will fall in love with her.

Daria has good reason to be concerned about the consequences of removing her glasses. She is surrounded, for the most part, by well-meaning but idiotic characters. Her mother and sister are image-obsessed, her teachers vapid and self-involved, and her peers, save Jane and a few others, idiotic and fixated on popularity. They encourage Daria to wear contact lenses not to enhance her peripheral vision, but as a way of changing her personality and softening her intelligent but sharp demeanor. Her teacher, the hippy dippy and easily distracted Mr. O'Neill, says to her that it is good that she has tried life without her glasses and is taking a positive step by "taking command" of her appearance. When Daria replies, "Actually, I'm not sure that I want an identity based on appearance," he responds, "Of course not. The inner you, that's what's important. I just meant that a revised outer you is an even more confident manifestation of the unchanged inner you . . . the real you . . . the you-ness inside."[27] The idea of the internal becoming external is a major goal of practitioners of the "self-esteem" movement, such as Mr. O'Neill. He believes that if Daria looks less intimidating and displays her intelligence less fiercely, she will demonstrate a more feminine and amiable core that will make other students like her, so she will feel better about herself. The fact that this core barely exists is one of the characteristics that makes her such a groundbreaking heroine.

Bowing to the pressure, Daria finds the contact lenses painful and her vision blurry. However, instead of returning to her glasses, she goes to school with impaired vision. She bumps into walls and people and has to be led around by Jane. Daria ends up hiding in the bathroom, ashamed because, although she considered herself above all that, she caved to societal pressure. But she learns from the experience. Her glasses are actually good and are, in fact, a huge part of her personality. In her words, she "can see things that other people can't."[28] This is a far cry from the girl who has to remove her glasses before she can make an impact. Daria's acceptance of her glasses and her essential self marks a change that could only occur because some important changes had occurred in society.

Many smart girls on television, and in literature and movies, have gone through a makeover that changes their lives, often beginning with the removal of glasses. Once the glasses are removed, the hair is changed, the clothes are changed, and then the girl's life is ultimately changed. Popularity for girls in real life is a different animal. Rachel Simmons writes that it "requires strategy and calculation" and that "the rules change from day to day."[29] Television is more predictable. The fact that Daria's life is not changed by the removal of her glasses is a significant departure from earlier depictions of smart girls on television, and it marks one of the first times viewers could admire a glasses-wearing girl without reservations.

Daria has seen the makeover story and wants no part of it because, she feels, it just might turn her into a "regular girl" who is susceptible to the allure of popularity. She is especially concerned that other people might make her feel as if she had not been measuring up before, when she still had glasses. Yet, at the same time, she is curious about what might happen. Girls grow up with this mythology in popular culture. Although she is fictional, a girl like Daria probably played with the traditional "girl" toys as a younger child and has probably seen movies like *The Big Sleep* and spent hours and hours watching television shows like *Gidget* and *The Brady Bunch*. The typical American girl has probably "seen at least one version of Cinderella, or owned a Cinderella Barbie, or played dress-up Cinderella with her friends. By the time she gets to be a teenager, the conventions of that old tale have become the familiar fabric of her life."[30] Despite her ironic detachment as a teenager, Daria would have been exposed to these trends and would be aware that many of the movies and television shows she has seen "are specifically designed to speak to teens with one thing in mind: attracting the ever-popular, always hunky, brutally hot Prince Charming."[31] Even the girl who considers herself completely immune to peer pressure is bombarded by messages that say romance is the most important thing. No one hears repeated messages that brilliance is valued for girls.

Daria's ability to resist these pressures is influenced, in large part, by the fact that she is animated. In live action shows, viewers see actresses who are already conventionally attractive. Prior to the makeover, a girl character's "before signifiers barely conceal the loveliness beneath. Even when the heroine doesn't acknowledge her beauty. . . . The audience accepts it without question."[32] Since animated characters do not age in the same way as actresses, do not have realistic bodies, and rarely change physically, to the point that they wear the same clothes in every episode, Daria faces different pressures than characters on live-action shows. Kathy Newman calls Daria "an animated girl without a bust line."[33] She can remain consistent in her attitude because she is drawn consistently from episode to episode, wearing her glasses with an intelligent look on her face.

Daria was not the first brilliant glasses-wearing cartoon girl. On Saturday mornings in the late 1960s and early 1970s, animated high school student Velma Dinkley of *Scooby-Doo, Where are You?* (CBS, 1969–1972) joined her four friends—handsome and popular Fred; his girlfriend, the pretty Daphne; Shaggy, a beatnik type; and Scooby-Doo, a talking Great Dane—as they rode around in a van and solved mysteries. Velma had short hair, was much less willowy than the conventionally attractive "Danger Prone Daphne," and wore glasses. She lost her glasses frequently, which provided fodder for the series when her friends had to help her find them while the crook of the week escaped. When the show originally aired, she was not the type of girl that most female viewers wanted to be like. It was not until the 1990s that women's braininess was valued and Velma would be embraced as an example of geek chic.[34] But Daria has been a role model for many smart girls since she first appeared. Unlike Velma, Daria would never have tolerated Daphne's silliness or Shaggy's irresponsibility and would probably have taken control of the whole operation.

Daria also resembles, at least in personality, cartoon girl Lisa Simpson (voiced by Yeardley Smith) of *The Simpsons* (Fox, 1989 to present). Even without the glasses, Lisa conveys the glasses-wearing girl persona. Like Daria, she is at times sarcastic. But Lisa is more of an outsider than Daria, having no Jane of her own. Although she is only eight, she sometimes shares Daria's cynicism, but at other times, is much more likely to be idealistic. Like Daria, Lisa is a product of the postmodern moment, when activism seems to have little result and many people have become complacent. Chris Turner observes that because of this, "Lisa is the most world-weary Simpson, the one with the greatest sense of what's wrong with the world, the one who vacillates between optimism and despair."[35] Lisa frequently takes a stand, even when it makes her unpopular. Although many smart girls and women love her, a 1998 online poll revealed that "Simpsons fans rated Lisa their fourth-favorite character,"[36] behind Homer, Bart, and Ralph. She is not an icon of hip and, in part because she is so young, not necessarily a role model for teen girls.

Daria, however, has inspired an entire subculture of witty, sarcastic girls and women. *Daria* "became a signature show for MTV."[37] Unlike the foolish Beavis and Butthead, who attracted mostly boys with dumb senses of humor, Daria represented a type of fan MTV wanted to attract. Van Toffler, MTV's General Manager at the time the show aired, commented, "[Daria] has the attitude about parents, school, siblings that is common to our audience. She is a good spokesperson for MTV . . . intelligent, but subversive."[38] Many viewers would rather be like Daria and wear their intelligence for all to see than be marginalized like Velma or disliked like Lisa.

Daria was only able to succeed, however, because she came along at the right time, and in part because in this period glasses lost a certain stigma of their own. The rise of geek chic in the early 1990s meant that glasses-wearing acquired a certain cachet. With the rise of the Internet industry, suddenly those who could do knowledge work on computers were wealthy and, therefore, chic. In the wake of this, a few figures became cool despite, or even because of, their glasses. In 1994 the glasses-wearing female singer Lisa Loeb's song "Stay" became a hit after it appeared in the film *Reality Bites*. The culture was finally ready for a glasses-wearing heroine who was almost entirely resistant to the pressure for girls to remove their glasses.

But there is a secondary reason that Daria is an important representative for smart girls. *Daria* was one of the earliest shows in which the main character was a smart girl, and she dealt with the pains of adolescence through a bracing humor, much the way the characters on *Buffy the Vampire Slayer*, which debuted the same year, did. Daria's sarcastic wit and her general air of not caring about anything are in sharp contrast to the earnestness of brainy girls like Becca and Andrea, or Lisa Simpson. This situational shift in the way a smart girl could be portrayed came about because of a major change in culture. Starting in the 1980s, humorists like David Letterman had begun to demonstrate smart humor through ironic detachment. He was transformative because he "replaced the politics of confrontation represented by the satire of such shows as *Saturday Night Live* and *SCTV* with a politics of accommodation, removal, and irony. His ironic stance was increasingly acknowledged as capturing the 'voice' of his generation."[39] One of many comedians who shared Letterman's ironic detachment, along with Ben Stiller, Jerry Seinfeld, and the writers of *The Simpsons*, was the glasses-wearing comedian and actor Janeane Garofalo, who appeared in the Generation X movie *Reality Bites* (1994), in which she and Winona Ryder shared sardonic smart-girl quips. Garofalo's persona was very influential to the writers of *Daria*.[40] In her humorous dating guide *Feel This Book* (written with Ben Stiller), she wrote that considering "the public's regrettable lack of taste, it is incumbent upon you not to fit in."[41] She became the reigning example of geek chic for young women who like to wear a lot of black, make sarcastic comments, and wear large, black-framed glasses.

At graduation, Daria is given the "Diane Fossey Award for Dazzling Academic Achievement in the Face of Near-Total Misanthropy." Her speech echoes Garofalo's tone when Daria says, "High school sucks," but also asks her listeners to "stand firm for what you believe in, until and unless logic and experience prove you wrong; remember, when the emperor looks naked, the emperor is naked; the truth and a lie are not 'sort of the same thing'; and there's no aspect, no facet, no moment of life that can't be improved with pizza."[42]

Like the glasses-wearing Garofalo, Daria is almost entirely immune to the allure of popularity, "lookism," or efforts to change her clothes or hair or to remove her glasses. And a main part of the show involves her commenting on the fact that practically everyone else at school, save Jane, does not see what she sees through her glasses. Daria, writes Kathy Newman, "was verbally disdainful of the corruption, consumerism, and commercialism that surround[s] her."[43] Daria's position as a happy marginal outsider is made clear in the first episode, "Esteemsters," when she is assigned to take a self-esteem class. She meets Jane, who has taken the class six times already, and who says, "I like having low self-esteem. It makes me feel special." Daria suggests that they both simply memorize the answers to the test and be done with the class early. "I don't have low self-esteem," she says. "I have low esteem for everyone else."[44] The girl with glasses recognizes that modern-day buzzwords and programs are a complete waste of time; they simply allow the school to say "We tried," before some student or "trench coat Mafia" comes to school with weapons.

Daria's mother is a corporate lawyer so obsessed with work that she frequently has no time for her daughter, and her father is so traumatized by his childhood and marketing job that he is completely out of touch and easily alarmed. While her sister Quinn is easily excited by perceived slights among her friends in the fashion club, Daria generally stays calm and comments ironically on the absurd doings that surround her every day. For example, in the episode "This Year's Model," practically every other girl at school is absolutely thrilled when a modeling representative comes to visit and offers free modeling classes and a modeling contract for one lucky student. Daria wants no part of it. When asked to remove her glasses, she replies, "I can't take my glasses off. I need them to see scam artists." She sees more clearly than anyone else at school that something is wrong. And it turns out that her corrupt principal has taken kickbacks from both the modeling agency and the military. Although her mother and one of her teachers are against the modeling industry in general, most other people in her life just want to ogle the aspiring models, and Daria is presented as the only one who actually sees what is going on. Her brilliance is translated into perceptiveness.

As a glasses-wearing girl, however, the one thing Daria is still not allowed to have is social skills. She has no more ability to navigate the world of conventional friendship and romance than Gidget's and Marcia's protégés. That last vestige of nerdiness may always cling to the bespectacled girl, no matter how contentedly aloof she may seem. When, in the fourth season, Jane's boyfriend, Tom, decides that he likes Daria better and kisses her, Daria's chosen tactic is avoidance. She refuses to believe that she likes him and does not discuss it with either Tom or Jane. When she and Tom do go out together, people simply refuse to believe that he and Daria are together.

Daria cannot deal with this. As a girl with glasses, the one thing she has always been able to be is inconspicuous. Being the subject of gossip is completely unfamiliar to her and makes her feel *seen* in a way that most people her age, used to behaving in ways that are embarrassing or notable, would not. Although she is still wearing her glasses, she has been unmasked as a girl who has feelings and needs and who, rather than standing by and commenting on the rest of the world, would actually take the action of stabbing her best friend in the back. Yet she still acts as if all of this is happening *to* her and as if she has no control over the situation and her own behavior. One of the cultural markers of being intellectual on television is the inability to have a smooth social life. Daria and Jane take much longer to become friends again (although they do, after a summer apart) than would those caught up in the ever-turning wheels of popularity, in which other teenage girl characters on television live.

Daria and Tom do ultimately break up when he gets into a prestigious college because of his family connection. She is rejected by that school but gets accepted into another that is considered *almost* as good. The breakup is on her terms.[45] She and Jane, who is going off to art school in the same city as Daria, seem to be headed toward a future in which there will be lots of eligible boyfriends for both of them, and from whom they will have their pick. While Daria getting engaged to Tom or both of them going off to the same college might have been a more typical television ending for a popular girl, this is the best possible ending that television offers for the girl with glasses: they do not try a long-distance relationship that will inevitably fail and she does not get dumped (both of which happen to Lane in two separate relationships on *Gilmore Girls*); no one dies (like Jesse on *Life Goes On*); no one gets pregnant (like Andrea on *90210*); and Daria does not have to give up anything. She keeps her glasses on and goes off to a future that, the show is quick to assure us, will be just as successful as if she had been accepted by the slightly more prestigious school.

Framing Glasses

The changing image of the girl with glasses matters because television influences what viewers believe about culture and themselves. Young people, in particular, are susceptible to its messages. Television characters on teen shows live charmed lives. If removing their glasses leads to popularity and romance, many teenage viewers reason that they will also be popular and have romance if they remove theirs. Most recent smart girl characters on television have not even worn glasses. These girls instead experience metaphorical glasses removal, such as Angela's dying her hair "crimson glow" on *My So-Called Life*, Willow's turning from computer hacking to witchcraft on *Buffy the Vampire Slayer*, and Lindsay's wearing a green army jacket and disavowing the "mathletes" on *Freaks and Geeks*.[46] Once they make these changes, they too make new friends, find cool boyfriends, and start to forget the importance of school.

The representation of the glasses-wearing girl on television is improving, although in baby steps. In 2004, the WB show *Everwood* demonstrated the old stereotype when the character of Hannah, a shy girl who liked to write, had to take off her glasses before a boy would see her. However, she referred sarcastically to the traditional makeover story as she did it, making the action into parody. Then, in 2005, Lane Kim of *Gilmore Girls*, who is clearly as sharp as Rory Gilmore, but who chooses to play the drums in a band rather than attend college, removed her glasses, only to have her dim but talented musician boyfriend tell her to put them back on because she was "the first smart girl I've ever gone out with, and the glasses are a big part of that." He was concerned that she had lost "that initial impact. Now people will have to talk to you for a few minutes to figure out that you're smart."[47] Characters like this can give bespectacled girls hope that they can have glasses and romance, too.

Progress like this means that there could some day be a glasses-wearing girl on television who is actually cool from the start, even to her peers. Although the primary characters of many teen shows still comply with the "vapid but pretty" stereotype, some female characters on television have no trouble demonstrating how smart they are, and embrace intellectual pursuits and clever repartee. Most bright girls on teen shows these days speak in a way that indicates not only that they are smart but also that they believe they are smarter than everyone else, though almost none wear glasses. Rory, Paris, and, of course, Lane, of *Gilmore Girls*, and the extremely clever Veronica Mars of her eponymous show, frequently drop allusions to both popular and high culture into ordinary conversation. Yet they are surrounded by friends and love interests.

Their influence has spread to a subculture of real-life girls, inspired in part by Daria, who wear big black-framed glasses and speak in a sarcastic, knowing tone. Ironic detachment may be a defense mechanism, but it is a much smarter one than Molly's enormous dress. Brilliant girls now occupy a niche in high school, and in culture, that they could not in earlier years. Girls like the bespectacled Enid of the comic and movie *Ghost World*, or bloggers like Ana Marie Cox, the creator of *Wonkette*, show that there is a whole world of girls and young women who shop at thrift stores, collect old LPs, read and write for pleasure, comment ironically on the vapid doings of those in power, demonstrate their brilliance without reservation, and wear their glasses with pride.

Notes

1. Elizabeth A. Ford and Deborah C. Mitchell, *The Makeover in Movies* (Jefferson, North Carolina: Mcfarland Press, 2005), 23.
2. Ford and Mitchell, 35.
3. "A Historical Tour of Opthamology," *MRCOphth*, 2000, http://www.mrcophth.com/Historyofophthalmology/spectacles.htm (accessed 17 December 2005).
4. Richard Corson, *Fashions in Eyeglasses* (London: Peter Owen, 1980), 47.
5. Diana Pemberton-Sikes, "The History of Eyeglasses," *The Sideroad*, http://www.sideroad.com/Beauty/history-of-eyeglasses.html (accessed 19 December 2005).
6. Corson, 142.
7. Dorothy Parker, *Enough Rope* (New York: Viking Penguin, 1944), 109.
8. Corson, 199.
9. Pemberton-Sikes.
10. Lisa Tant, "No More Glasses," *Chatelaine* 72. 10 (1999): 76, http://0-search.epnet.com.maurice.bgsu.edu:80/login.aspx?direct=true&db=f5h&an=2356030 (accessed 20 December 2005).
11. *Review of Optometry*, "Kids Who Wear Glasses are Bully Magnets," 142. 5 (2005): 6, http://0-search.epnet.com.maurice.bgsu.edu:80/login.aspx?direct=true&db=aph&an=17177607 (accessed 31 October 2005.)
12. Timothy Shary, "The Nerdly Girl and Her Beautiful Sister," in *Sugar, Spice, and Everything Nice: Cinemas of Girlhood*, ed. Frances Gateward and Murray Pomerance (Detroit: Wayne State University Press, 2002), 236.
13. Charles Taylor, "Sexy Specs," *Salon*, 2002 http://www.salon.com/sex/feature/2002/04/17/glasses/index.html (accessed 14 December 2005.)
14. This episode was not available while this chapter was being written, however, it recently became available on DVD. Although I remembered glasses, surprisingly, Inge does not wear any. However, the fact I mentally filled them in reinforced the ubiquity of glasses in such makeover stories.
15. Ilana Nash, "'Nowhere Else to Go': *Gidget* and the Construction of Adolescent Femininity," *Feminist Media Studies* 2.3 (2002): 342.
16. Nash, citing Douglas, 343.
17. Susan J. Douglas, *Where the Girls Are: Growing Up Female with the Mass Media* (New York: Times Books, 1994), 110.
18. Douglas, 111.
19. The episode in which Jan gets glasses, "The Not So Rose Colored Glasses," involves her taking the wrong bike from the playground. The family concludes that she needs glasses, which she resists because she'll "look positively goofy." The bulk of the episode, however, is concerned with getting a large photo of the family retaken after Jan, not wearing them, rides a bike into it. Unlike a similar episode in which Marcia gets braces on her teeth, or another in which Cindy attempts to rid herself of a lisp, this episode does not focus on Jan's attractiveness to a boy.
20. "My Fair Opponent," *The Brady Bunch*, first broadcast 3 March 1972 by ABC, written by Bernie Kahn and directed by P. Baldwin.

21. Barry Williams and Chris Kreski, *Growing Up Brady: I Was a Teenage Greg* (New York: Harper Perennial, 1992), 278.

22. John Leonard, "Grace Notes," *New York Magazine*, 18 September 1989, 67.

23. My doctoral dissertation is called *Girls Who (Don't) Wear Glasses: The Performativity of Smart Teenage Girls on Television (1990–2006)*. It traces the changes in representations of smart teenage girls on television dramas and what messages they send to girl viewers. Primary subjects are characters on these three shows, as well as *Beverly Hills, 90210* (Fox, 1990–2000), and *Gilmore Girls* (WB, 2000 to 2006; CW, 2006 to present).

24. Anita Gates, "*Daria*: In Praise of the Most Unpopular Girl at Lawndale High," *New York Times*, 16 May 1999, http://www.outpost-daria.com/media_art23.html (accessed 7 February 2006).

25. "Through a Lens Darkly," *Daria*, first broadcast 24 February 1999 by MTV, written by Glenn Eichler and directed by Guy Moore. All quotations taken from transcripts at the Web site Outpost Daria, http://www.outpost-daria.com (accessed 18 January 2006).

26. Ford and Mitchell, 28.

27. Eichler.

28. Eichler.

29. Rachel Simmons, *Odd Girl Out* (New York: Harcourt, 2002), 160.

30. Ford and Mitchell, 65.

31. Ford and Mitchell, 67.

32. Ford and Mitchell, 75.

33. Kathy M. Newman, "Misery Chick: Irony, Alienation and Animation in MTV's *Daria*," in *Prime Time Animation: Television Animation and American Culture*, ed. Carole A. Stabile and Mark Harrison (London: Routledge, 2005), 195.

34. There is currently a Web site devoted to Velma. It is at http://www.velmadinkley.com/ and contains fan fiction, fan art, trivia, and speculation about Velma and the show.

35. Chris Turner, *Planet Simpson: How a Cartoon Masterpiece Defined a Generation* (Cambridge, MA: Da Capo press, 2004), 203.

36. Turner, 191.

37. Newman, 187.

38. Newman, 186.

39. Robert Erler and Bernard Timberg, "Talk Shows," Museum of Broadcast Communications, http://www.museum.tv/archives/etv/T/htmlT/talkshows/talkshows.htm (accessed 10 January 2006).

40. Garofalo was not involved in the show at all; however, she hosted a Daria special, *Behind the Scenes at Daria*, in 2000.

41. Janeane Garofalo and Ben Stiller, *Feel This Book: An Essential Guide To Self-Empowerment, Spiritual Supremacy, and Sexual Satisfaction* (New York: Ballantine Books, 1999), 117.

42. "Is It College Yet?" *Daria*, first broadcast 21 January 2002 by MTV, written by Glenn Eichler and Peggy Nicholl and directed by Karen Disher.

43. Newman, 187.

44. "Esteemsters," *Daria*, first broadcast 3 March 1997 by MTV, written by Glenn Eichler and directed by Ken Kimmelman.

45. The names of the schools are all made up for the show, but it sounds like a Harvard/Yale sort of choice, with her parents' alma mater, where she does not apply, to the distress of her father, as more of a mid-tier school.

46. For more on this topic, see Cindy Conaway, "Cinderella in the High School Hallways: The Place of Smart Girls on Teen TV," *Mid-Atlantic Almanack* (2004): 75–83.

47. "Come Home," *Gilmore Girls*, first broadcast 1 February 2005 by the WB, written by Jessica Queller and directed by Kenny Ortega (transcribed by Kristina Smith for TWIZTV.COM).

CHAPTER 4

"Pretty Smart": Subversive Intelligence in Girl Power Cartoons

Rebecca C. Hains

Who says a girl cannot be pretty and smart at the same time? In girl power cartoons, girls who are both brilliant and beautiful abound. Preteen and teenage girls star as action-adventure cartoon heroines, using their physical strength and keen intellectual abilities to fight crime and save the world. They also succeed academically and socially in school, earning good grades, wearing the latest fashions, enjoying the attention of boys, and sporting enviably perfect hair. Through such depictions, girl power texts offer girls cultural support by suggesting that they can be feminine, intelligent, strong, and empowered—they can have it all. This is a significant change, as earlier cartoons rarely focused on powerful, smart girls. Now, pro-girl cartoons proliferate across children's cultural landscape. After exploring the growth of the girl power movement, this chapter focuses on girl power cartoons' contributions to changing representations of intelligent girls. Girl power is, in part, a response to cultural concerns about adolescent girls' plummeting intelligence, self-esteem, and self-image. The brilliant girls depicted in these cartoons are not victims of this crisis. Instead, they subvert the cultural expectation that girls should avoid displaying their intelligence. The characters model the use of "niceness" as a subversive strategy to make female intelligence palatable. By acting nice, smart girls are also able to positively change the world at large.

"Girl power" became a household term in the late 1990s when it was the rallying cry of the Spice Girls, an all-female pop music group whose devoted preteen fans catapulted it to international stardom. Girl power suggests that girls are strong, smart, and capable of anything, and that playing with femininity can be positive and empowering. As girls embraced the concept of girl power, marketers emblazoned the slogans "Girl power!" and "Girls rule!" upon notebooks, T-shirts, packaging for dolls, and other commodities that appeal to preteens and teenagers. The concept has such appeal that some women also claim girl power. The girl power ethos permeates television shows such as *Buffy the Vampire Slayer* (1997–2003) and movies such as *Legally Blonde* (2001 and 2003), which star feminine yet strong and intelligent heroines.

My first direct encounter with girl power came in 2002, when an episode of Cartoon Network's *The Powerpuff Girls* (1998–2004) caught my attention. I had never watched the cartoon, which had a strong following among both children and adults, but I recognized the wide-eyed superheroes from the stickers, decals, plush dolls, and other kitsch items that my twenty-three-year-old sister and some friends owned. As the episode unfolded, I was surprised by its empowering overtones: The three kindergarten supergirls sought admission to a men's superhero association, and they outperformed the men in every test they were given—strength, speed, and problem-solving. Despite their triumphs, the girls were then denied membership because of the men's overt chauvinism, but by the episode's end, the girls had saved the men from an otherwise unbeatable foe.

The Powerpuff Girls claimed millions of fans in the late 1990s and early 2000s. At its zenith, its viewership was approximately 50 percent male and 50 percent female and comprised roughly 75 percent children and 25 percent adults.[1] It established a $1 billion merchandising empire.[2] Tweens, or preteen girls aged eight to twelve, who are "between" childhood and the teenage years, were an important target audience for the show. Now airing in reruns, *The Powerpuff Girls* is still going strong, and its merchandising enjoys continued success among younger children.

The Emmy Award-winning show paved the way for more girl power action-adventure cartoons, whose heroines are pretty, powerful, and adored by tween girls. These shows include Cartoon Network's *Totally Spies* (2001 to present), *Atomic Betty* (2004 to present), and *The Life and Times of Juniper Lee* (2005 to present); the Disney Channel's *Kim Possible* (2002 to present) and *W.I.T.C.H.* (2005 to present); Nickelodeon's *My Life as a Teenage Robot* (2003 to present); and Fox Television's *Winx Club* (2004 to present). These shows feature lead characters who are intelligent, strong, and independent, and their publicity indicates that they are intended to offer positive role models for girls. For example, Disney's *Kim Possible*'s executive producer, Bob Schooley, claims, "Kim's mix of tenacity, intelligence and heart makes for a very strong female role model for kids."[3] Likewise, Christy Carlson Romano, who voices Kim Possible, often speaks about Kim as an empowering role model for girls. Romano has explained, "She's a teenager, she's a cheerleader, she's perky, and I'm a little like that. . . . [Kim] is brave and is a good role model."[4] Romano also describes how animation changes Kim's role, explaining, "With animation it is great because you can reach a younger audience and it isn't an actual person so they don't have to try to look like her."[5] According to this kind of discourse, girl power cartoons empower girls in ways that other television genres cannot: their roots in animation and fantasy make anything possible.

However, preadolescent girls have not always been an important audience for television programming. In fact, television programmers have often treated girls as second-class citizens. Here's why: programmers target an audience only if certain market conditions are met. From a political economic perspective, the function of the mass media is to deliver viewers to advertisers, who pay large sums of money to advertise their products and services during programming that is viewed by people in their target audience. Targeting audiences is big business in modern capitalist societies. In years past, the very limited number and types of girls' programming made it clear that girls themselves had little "value" in the U.S. economy: they were too inconsequential for the industry to construct a homogenized "girl" audience to deliver to advertisers. Conventional wisdom was that whatever boys would watch, girls would watch, too— but not vice versa. Therefore, for years, boy characters dominated children's television landscape.[6]

But as marketers continued to forage for new audiences to sell to advertisers, they made a "discovery": preadolescent girls are a lucrative market, and marketers have dubbed them "tweens." Tweens now constitute a powerful target audience, and with tween girls' newfound value as consumers and viewers, girl power cartoons and commodities have proliferated, filling the airwaves and shelves across the marketplace.

The mass media now tailor numerous productions to the tastes of the preteen set, such as *The Powerpuff Girls*, Disney's *Kim Possible*, and *Totally Spies*. What appeals to girl viewers? According to Peggy Tally, tweens so eagerly aspire to become teenagers that media targeting them, such as tweenie films, often feature teenagers as their protagonists.[7] In addition to carefully themed films and television shows, companies offer innumerable material culture commodities for tween girls. Girlie kitsch includes clothing, makeup, accessories, Bratz dolls, and electronic gadgets like Tamagotchis that come decorated with hearts and purple swirls. Some of these items are sold under the banner of girl power, featuring slogans like "Girls rule!" Critics have been harsh on this commodification of girl culture and girl power. Ellen Riordan notes that as companies created increasing quantities of girl power commodities, they sought as large an audience as possible.[8] As a result, "the original meaning of girl empowerment became watered-down so that it meant something to everyone," which caused it to lose potency and infused it with conflicting messages.[9] For example, the Spice Girls' sexy appearances contradicted the feminist-sounding, respect-demanding lyrics to their hit song "Wannabe," thus reducing girls' empower- ment to the freedom to gain power by looking good.[10] Anita Harris also laments that tween girl power products reduce feminist ideals of empowerment and female solidarity to the freedom merely to consume products.[11] Harris's criticisms of the " 'girls rule' ethic" echo feminist criticisms of the earlier commodification of a feminist ethic, such as the Virginia Slims's "You've Come a Long Way, Baby" advertisement, which Douglas notes co-opted feminist progress to sell cigarettes.[12]

Because of this context, there are many problems with the girl power cartoons that seek to empower girls, despite their pro-girl rhetoric. For example, the girls in these shows are always middle to upper-middle class, and they are nearly always white. Their privileged positions give them access to incredible resources that make their status as "role model" suspect, as most girls will never have lives of such privilege. For example, the Powerpuff Girls' father is a professor and scientist, and they live with him in a spacious home in the suburbs of the city in which they fight crime. The Powerpuff Girls' privilege and their foes' status as marginalized city dwellers has class and race implications. Likewise, the spies on *Totally Spies* live luxurious lives in Beverly Hills; for example, Clover lives in a mansion. Kim Possible's status as a crime fighter is similarly rooted in class and privilege that are beyond the reach of most people: As a playful explanation of Kim's intelligence, much is made of the fact that her father is a rocket scientist and her mother is a brain surgeon. Given Kim's privilege, it seems disingenuous that the lyrics of Kim's theme song state, "I'm your basic, average girl, and I'm here to save the world." There is little that is either basic *or* average about Kim. Does this imply to the tween audience that girl power is only available to girls who belong to a privileged race and class?

Action-adventure girl power cartoons are riddled with other problems as well. For example, although such cartoons suggest that girls can do anything they choose, they are also taught that they must look just right in order to do so—conforming to the slender, long-legged, light-skinned ideals or normative femininity. Girl power cartoons suggest that purchasing commodities to create normatively feminine appearances is essential to a girl's identity, for girl power heroes on Disney's *Kim Possible* and *Totally Spies* are shown engaging in consumer culture in ways that boys are not. The girls spend time shopping and creating their girlish appearances as part of the cartoons' stories. By placing such an emphasis on their heroines' appearances, girl power cartoons, like other girl power texts, imply that normative femininity is a *prerequisite* for girl power. In other words, only girls who look "girlish" may receive girl power's cultural support.[13] Because they meet dominant beauty ideals, the girls' tiny bodies do not reflect their immense physical strength, thus making the girl power movement more palatable and less threatening to patriarchal norms. Is girl power genuine, or has it merely co-opted feminist ideals to sell prepackaged "empowering" commodities to girls? If so, does this mean girl power is simply the power to . . . shop?

Further lessening girl power's feminist potential, the heroines tend to be pitted against other girls in ways that boy cartoon characters are not pitted against one another. There is usually another girl in each girl hero's school who is mean, arrogant, and a threat to her social status. While other cartoons typically depict boys who are friends with other boys outside their immediate circle, such as Jimmy in *Jimmy Neutron: Boy Genius*, the girls in these programs tend only to be friends with girls from their crime-fighting group. The girls who are heroic on a solo basis—like Kim Possible and Jenny, the Teenage Robot—mostly surround themselves with boys, rather than female friends. Such divisive depictions contradict the messages of female solidarity suggested by the all-girl fighting teams that so frequently populate girl power cartoons.

Concerns about media representations of class, race, beauty standards, commodification, and a lack of female solidarity are nothing new. Scholars have repeatedly cited these issues in their analyses of media targeting women, including prime-time television, soap operas, magazines, advertisements, and books. For thirty years, feminist scholars have railed against the media's limiting depictions of middle-class white women, who meet every American beauty standard and whose "empowerment" is merely a co-opted, commodified, and watered-down version of feminism. The very same complaints apply to girl power cartoons. Although these issues are highly problematic, they should not be used to condemn tween girl culture or girl power cartoons as a whole.

Cultural studies scholars, such as Celeste Condit and Stuart Hall, have demonstrated that despite popular culture's problems, it is worth exploring its positive aspects, too. For example, Condit has argued that media texts contain multiple messages, some of which may not be intended by producers, and that individual viewers' responses to media messages can vary somewhat.[14] Thus, there is the potential that even media messages that would seek to indoctrinate girls into the cult of femininity can be empowering to viewers. Furthermore, Hall claims that viewers are not uniformly passive, unintelligent receivers of media messages. Many viewers are aware of the messages delivered in their media content, but they will take exception to those messages they disagree with.[15] This suggests that despite the problems with girl power's emphasis on consumption and normative femininity, girls are not cultural dupes. Their ideas about femininity, empowerment, strength, and intelligence do not simply parrot what they learn on-screen.

Therefore, although we recognize serious problems with the commodification, consumption, and normative femininity intertwined with girl culture, we must not dismiss girl culture out of hand. It is worthwhile to look at the positive aspects of girl culture, too—such as the empowering themes within girl power shows. Rather than exploring the ways in which girl power is "business as usual," let us temporarily accept its problems as ongoing issues with the broader media and cultural environment. By moving beyond these complaints, maybe we can tease out what's *good* about girl power.

From Girl Crisis to Girl Power

The very existence of girl power cartoons seems revolutionary. In earlier television programming, girls were victims of the same symbolic annihilation that Gaye Tuchman pointed to in mediated depictions of women.[16] Over the past thirty years, studies have consistently found that children's programming depicts its characters in limiting gender stereotypes, with boys featured more frequently, more prominently, and in a wider range of settings and activities than girls.[17] The same is true of advertising directed at children, so that, taken altogether, the content directed at children perpetually reinscribes restrictive female sex roles for girls.[18]

This is exemplified by the general exclusion of girls from action-oriented children's programming, which has varied over time. For example, as Ellen Seiter observed, in the 1970s, girls were included on at least a token level as heroes in action-adventure shows (i.e., *Scooby-Doo*), whereas in the 1990s, they were often excluded (i.e., *Teenage Mutant Ninja Turtles*).[19] But now that girls are recognized as a valuable target audience, they are depicted everywhere, doing everything. These girls are gendered exaggeratedly in a visual sense, marking them clearly feminine, which is supported by the shopping and consumption they are shown engaging in, but unlike many of their cartoon girl predecessors, they are intelligent, active, and strong. Leaders, fighters, and advocates, they know right from wrong, and they make sure that justice is served by serving it themselves. They are supergirls.

Although some might dismiss these depictions as a two-faced capitalist effort to get girls to open their wallets, and perhaps rightly so, marketers could take any number of approaches to a target audience. The mass media do not *have to* depict action-adventure girl heroes who are strong, self-sufficient fighters. Pro-girl rhetoric did not develop in a vacuum or by the grace and goodwill of programmers alone; what is the sociohistorical context in which girl power emerged?

Girl power emerged on the heels of a concept that arose in the early 1990s: the crisis of female adolescence. This topic led to major handwringing among parents, educators, government officials, and scholars alike, as they agonized about what was wrong with our girls. Thanks to landmark books such as Mary Pipher's *Reviving Ophelia: Saving the Selves of Adolescent Girls* (1994),[20] a number-one *New York Times* bestseller, and Peggy Orenstein's *School Girls: Young Women, Self-Esteem, and the Confidence Gap* (1994),[21] a *New York Times* notable book of the year, girls were on everyone's radar screens. Again and again, scholars and cultural critics cited three major concerns: as girls hit adolescence, their academic achievement dropped, their self-esteem plummeted, and their preoccupation with their appearances increased. Such concerns were sparked by a nationwide poll commissioned by the American Association of University Women, *Shortchanging Girls, Shortchanging America* (1991). The report cited popular culture's symbolic annihilation of women as a root cause of girls' plummeting self-esteem that is reinforced by the educational system in the United States.[22] The report's authors argued that classroom texts are "devoid of women as role models," and "unconsciously, teachers and school counselors also dampen girls' aspirations, particularly in math and science."[23] They called for change across all institutions—family, education, government, and mass media—that contribute to girls' sense of self-worth.[24]

How were people within these institutions to effect this change? Parents and educators could tell any girl they encountered that she was smart, valued, and beautiful. They could repeat this like a mantra and hope it counteracted the female adolescent crisis. But as every writing teacher knows, telling is not nearly as effective as showing.

When girl power cartoons like *The Powerpuff Girls* began airing, they served an important function. They *showed* preadolescent girls that being a girl is culturally valuable. Their producers did not necessarily intend this function; for example, Craig McCracken has said that he was inspired to create *The Powerpuff Girls* because "I just thought it was cool to see these cute little girls being really tough and really hardcore."[25] However, thanks to the Powerpuffs paving the way, girl power cartoons are still proliferating, and they still show girls that they are culturally valued. They show girls with superpowers, who do not let chauvinistic associations of supermen stop them from saving the world. They show girls who do not have superpowers but who save the world anyway. They show girls displaying their intelligence in school without being negatively judged by others; instead, these girls receive compliments on their smarts. They show the norms of femininity that have restricted girls reimagined as a weapon that subversively makes all of the above possible.

That is what is good about girl power. In fact, that is revolutionary. That is surely why we are in the midst of a girl power deluge. The ideas communicated in girl power texts have cultural resonance. Because of this, girl power cartoons have the potential to function as an inoculation against the crisis of female adolescence. If supplemented by other cultural support for girls—in the home, at school, in extracurricular activities—maybe girls can get through the crisis of female adolescence relatively unscathed, with their intelligence, self-esteem, and self-image intact. In the late 1990s, the broad awareness of the issues girls face in adolescence, combined with the dearth of girl-centered programming, sealed girl power's fate. Girl power is more than a fad or a trend: it is a cultural phenomenon.

Redheads and Ratings

Over the past three years, I have watched nearly 300 episodes of girl power cartoons. I have enjoyed many of these shows, especially *The Powerpuff Girls*, which deliberately and skillfully targeted both child and adult viewers. During my fieldwork on girls' viewing of girl power cartoons, I have also watched over thirty girl power episodes with groups of working- to middle-class white and African American girls. I have witnessed *The Powerpuff Girls* decline in popularity, becoming perceived as being more for younger children, while new shows like Disney's *Kim Possible* and *W.I.T.C.H.* surpass the Powerpuffs in coolness. I have also observed that just as each of the Spice Girls had a distinct look and personality, from which their preteen fans could select to identify with, so do the cartoons featuring teams of crime-fighting heroines.[26] Girls in the viewing audience often look to a specific girl hero within each team as being the one with whom they most relate. Thus, girl power heroes' depictions inform their tween fans' identity constructions.

What types of girls are depicted in girl power texts? Visually, the girls meet dominant beauty standards for the female body (reinforcing the cultural ideals so detrimental to girls' self-images). Their hair styles may range from short bobs to long, flowing tresses, but shows featuring a single girl hero usually star a white girl with red hair, as on Disney's *Kim Possible* and *Atomic Betty*. (Even the robotic Jenny on *My Life as a Teenage Robot*, who is metallic with blue metal "hair," has an "exoskin" that makes her look like a Caucasian redhead.) In shows featuring all-girl crime-fighting teams, like *The Powerpuff Girls*, *W.I.T.C.H.*, and *Totally Spies*, there is usually one girl who is blonde, another who is a brunette, and a single redhead who is the team's intelligent, levelheaded leader.[27] Despite these differences, the girls share one overarching visual trait: they are all appealing, described by others as cute, or pretty, or beautiful. They are also quite strong, although their bodies are so slight that they never visually reveal this physical strength.[28]

The girls' behaviors and character traits are similar. In addition to fighting crime and saving the world on a routine basis, they have the intelligence, self-esteem, and positive self-images that girls facing the crisis of female adolescence lack. Intelligent leaders, respected for their brains, include Blossom on *The Powerpuff Girls*, Betty on *Atomic Betty*, and Sam on *Totally Spies*. Girls like Buttercup on *The Powerpuff Girls* and Irma on *W.I.T.C.H.* display their self-esteem by reveling in being tomboyish, feeling good about themselves just the way they are. Girly girls, such as Clover on *Totally Spies* and Cornelia on *W.I.T.C.H.*, are into fashion and boys. They successfully negotiate the normative feminine appearance that so many adolescent girls pursue, but without giving up their brilliance.

Interestingly, the girl heroes who are intelligent, who excel in school and are tremendously levelheaded, are also exceptionally nice. The traits—intelligence and "niceness"—appear to be insolubly bound together in certain girl heroes, specifically those who are considered leaders. What does this say about popular conceptions of female intelligence? The remainder of this chapter explores this question through a discussion of *The Powerpuff Girls*, *Totally Spies*, and Disney's *Kim Possible*. They are three of the original girl power action-adventure cartoons, and, with tween audiences, they have been among the most popular girl power shows. Indeed, like

The Powerpuff Girls, Totally Spies and Disney's *Kim Possible* boast fantastic ratings and product sales.

Totally Spies is an international hit, garnering over one million viewers daily in the United States alone and claiming to be France's most-watched show.[29] The program's appeal is not limited to tween girls; it boasts a strong boy viewership as well.[30] It is produced in France by Marathon, at a cost of $300,000 per episode.[31] It is scripted by former Nickelodeon writers located in Los Angeles, voiced by U.S. actors, and animated in South Korea.[32] As the show's marketing is geared toward tweens, among whom clothing is a major interest, both the show and its merchandising emphasize fashion. In developing the show, Marathon hired a French fashion agency, Promostyle, to design over 1,200 outfits in which animators could depict the spies.[33] The show's merchandising plans included marketing clothing to seven- to eleven-year-old girls.[34] Disney's *Kim Possible* also fares well in the ratings game: of all programming on the highly successful Disney Channel, *Kim Possible* boasts the largest draw of children in the six-to-eleven- and nine-to-fourteen-year-old age groups.[35] It also has a successful licensing agreement with the Wal-Mart stores, which offer a variety of *Kim Possible* products.[36] Such facts and figures demonstrate the popularity of the girl power cartoon genre, suggesting that they are significant cultural texts for the tween girl viewers who are their biggest fans.

Perfectly Intelligent: Being Nice and Smart

Considering the smart girls on *The Powerpuff Girls, Totally Spies*, and Disney's *Kim Possible* means focusing on three characters in particular: Blossom, Sam, and Kim, respectively. Each of these heroic girl leaders is strong, pretty, nice, and intelligent. However, they must be understood within the contexts of their shows, which depict a range of strong and feminine female characters, from the tomboyish Buttercup to the fashion-forward Clover. Therefore, let us turn to a brief overview of each cartoon.

The Powerpuff Girls first aired on Cartoon Network in 1998. It features the crime-fighting five-year-old Powerpuff Girls, who were the unintentional creation of their inventor/father, Professor Utonium. Attempting to create the perfect little girl through a laboratory experiment, the professor mixed together sugar, spice, and everything nice. However, a drop of "Chemical X" fell into the mixture, creating an explosion from which the Powerpuff Girls were born—with "ultra-superpowers."[37] Bubbles, the blonde, is the cutest Powerpuff; she enjoys coloring and playing with her stuffed animals. She represents "sugar." Buttercup, the brunette, is a tomboy; she enjoys fighting and hates taking baths. She represents "spice." Blossom, the redhead, is the leader of the group; she is intelligent, logical, and calmly pleasant. She represents "everything nice." (See figure 4.1).

The girls attend kindergarten, but much of their time—even during school hours—is consumed fighting monsters and villains that constantly threaten the City of Townsville. They engage their foes in fistfights involving frenetic action sequences, while they wear cute little dresses, white tights, and Mary Jane shoes. When *The Powerpuff Girls* first aired, this combination of "power" and "puff" made the show unique. A wealth of press coverage has hailed the Powerpuff Girls as new feminist icons.

Since 2001, Cartoon Network's *Totally Spies* has followed the adventures of three teenage girls from Beverly Hills who lead a secret double life working as spies for WOOHP, an international crime-fighting agency. The teens go to the same high school

Figure 4.1 Blossom, the leader of the Powerpuff Girls, prefers toys like chemistry sets and the Doctor Didi doll.

and are close friends. *Totally Spies* was conceived by Marathon president Vincent Chalvon-Demersay, who used girl power icons the Spice Girls and the hit movie *Clueless* as inspiration for this *Charlie's Angels*-like show. Sam, the redhead, is the most logical; Clover, the blonde, acts like a stereotypical "Valley Girl," obsessed with shopping and dating; and Alex, the brunette, is the youngest and most impulsive. All three are tall, slim, and beautiful and spend a lot of time together at the mall.

The girls are sent on missions by Jerry, WOOHP's director. Whenever he needs them to go on a mission, an everyday-looking object (such as a phone booth, locker, or changing room in a store) opens up and—without warning—drops them down a complex series of secret tunnels and into Jerry's office. He then briefs them on the situation and presents them with an array of gadgets to use on the mission. During their missions, the girls are more or less autonomous, but they report back to Jerry regularly. In everyday life, many of the problems Sam, Clover, and Alex face are fueled by interpersonal conflicts with the snobby and mean Mandy, a teenage girl at their high school who hates them—and whom they hate in return∏.

Sam is clearly the smartest of the spies, which is demonstrated in many episodes. A key example is found in "S.P.I.," in which Sam single-handedly brings down a crime-fighting organization that was so successful at fighting crimes, it put WOOHP out of business. Being more observant and a better critical thinker than the other spies, including Jerry, she independently investigates and determines that they were setting up the crimes to make themselves look good. In contrast with Clover, the self-absorbed fashion-conscious shopaholic, and Alex, whose naïveté makes her seem not

Figure 4.2   In the opening sequence of Cartoon Network's *Totally Spies*, the intelligent Sam is depicted as both a reader and a fighter.

so bright, Sam stands out as being particularly intelligent. Her logical, level-headed crime-fighting and problem-solving abilities are often responsible for the success of the entire team, making Sam less stereotypical than her teammates (see figure 4.2).

Kim Possible, another smart and pretty action hero, is the principal character on the Disney Channel's *Kim Possible*. Since 2002, *Kim Possible* has depicted Kim and her sidekick, Ron Stoppable, as they juggle the demands of high school and crime fighting. At school, Kim's best girlfriend is Monique, and her nemesis is Bonnie, a snobby cheerleader who strongly dislikes Kim. In fighting crime, Kim and Ron rely on Wade, a boy-genius friend who provides them with various gadgets. Kim and Ron are always together, and Kim is clearly the more intelligent of the two: Kim earns good grades, while Ron is at risk of failure, and Kim's serious, intelligent approach to fighting crime is offset by Ron's goofy comic relief. At school and in saving the day, Ron stumbles, but Kim soars (see figure 4.3).

As these overviews indicate, Blossom, Sam, and Kim are clearly the smartest girls in their worlds. Significantly, they are the nicest girls around, too. They are not prone to bickering, like Buttercup and Clover, nor are they likely to complain about being left out, like Bubbles and Alex. They are perfectly sweet and kind, and nice to everyone around them. For example, Kim has a pleasant rapport with her clients, who often return her kindness by helping her travel the world to fight villains in their exotic locations. While ferrying her across continents or oceans, such clients will invariably reaffirm just how grateful they are to her for her assistance—to which she usually smiles and replies, "No big." Her niceness charms those around her.

Figure 4.3 Disney's *Kim Possible* outwits her foes with a mix of intelligence and martial arts moves. © Disney

While reflecting on the implications of the most intelligent girls being the nicest girls, I came to a realization: perhaps owing to their greater intelligence, these girls surpass the other girls in their pursuit of social acceptability, through the nice behavior that adults encourage in girls and that their peers reinforce. "Niceness" is a concept related to class and sex. Specifically, in the United States, middle-class girls learn that being "nice" is highly desirable.[38] As Joseph Tobin notes, adults more often tell girls than boys to be nice, which pressures them "to be nonaggressive, obliging, and modest in their desires."[39] As children internalize this lesson, they begin to police one another, noting who is nice and tattling on those who are not;[40] and when asked what the perfect girl would be like, girls frequently offer "nice" as a description.[41] Gifted girls are more likely than their peers to internalize gendered social norms,[42] so by matching their superior intelligence with perfect niceness, the cartoon girl heroes conform to the ideal that girls should be sugar, spice, and everything nice. By choosing to play this game, they come out as winners, reaping social rewards such as adult and peer approval—which is problematic, of course, as it is a choice society expects girls to make.

In fact, niceness is an important factor in popularity, and popularity bestows social power upon girls.[43] By being agreeable and nice to everyone, these smart girls are avoiding being labeled snobs, which is considered "one of the most reviled descriptors of girls at this age and a factor in losing popularity."[44] In avoiding snobbishness, however, the smart girls in girl power cartoons sometimes take niceness to extremes. For example, in the *Totally Spies* episode "Eraser," the insufferable Mandy decides that Sam is her new best friend, but Sam wants nothing to do with her. She has a hard time shaking Mandy off, however. Unlike Alex and Clover, Sam cannot bring herself to be mean to another girl—which is what it would take to make it clear she is not interested in Mandy's friendship. In this way, the intelligent girl power heroes avoid abusing even those they dislike.[45] Unlike real girls who alternate between being nice and mean to others around them, they are unrealistic model citizens. By modeling the "nice" behavior that wins so many girls their peers' acceptance and admiration, brilliant girls like Blossom, Sam, and Kim suggest that girls can be intelligent and popular at the same time. In other words, they can overcome the stereotype of the bookish wallflower that plagues smart girls everywhere.

If social rewards translate into social power, it makes sense that intelligent girls like Blossom, Sam, and Kim would recognize this and take their niceness a step further than do their peers. Through cartoon girls' saccharine behavior and pleasant appearances, they win the unflagging approval of those around them, especially of adults. This reflects the experiences of real girls. Thus, in the *Powerpuff Girls* episode "Ice Sore," Blossom pleases her kindergarten classmates by using her ice breath power to help them all beat the intense summer heat. However, the professor had told her not to use that power too much, so Bubbles tattles to their kindergarten teacher, Ms. Keane. She replies, "What are you talking about? Blossom never does anything bad." Ms. Keane then praises Blossom's kindness toward the other children, saying, "Blossom, what a nice thing you're doing." When Ms. Keane singles out Blossom for being so nice, she suggests that niceness is a valuable trait that results in acceptance from authority figures, and Blossom is permitted to carry on with her peer-pleasing behavior. She gains popularity points among her classmates and brownie points from Ms. Keane. This vignette demonstrates the power that niceness can bestow upon the intelligent girls who master it, setting a good example for girls who want to use this tactic—and a bad example for girls who would prefer not to mitigate their intelligence in this way.

In addition to behaving the nicest, these intelligent girls also *look* the nicest. Blossom and Sam take their normative femininity a step further than do their teammates: they both have long hair, whereas the girls around them have shorter hair. Long hair is an obvious signifier of femininity, and the fact that they have flowing red tresses in opposition to their teammates' short blonde and brunette bobs indicates that their appearances are the most conventionally feminine. Kim Possible also fits this mold, with hair that is the envy of many little girls. Tobin found that children used niceness to discuss the appearance and behavior of film characters that they liked: "nice" meant "kind" in some instances and "attractive" in others.[46] This suggests that the intelligent girl heroes' nice behaviors and appearances are important both in their cartoon worlds and in the minds of the girl audience members who view them.

Subversive Smarts

So, what is new about these portrayals of nice, intelligent girl heroes? They represent progress. As Lyn Mikel Brown notes, traditionally "Girls are supposed to *be* smart and *appear* dumb."[47] Bucking this cultural expectation, cartoon girls like Blossom,

Sam, and Kim show their brilliance openly; everyone knows they are smart. It is the way the girl heroes wield their niceness that allows for open demonstrations of their intelligence. In addition to looking nice and acting nice, these girls strategically deploy niceness to make their open displays of intelligence less of a threat to social norms. In other words, girl power cartoons suggest that niceness—which is primarily a patriarchal dictate—can also be a subversive strategy. It can make intelligence and power acceptable, even though broader social forces encourage girls' passivity and apparent disinterest in book smarts.

Blossom, Sam, and Kim show that niceness is a subtle but effective subversive strategy. Responding to compliments in stereotypically nice ways, they carefully deflect attention from their open displays of intelligence. For example, in *The Powerpuff Girls* episode "Power-noia," Buttercup praises Blossom by saying, "You really are the smartest girl in Townsville!" Blossom downplays this praise with characteristic niceness, replying, "Aw, shucks. I was just being resourceful." Similarly, in the *Totally Spies* episode "Brain Drain," a boy in Sam's class compliments her for being so good at science, and asks how she does it. She too downplays her accomplishments, replying, "I dunno! I just read it and then it's, like, stuck in my mind forever. Kinda dorky, huh?" Likewise, in the episode of Disney's *Kim Possible* "Kimitation Nation," when Kim's friend Monique praises her for so frequently saving the world—a job that relies on her keen intellectual abilities—Kim replies, "Oh, stop, Monique. I'm no better than anybody else." The subtext of such responses is that the girls are not seeking attention or glory—after all, that is not something that "nice" girls do. The girls demonstrate that they are not conceited or self-absorbed about their intelligence, which makes their brilliance seem perhaps less central to their effectiveness than it is.

This pattern in girl power cartoons could suggest that girl power reinforces culturally repressive ideas about girls' intelligence—that smart girls should play dumb. However, on closer inspection, it is clear that something unusual is going on. These girls are neither playing dumb nor hiding their intelligence. They do not succumb to the cultural pressures to do so. They are overtly intelligent on an everyday basis, excelling in school and demonstrating their knowledge when fighting crime outside of school. By being supremely nice to others and downplaying but never hiding their smarts, Blossom, Sam, and Kim minimize the threat they pose to restrictive cultural ideals for girls. Instead of having to play dumb, they can use their intelligence freely and openly. Their pretty, nonthreatening looks, combined with sweet, nonthreatening behavior, makes their intelligence seem less important than it is. What real girls take away from these depictions in an important question for future research.

When today's cartoon smart girls use niceness as a subversive strategy, they are following in the footsteps of televisual predecessors from the early 1960s. On the cusp of second-wave feminism, television shows about teen girls, such as *The Patty Duke Show* and *Gidget*, depicted girls who also subverted cultural expectations of them. As Douglas explains, Patty and Gidget cleverly deployed a strategy that let them be assertive and have their way, without being thought unappealing by the boys around them: perkiness.[48] Perkiness, or "assertiveness masquerading as cuteness," allowed these girls to behave as they pleased.[49] The smart girls of today's girl power cartoons achieve the same end result through their use of niceness. For example, in the *Totally Spies* episode "S.P.I.," the girls are caught in a machine intended to kill them, and cannot find a way out. Alex fears it is hopeless and cries, "All we have left is a laser lipstick!" Sam immediately replies, "Alex, that's perfect! Point the laser at the cockpit panel and fire." Despite the stress they are under, Sam gives this instruction in a calm, supportive way. Her intelligent idea saves them all, but in a way that is cheerful and thus not assertive. She is able to command those around her without appearing bossy, mean, or conceited. Thus, niceness, like perkiness, gives girls more agency in the world around them.

Because they are nice and smart, girl heroes like Blossom, Sam, and Kim share another trait: within their crime-fighting teams, each of these girls is the leader. Their cartoons do not make it clear how each girl came to her leadership position; in fact, their leadership positions are implied through behavior, rather than elected and recognized through title or rank. They are what Cynthia Allen Edwards called "informal leaders."[50] The girl power heroes' pleasant personalities and intelligent command of tricky situations make them natural leaders. They model leadership behavior for their preteen viewers, demonstrating that leading calls not for dominating others, but for abilities that require the use of one's intellect. For example, in the *Powerpuff Girls* episode "Three Girls and a Monster," Blossom spends her spare time devising new plans of attack for her and her sisters to use when fighting crime. These positive portrayals of girls using their intelligence to effect change highlight girl power.

The fact that these girls both look and behave nice resonates with other studies of real girls' leadership. For example, Dawn Shinew and Deborah Thomas Jones found that only girls with a pleasant physical appearance are considered leaders, and in asking girls to describe the informal leaders in their communities, kindness, caring, and nurturing emerged as key qualities.[51] Shinew and Jones argued that although some might dismiss this finding as important because the girls assumed "traditional gendered roles as caregivers and nurturers—societal scripts that have been written upon girls," being "nice" truly brought girls "a certain recognition and sense of power among their peers."[52] In the context of the crisis of female adolescence, girl viewers may be reassured by depictions of intelligent girls who successfully negotiate a pleasant appearance and are admired by their peers. Thus, girl power cartoons seem to culturally support intelligent girls by suggesting niceness as a strategy for not only displaying intelligence, but for being welcomed as leaders among their peers.

Smart-Mouthed Brats

The flip side to the beloved nice girl is the socially outcast mean girl. The importance of intelligent girls' conformity with placid niceness is heightened when compared with intelligent cartoon girls who, refusing to conform, enjoy being mean rather than nice. Examples of such girls include Daria in MTV's *Daria* (1997–2001), a girl power cartoon that targeted a teen audience, and Shego, a supervillain on Disney's *Kim Possible*. Although Daria and Shego are highly intelligent, they face serious consequences as a result of their refusal to conform. Daria, who is not an action-adventure hero, is the central character in a cartoon about her everyday life. She dislikes many things about the world in which she lives and has a pessimistic view of the social life and quality of education at her high school. As a result, she is quietly sarcastic. She frequently makes highly articulate barbed remarks in a monotone voice that masks her harshness, leaving the people they were directed at sometimes uncertain as to whether she was actually insulting them. Because of such deliberately "not-nice" behavior, she is a social outcast at her high school, where she has few friends. Neither her parents nor her fashion- and popularity-focused sister understand her displeasure with the status quo at her high school. Daria is an illustration of the consequences of being intelligent but failing to conform in appearance, attitude, or behavior: holding true to her ideals, she is a social outcast. Although she is content with her lot, many girls would not be.

A similar moral is offered through the example of Shego, a supervillain who is one of Kim Possible's major nemeses. Shego looks similar enough to Kim that on my first viewing of the show, I wondered if she was Kim's evil twin. Like Kim, Shego is tall and slender and has big round eyes and full, flowing, gorgeous hair. However, Kim is a redhead and Shego is a brunette, and Shego only wears one outfit: a green and black jumpsuit. Although both are more intelligent than most of the people they work with, their personalities are inverse to one another. While Kim is the embodiment of the nice girl, who is polite and sweet, Shego is incessantly sarcastic and outspoken (see figure 4.4).

Figure 4.4 Shego of Disney's *Kim Possible* is a smart and sarcastic villain. © Disney

In the episode "Go Team Go," Shego's backstory is revealed. She was once part of a superheroic crime-fighting team, comprising herself and her four brothers. However, she is so intelligent and strong-willed that she grew tired of putting up with her brothers. After all their do-gooding together, Shego grew attracted to the prospect of using her powers for evil rather than good. She defiantly quit their superhero team and set to work as a mercenary supervillain, using superpowers, martial arts skills, and intelligently sarcastic barbs to fight the people who try to stop her evildoing. Shego revels in this behavior.

Daria and Shego's habit of saying mean things seems to be at the root of their status as outcasts. Just as Daria's parents do not understand her attitude, Shego's older brother reveals to Kim that Shego was always difficult—always a "smartmouth." His comment implies that her verbal assaults were the start of a slippery slope into supervillainy. The outcast status of intelligent but "smartmouthed" girls like Daria and Shego serves as a problematic cautionary tale, suggesting that if intelligent girls want to be accepted, they had better temper their intelligence with ample doses of niceness. If Shego is a former superhero gone bad, and if she is one of the few villains whose intelligence and skills are a match for Kim's, Shego implies by example that intelligent girls must be nice, or their displays of intelligence will be unwelcome.

This implication is made by Kim and Shego's binary opposition to each other. Thus, Kim's traits (niceness and goodness) are dichotomous to Shego's traits (antisocialness and evilness). Binding these traits together, as though they are inextricably linked, suggests that intelligent powerful girls *must* be nice, if they want to be perceived as being good. Otherwise, if they are antisocial in their objections to the status quo, speak sarcastically, and openly air their negative opinions of others, they may be perceived as being evil or as failing at femininity, which could be just as bad. Girls' power and intelligence are only acceptable if girls are nice, sweet, and normatively feminine, acting in accordance with the mythological archetype of the "good mother."[53] Compared with girl power cartoons' positive messages about displaying intelligence, this message is regressive and untenable from a feminist perspective. I wonder when we will see an intelligent girl hero who walks a middle ground—who can speak her mind freely, without being rendered a social outcast like Daria or Shego.

Resistance and Role Models

It is troubling to see intelligent cartoon girls circumscribe their behaviors and appearances within culturally accepted standards of niceness. They jump through incredible hoops to make their intelligence palatable. At a glance, they do not differ from the types of females depicted before them. They fit within narrowly defined standards of acceptability in popular culture. They are of a privileged race, class, and body type, and their "nice" behavior aligns with cultural expectations of girls. Smart girls' use of niceness allows them to have agency and power in their cartoon worlds. However, when compared with being "smartmouthed," and therefore socially outcast, being strategically nice is reinforced as the smart girl's only socially acceptable choice. Although Daria is presented in a positive light to viewers, it is clear that she is misunderstood by those in her cartoon world, which would surely dissuade real girls from following in her footsteps—and Shego is just plain villainous.

When the smart girl power heroes' nice behavior and appearances are considered in terms of resistance, as problematic as that may be, they seem truly brilliant. These smart girls comprehend normative femininity and the imperative for girls to be nice. Instead of merely falling in line with female norms, they intelligently use those norms to their advantage. They subvert the cultural expectation that if a girl is smart, she should not show it. Instead, they use their brilliance to their full advantage but use their nice appearances and behaviors to avoid intimidating others, thus bringing a whole new meaning to the phrase "pretty smart." Because of their feminine looks and their pleasant natures, when these girls use their intelligence to change the world around them, their efforts are warmly received. They are praised by adult authorities and emerge as leaders among their peers.

By depicting intelligent, empowered girl leaders, girl power cartoons react against the idea that girls are victims. Instead, the shows offer tween girls role models that at least some might find useful as they approach the crisis-ridden female adolescence.[54] Read against the context of the early 1990s fears about girls' declining self-esteem and academic performances, girl power cartoons are a valuable source of support for girls, especially those who are willing to engage in normative femininity. Following the recommendations of the American Association of University Women's report—intentionally or not—these cartoons suggest that society values girls' lives and culture, and that girls can weather the storms of their teenage years. The shows demonstrate that smart girls need not be stereotyped as socially inept bookworms; they can be heroes. Intelligence in females does not equate with ugliness; smart girls can be pretty, too. Like the perky Gidget types of 1960s television, today's nice, brilliant girl power heroes behave mostly as they please, and they are loved for it.

When intelligent cartoon girls like Blossom, Sam, and Kim use their superpowers or jet packs to fly around on-screen, they are not just taking flight. They are spreading their "wings" and flying away from oppression, low self-esteem, and poor test performance, heading instead toward a bright future where girls are not victims: they are intelligent, compassionate leaders. Let us hope that for real girls, that future is not too distant.

Notes

1. Advertiser Staff and Wire Services, "For Powerpuffs, Whomping the Bad Guys is Girl Stuff," *Honolulu Advertiser*, 29 August 2000; http://the.honoluluadvertiser.com/2000/Aug/29/829islandlife14.html (accessed August 25, 2005); Lisa Hager, "What Little Girls Are Really Made Of: The Powerpuff Girls, Citizenship, and Quantum Mechanics or, 'Better Pray for the Girls' " (paper presented at *Cultivating Knowledge(s): A Conference and a Celebration* [Center for Women's Studies and Gender Research 25th Anniversary Symposium, The University of Florida, Gainesville, FL, 24–26 October 2002]), 2.

2. Nancy McAlister, "Powerpuff Girls Battle Villains on Big Screen," *Florida Times-Union*, 2 July 2002, C 1.

3. Quoted from "Show Description: Disney's *Kim Possible*," ABC Medianet, http://www.abcmedianet.com/showpage/showpage.html?program_id=001173&type=lead (accessed 25 August 2005).

4. Quoted in Dave Mason, "Kim Possible Tackles Time Travel: Popular Hero Goes to Yesterday and Tomorrow to Save the World in New Movie," *Ventura County Star*, 23 November 2003, K 6.

5. Quoted in Sara Fiedelholtz, "Impossible? Not For *Kim Possible*," *Chicago Sun-Times*, 29 August 2003, Kid Zone, 8.
6. Political economists, feminists, and other scholars have criticized how the media industries put an exchange value on the viewing of audience members, so from some perspectives, the lack of media attention to girls may not have been so bad. Cultural critics would not exactly fight for the homogenization and selling of a "girl" audience to greedy commodity producers, who wish to line their deep corporate pockets with little girls' allowance money.
7. Peggy Tally, "Re-imagining Girlhood: Hollywood and the Tween Girl Film Market," in *Seven Going on Seventeen: Tween Studies in the Culture of Girlhood*, ed. Claudia Mitchell and Jacqueline Reid-Walsh (New York: Peter Lang, 2005), 314.
8. Ellen Riordan, "Commodified Agents and Empowered Girls: Consuming and Producing Feminism," *Journal of Communication Inquiry* 25.3 (2001): 290.
9. Riordan, 290.
10. Riordan, 290.
11. Anita Harris, "In a Girlie World: Tweenies in Australia," in *Seven Going on Seventeen:* Mitchell and Reid-Walsh, eds., 218.
12. Susan J. Douglas, *Where the Girls Are: Growing Up Female with the Mass Media* (New York: Times Books, 1994), 245–246.
13. Rebecca C. Hains, "The Problematics of Reclaiming the Girlish: *The Powerpuff Girls* and Girl Power," *Femspec* 5.2 (2004): 1–39.
14. Celeste Condit, "The Rhetorical Limits of Polysemy," in *Critical Perspectives on Media and Society*, ed. Robert K. Avery and David Eason (New York: Guilford Press, 1991), 383–384.
15. Stuart Hall, "Encoding, Decoding," in *The Cultural Studies Reader*, ed. Simon During (New York: Routledge, 1993), 102.
16. Gaye Tuchman, "Introduction: The Symbolic Annihilation of Women by the Mass Media," in *Hearth and Home: Images of Women in the Mass Media*, ed. Gaye Tuchman, Arlene Kaplan Daniels, and James Benét (New York: Oxford University Press), 3–38.
17. See, for example, the following: Mark R. Barner, "Sex-Role Stereotyping in FCC-Mandated Children's Educational Television," *Journal of Broadcasting & Electronic Media* 43 (1999): 551–564; Beverly A. Browne, "Gender Stereotypes in Advertising on Children's Television in the 1990s: A Cross-National Analysis," *Journal of Advertising* 27 (1998): 83–96; Nancy Signorielli, "Television and Conceptions about Sex Roles: Maintaining Conventionality and the Status Quo," *Sex Roles* 21 (1989): 341–360; and, Sarah H. Sternglanz and Lisa Serbin, "Sex Role Stereotyping in Children's Television Programs," *Developmental Psychology* 10 (1974): 710–715.
18. M. S. Larson, "Interactions, Activities, and Gender in Children's Television Commercials: A Content Analysis," *Journal of Broadcasting & Electronics* 45.1 (2001): 41–56.
19. Ellen Seiter, "Semiotics, Structuralism, and Television," in *Channels of Discourse, Reassembled*, ed. Robert C. Allen (Chapel Hill: University of North Carolina Press), 60.
20. Mary Pipher, *Reviving Ophelia: Saving the Selves of Adolescent Girls* (New York: Random House, 1994).
21. Peggy Orenstein, in association with the American Association of University Women, *School Girls: Young Women, Self-Esteem, and the Confidence Gap* (New York: Anchor Books, 1994).
22. American Association of University Women, *Shortchanging Girls, Shortchanging America: Executive Summary* (Washington, DC: American Association of University Women, 1991), 5.
23. American Association of University Women, 5.
24. American Association of University Women, 17.

25. Quoted in Gregory Weinkauf, "Powerpuff 'n' Stuff: Animator Craig McCracken Discusses His Little Whoopass Chargettes," *New Times Los Angeles*, 4 July 2002 (retrieved 6 May 2003, from Lexis-Nexis database).
26. Dafna Lemish, "Spice Girls' Talk: A Case Study in the Development of Gendered Identity," in *Millennium Girls: Today's Girls Around the World*, ed. Sherrie A. Inness (Lanham, MD: Rowman & Littlefield, 1998), 145–168.
27. They lack racial diversity, but recent shows such as *The Life and Times of Juniper Lee*, which features an Asian American girl, and *W.I.T.C.H.*, with its team of five girls, offer more racial diversity.
28. For more on this subject, see Meenakshi Gigi Durham, "The Girling of America: Critical Reflections on Gender and Popular Communication," *Popular Communication* 1.1 (2003): 23–31.
29. "*Totally Spies:* New Episodes Available," New at MIPTV, Marathon, http:// www. marathon.fr/news.php?lg = uk&cn = 179 (accessed 25 August 2005).
30. Jocelyn Longworth, "Winner—Girls: Totally Spies!" *Kidscreen*, 1 July 2002.
31. Alison James, "Give 'Em an Eiffel: U.S. Cabler's Bev Hills-Set Toon Has a Lot of Gaul," *Variety*, 11–17 March 2002, 25.
32. James, 25.
33. Amanda Burgess, "Marathon Totally Spies Global Music and Merch Potential in Its Tween Girl Toon," *Kidscreen*, 1 April 2002, 51.
34. Lana Castleman, "Marathon Has U.S. Retail Opps for Totally Spies! in Its Crosshairs," *Kidscreen*, 1 May 2004, 27.
35. Brent Hopkins, "Disney Brokers *Kim Possible* line at Wal-Mart," *Daily News of Los Angeles*, 11 June 2003, B 1.
36. Hopkins, B 1.
37. In the creator Craig McCracken's original conception, the accidental ingredient was "a can of whoopass," and the girls were "The Whoopass Girls."
38. Joseph Tobin, *"Good Guys Don't Wear Hats": Children's Talk About the Media* (New York: Teachers College Press, 2000), 118.
39. Tobin, 119.
40. Lyn Mikel Brown and Carol Gilligan, *Meeting at the Crossroads: Women's Psychology and Girls' Development* (Cambridge, MA: Harvard University Press, 1992), 45.
41. Rachel Simmons, *Odd Girl Out: The Hidden Culture of Aggression in Girls* (New York: Harcourt, 2002), 67.
42. Barbara A. Kerr, *Smart Girls: A New Psychology of Girls, Women, and Giftedness* (Scottsdale, AZ: Gifted Psychology Press, 1994).
43. Pamela J. Bettis, Debra Jordan, and Diane Montgomery, "Girls in Groups: The Preps and the Sex Mob Try Out for Womanhood," in *Geographies of Girlhood: Identities In-Between*, ed. Pamela J. Bettis and Natalie G. Adams (Mahwah, NJ: Lawrence Erlbaum, 2005), 68–84.
44. Bettis et al., 73–74.
45. Lyn Mikel Brown, *Girlfighting: Betrayal and Rejection among Girls* (New York: New York University Press, 2003), 109.
46. Tobin, 118.
47. Lyn Mikel Brown, *Raising Their Voices: The Politics of Girls' Anger* (Cambridge, MA: Harvard University Press, 1998), 159.
48. Douglas, 108.
49. Douglas, 108.
50. Cynthia Allen Edwards, "Leadership in Groups of School-Age Girls," *Developmental Psychology* 30.6 (1994): 920–927.

51. Dawn M. Shinew and Deborah Thomas Jones, "Girl Talk: Adolescent Girls' Perceptions of Leadership," in *Geographies of Girlhood*, Bettis and Adams, eds., 61–63.

52. Shinew and Jones, 61.

53. Simmons, 17.

54. As I have argued elsewhere, girl power primarily offers empowerment to girls who are willing and able to successfully perform normative femininity. Girls who cannot or choose not to do so are excluded. In this chapter, I have set aside this issue to explore girl power's positive aspects, but the problematic aspects continue to concern me greatly. For a through explanation of my perspective, see Hains, 15–30.

CHAPTER 5

Super Slacker Girls: Dropping Out but Divinely Inspired

Michele Paule

Generation X, Generation Y, post-boomers, Border Youth, slackers. Marketing mandarins and cultural theorists alike have invented names and identified characteristics of the generation of youth who just cannot be bothered.[1] I identify a variation on the theme, a short-lived phenomenon lounging on the millennial cusp, born out of unique conditions within the culture and the industry that produced her—the super slacker girl.

Super slacker girls are smart young women in television dramas who reject academic success and traditional career trajectories. Instead, their lives are shaped and given meaning by some form of supernatural prompting toward philanthropic acts. In this group is Georgia of *Dead Like Me*, Jaye of *Wonderfalls*, and Joan of *Joan of Arcadia*. There are others, too, who fit the bill enough to identify the phenomenon as a trend. For example, Tru of *Tru Calling* ends up working in a mortuary and saving the dead, who speak only to her, rather than training as an intern in a hospital; *Dark Angel*'s genetically engineered Max opts out of what could be described as an extreme form of gifted program to work for the underground resistance in a dystopian Seattle, and *Smallville*'s Lana Lang rejects college in the same season in which she acquires her own supernatural identity. However, Tru only works in the morgue because her internship was canceled, but does not abandon her ambitions to become a doctor; Max's powers are a result of human rather than divine intervention; and Lana's supernatural powers are a form of evil possession rather than a "gift." So for the purposes of this analysis I shall concentrate on the first three. As well as fulfilling the criteria described above, the heroines I have chosen also provide insights into the different issues of the smart slacker's progress at different ages, while remaining within the protracted trajectory of adolescence, as experienced within late capitalist Western culture.

A range of factors makes these reluctant heroines highly interesting variations on the themes of girlhood and smartness. Considered together, these factors would indicate that the smart girl as a cultural construct is very much a work in progress. Using the cultural studies approach that Laurie Ouelliette describes as "symptomatic analysis," in which a television text can be analyzed within both its broader cultural context and interpretative discourses, I argue that Georgia Lass, Jaye Taylor, and Joan Girardi offer particular insights into the conditions producing the youth of the twenty-first century, who are shaped by a postfeminist consciousness and subject to some deeply ingrained conceptions of not only gender but also giftedness.[2]

The Super Slacker Girl as Subgenre

The super slacker phenomenon is located in media as well as in cultural development; in these days of cable channels and niche markets, it is clear that, in industry terms, Jaye, Joan, and Georgia owe their existence to *Buffy the Vampire Slayer*. The rush to cash in on *Buffy*'s cult success and the attendant marketing opportunities led to a flurry of new productions featuring heroines with a supernatural slant. It is hard to follow an original; not one among *Dead Like Me, Wonderfalls*, or *Joan of Arcadia* was as successful as its inspiration. Despite collecting an Emmy, even *Joan of Arcadia* ran for only two seasons. In the words of a Slayer, perhaps "there can be only one, and I am she" (*Buffy the Vampire Slayer*, 2.2). But there may be more to it than this. As interesting as the newer heroines may be, and as well-crafted as some of the shows are, super slacker girls may present too discomfiting a vision of what it means to be a brilliant young woman today to have succeeded. This challenging vision may in part account for their lack of broad appeal and their commercial failure, and the underlying reasons can be traced in part through some developments in the genre they represent.

It would seem relatively simple to locate super slacker shows, which blend the experience of girlhood with the supernatural, within the teen sci-fi continuum. As Rachel Mosely has pointed out, there are strong links between this genre and aspects of the adolescent condition in the centrality of otherness and alienation. Mosely also describes the adolescent's access to increased power and the impact of this on the community and relationships.[3] Thus, we can understand the teen superheroine as embodying and enacting experiences central to adolescence, even if this is the prime-time television version of a white, privileged female experience often noted in postfeminist analysis. However, the final seasons of *Buffy* marked the beginning of an important divergence from the conventions of this science-fiction subgenre, a divergence that the super slackers continue. If, as Leonie Rutherford claims, science fiction is "culturally constituted as a young adult product" that celebrates "the pleasures of possibility," what then do we make of science-fiction heroines whose response to the possibilities on offer is to turn off and drop out?[4] Again, we can see some of the roots of this development in *Buffy*. The seven seasons of *Buffy* saw the eponymous heroine grow from a perky high school sophomore to a thoughtful and committed college student, but then gradually descend into a depressed and increasingly solitary adulthood, dropping out of college and working in a minimum wage job with family and other burdens too heavy at times for one young woman's shoulders. It is only at the end of the final season's final show that her burden is lifted and she can smile at the prospect of her future, because *all* girls with potential are going to share her load. There was fan dissatisfaction at the gloomy nature of the later seasons, but it was this dark view of the condition of the gifted young woman that the super slacker girl dramas picked up and developed.

In the details of character and plot, one can see ways in which Buffy Summers is the antecedent of the super slacker girl: Like Buffy, she is subject to a supernatural calling; she finds herself abandoning or compromising personal ambition and desire in order to serve a wider common good; she has to keep her particular calling or ability a secret, and finally, her career prospects are grim. Georgia in *Dead Like Me* drops out of college and works in a temping agency, a fate from which not even death can save her despite her new role as a "Reaper." Jaye in *Wonderfalls* earns a degree in philosophy from the high-status Brown University, only to take a job in a souvenir shop, while Joan in *Joan of Arcadia* joins advanced science classes, the debate team, and the chess club because she is ordered to do so by God, and even then does so extremely reluctantly. Ultimately, however, it does her no good, because she still fails to get into a good college.

However, while Buffy is at least allowed the relief of kicking some demon derrière in the course of seven years of saving the world, the super slacker, in general, has less clout, less fun, a smaller audience, and a shorter run. It seems the viewing public finds it hard to love a girl who does not just want to have fun. But while the audience may not love her, they recognize her. The very fact that the underachieving smart girl should appear at the center of so many dramas is noteworthy. It is in the nature of popular television drama that it must employ recognizable cultural models in order to enlist the sympathies of its audience; we must be able to recognize the Jayes, Joans, and Georgias and to position ourselves to encounter the world from their perspective and engage with their dilemmas. It is therefore troubling that these intelligent young women should be so compromised in their ambition and motivation, and yet so able to hail their audience with the ease of the familiar.

The slacker girl is familiar because she is ubiquitous, a small-screen manifestation of a deeply troubling and persistent phenomenon that finds our most able girls failing to fulfill their promise. Brilliant but underachieving, she is the embodiment of what the psychologist Carol Dweck describes as a sort of paralyzing instinct that drives some able young women to avoid the unknown, question their abilities, and limit their ambitions.[5]

In her popular and seminal book *Smart Girls: A New Psychology of Girls, Women and Giftedness* (1997), Barbara Kerr argues that the academic and professional aspirations of brilliant girls continue to be too often influenced by expectations associated with gender rather than ability, so that they aim low or opt out entirely, and finds that the theme of many gifted females' lives is one of declining involvement with former achievement goals.[6] More recent studies in the field of female talent development, such as Sally Reis's "Internal Barriers, Personal Issues, and Decisions Faced by Gifted and Talented Females" (2002), continue to suggest that this is the case for many.[7]

The perspective that the super slacker girls offer us is a depressing one, not just because they are wasting their talents in temp agencies, retail outlets, and morgues, but also because it does not surprise us that they should do so. Nonetheless, the dramatization of the bright girls' dilemma on popular television can offer us insights and perspectives on the conditions that being both gifted and female creates for them in contemporary culture.

Teen television, Douglas Kellner asserts, can offer "an allegorical spectacle about contemporary life" and illuminate aspects of the situation of contemporary youth.[8] It is particularly fantasy television, a genre much overlooked if not derided by the arbiters of quality (see, for example, Rhonda Wilcox's *Why Buffy Matters* [2005] for further discussion[9]), that Kellner suggests provides us with "access to social problems and issues and hopes and anxieties that are often not articulated in more 'realist' cultural forms."[10] The issues, hopes, and anxieties articulated through Georgia, Jaye, and Joan are those surrounding contemporary issues for able youth and the tensions and intersections surrounding gender.

Why Georgia Lass Will Not Get Out of Bed

Dead Like Me's Georgia (George) Lass embodies the dilemma of youth, and particularly able, articulate youth, in late capitalist culture. A disassociated, disaffected college dropout, George is sent to a temp agency by her exasperated mother to find gainful employment. The randomness of life, and death, is dramatically illustrated when on her very first lunch break she is killed by a lavatory seat falling from a space station. To her surprise, immediately after her death she is recruited as a "Reaper," one of a team of beings whose role it is to take the souls of those about to die and conduct them on to the next stage. This odd team comes to constitute a replacement family for George, and through both her progress as a Reaper and the simultaneous need (much to her chagrin) to support herself financially, she achieves a sort of reengagement with life and a connectedness to others.

It is via George's voice-over of the opening scenes that her dilemma is established. Over a shot of herself awaiting an interview at the Happy Time employment agency, she tells us, "I excel at not giving a shit. Experience has taught me that interest begets expectation and expectation begets disappointment, so the key to avoiding disappointment is to avoid interest. A equals B equals C or A or whatever. I also don't have a lot of interest in being a good person or bad person, from what I can tell either way you are screwed" (*Dead Like Me* 1.1). She recognizes that the external pressure created by her abilities (clearly smart) and her situation (privileged, educated, white) conflict with what she sees the world as capable of delivering in terms of possibilities; even a moral compass becomes arbitrary in a hard world with few securities other than that hardness. And as a smart girl in particular, she is likely to recognize more easily and experience more acutely the dilemmas and limitations of her condition.[11] In a rare moment of perception, her mother diagnoses her daughter's malaise, commenting, "She was stubborn. I think that was only because she was smart, probably too smart" (*Dead Like Me* 1.1).

From the outset George is coded as privileged through her appearance, the establishment of her domestic situation, and the dialogue and voice-over, which fill in her background. The nature and style of her observations set the tone for the show: smart, sharp, and cynical. Given her privileged status, her cynicism seems needlessly pessimistic and self-dramatizing. However, even allowing for the exaggerations of teen angst, her dilemma is real and contemporary. Young people of her generation are the first to be more in doubt of their economic future than their parents were. The myth of progress and continued self-betterment has been exploded for them in a postmodern world where identities, job securities, and family structures are no longer stable. As Henry Giroux observes, "For many postmodern youth, showing up for adulthood at the fin-de-siecle means pulling back on hope and trying to put off the future rather than taking up the modernist challenge of trying to shape it."[12] He cites Andrew Kopkind's analysis, which is worth repeating here:

> The domestic and economic relationships that have created the new consciousness are not likely to improve. . . . The choices for young people will be increasingly constricted. In a few years, a steady job at a mall outlet or a food chain may be all that's left for the majority of college graduates. Life is more and more like a lottery. Slacking is thus a rational response to casino capitalism, the randomization of success, and the utter arbitrariness of power. If no talent is still enough, why bother to hone your skills? If it is impossible to find a good job, why not slack out and enjoy life?[13]

Steven Gibb puts it more succinctly: "Perhaps the cruelest joke played on our generation is the general belief that if you went to college, you'll get a job and be upwardly mobile."[14]

George, as we see in flashbacks of the day leading up to her death, tries to stave off the future by staying in bed and denying the day. The unfolding drama does not try to deny the validity of her vision of hopelessness and insecurity, but rather lends it credence. This is especially apparent in the portrayal of her supervisor and quasi-mentor at Happy Time, Dolores Herbig. She is terminally perky and relentlessly optimistic in the face of the banality of her job and the insignificance of her existence. She is both troubled by and critical of George's negative attitude and tells her, "A sunny disposition goes a long way in any line of work, especially here at Happy Time. Trust me, no employer is going to want a sad sack on their hands. Look at me; I certainly wouldn't have gotten far as that." Showing both her talent for perception and an ability to go for the jugular, George cruelly takes her up on her last comment, pointing out, "It's not like this is a corner office with a view and like every day, you have to find jobs for other people, mostly that are going to be better than yours and that has to suck and I bet they don't pay you much either"(*Dead Like Me* 1.1). Dolores here represents the end result of the pleasing behaviors demanded of girls while they are growing up, a set of behaviors that George, like may of the angry, bright young women described in Mary Pipher's *Reviving Ophelia* (1994), aggressively rejects.[15]

With the clever irony typical of the show, we later find that not only does George end up working (postmortem) for Happy Time itself under Dolores, but that her other "job" as a Reaper is, in essence, a variation on the same theme. Her role will be to conduct others on to other places while stuck in a kind of limbo herself, and she will not be paid at all. The fact that the Reapers have to live the lives of the marginal and the dispossessed, supporting themselves with minimum wage jobs or robbing the dead, squatting in the deceased's abandoned apartments, reinforces the precarious nature of existence for the clever girl born into Generation Y. The impersonal callousness of the career lottery is further underlined by the way in which Reapers are recruited. George happened to be the last soul "reaped" by her predecessor, who had filled his quota and could move on. George is recruited regardless of her own desires or suitability for the post; her character, aptitudes, and identity are all unimportant in fulfilling this cosmic McJob.

As well as embodying stereotypically pleasing feminine behaviors, Dolores is also important in representing the sources of satisfaction available to women in their professional lives as she demonstrates for George the art of engagement with the human minutiae of corporate life. It is Dolores who remembers the birthdays, organizes the leaving parties, and continues to demand George's participation in the face of her young protégé's cynicism. Ultimately, though, charmed as we may be by Dolores, the message is disturbing in two ways. First, it suggests that satisfaction at work is not to be expected from the work itself but from the contingent relationship opportunities; George's working routine is only varied by opportunities to file or to photocopy, to input data or to answer the telephone. This is a depressing view of professional life to be offered to the brilliant young woman. Her talents are unemployed because unrecognized, and her supervisor is more interested in developing her attitude that her aptitudes. Second, such satisfactions as Dolores represents, those of connectedness and nurturing, constitute a fundamentally gendered outcome, an issue I shall be exploring later.

Through George we also see how fragility of the contemporary nuclear family (via divorce, upheaval, problem children, and parents committed beyond the home) can have an impact on the gifted girl. The complications of the Lass's domestic situation clearly contribute to George's negative outlook. Like the depiction of her working life, this situation is not without its gendered message. In the pilot episode, George describes her mother, Joy, with contempt as a "career secretary" and manages to convey simultaneous disapproval of her both for working and for not having a high-status job. Here we get a further glimpse into the nature of George's paralysis; as a gifted individual, she is expected to have a successful career, but in doing so she may incur social disapproval as a working woman if that conflicts with other roles. In her very act of expressing contempt for her mother, we can see that she has absorbed and participates in the mixed messages aimed at smart women.

George's alternative Reaper family underscores the importance of parental care and modeling in the clever girl's development. Although the head Reaper Rube heartlessly refuses to support George, he is recognizably the patriarch of sitcom and myth, to be fought with and tricked but ultimately deferred to and respected. His success in reengaging her with life mirrors the findings of Kerr's study of successful women, which identifies the influence of a strong parental presence as a key factor in building ambition, resilience, and self-concept.[16] It is troubling that this presence is here decidedly patriarchal and that in George's previous life her mother is so cold and career-driven; are we to blame the working mother for her slacker daughter's disaffection? In fact, as the narrative progresses over its two seasons, Joy works to build a better bond with her younger daughter, and rather than staying home, she finds more personally fulfilling work after her divorce.

George's situation reflects another dilemma for contemporary youth—that of protracted adolescence. On her last day alive, her mother forces her out of bed, telling her, "Eighteen years of coddling is enough for you, young lady. You think you are going to spend the rest of your life suckling at my retirement fund. You've got another thing coming. You will get out of bed and you will work, you will collect a paycheck and you will move out of this house. Understood?"(*Dead Like Me* 1.1). After she is vigorously encouraged out of her family home, one of the shocks for George in her afterlife is the callous refusal of any of her new constituted Reaper "family" to give her temporary bed and board. For her, it is time to grow up, and while the viewer feels anxiety for George in having to cope with this enforced independence, there is also perhaps a degree of sympathy for the adults who refuse to accommodate this healthy, intelligent, active young adult. A sort of paralysis in the face of looming adult responsibility and the need for self-sufficiency is highlighted as a contributory factor to the slacker pathology. The cost and duration of education have kept the well-schooled young dependent on their parents for much longer than previous generations. While this may imply the luxury of continued care, protection, and even pampering, it is also ultimately incapacitating; it is as adults that our educated, brilliant young women are eventually turned out into a world that demands survival skills they may have never had the chance to develop.

George poses this question to us via her voice-over narrative: "Do you know what it is like, to be like, cusping on adulthood and not know who you are? What you want to be or even if you want to be? It's ten shades of suck, is what it is" (*Dead Like Me* 1.1). Here the postmodern nature of her dilemma is encapsulated; her crisis is one of identity and uncertainty. Being bright, she has the self-awareness to recognize her malaise; but, being unambitious, she has no solutions. In the face of unstable social, financial, and cultural structures, the solution offered is through connectedness; a sense of identity and self-actualization is achieved through caring for others and actively working for the good of the community. In *Dead Like Me*, as in each of the other dramas, the supernatural rehabilitation of the slacker girl through good works could be read as a moral and ethical transcendence of contemporary identities and cultural uncertainties or, more disturbingly, as a reinforcement of traditionally ascribed attributes for girls, a relegation of the woman's sphere of interest to the personal and the nurturing. Furthermore, it could be argued that the qualities nurtured in the super slackers via self-abnegating and generous acts are those that characterize the culturally subordinated—an issue that recurs in *Wonderfalls*.

Why Jaye Taylor Will Not Get in the Boat

Superficially, Jaye Taylor's identity as a smart young woman would appear as secure as George's should be. Both are what Angela McRobbie describes in "Post-feminism and Popular Culture" (2004) as the "A1 girls" of the affluent West: attractive, bright, and privileged, with access to an education that should guarantee professional opportunity and financial security.[17] However, through Kellner and Giroux, we have already recognized that an education no longer guarantees a secure, fulfilling future. Super slacker dramas also challenge the optimism of popular culture's postfeminist vision. The postfeminist era, if we acknowledge such a periodization, is one characterized by choice and by what Elyce Rae Helford describes as a "hopeful, positive tone."[18] Postfeminist representations also tend to focus on women of the white middle or upper classes, women with access to a wealth of opportunities.[19] All three of my super slacker girls belong to this group and should, in theory, identify with the images; however, they refuse to do this. For them, slacking is an act of resistance. Perhaps the slacker girl represents television's recognition of the reality gap between the optimism of postfeminist popular culture and the constraints of the reality experienced by bright women.

Despite her privileged and educated position, eighteen-year-old George drops out of college when she has barely begun ("some college seemed like enough," *Dead Like Me* 1.1). And Jaye, although successfully graduating college, refuses to participate further and takes a job in a souvenir shop at Niagara Falls. It is the shop's tourist knickknacks, stuffed animals, statuettes, and the like, that embody the supernatural voice on this show, a fitting medium for the message that engagement with the everyday, no matter how banal, may be the key to redemption.

The locating of the series at Niagara Falls is not accidental; Jaye is thus physically as well as developmentally located on the brink, of both a waterfall and of girlhood/womanhood. The prospect of both is terrifying, and like George, she is stuck in a kind of limbo while dealing all day with others who are passing through and moving on. From the outset, both Georgia and Jaye recognize the illusion of control of one's destiny, of the passport of education, and of the possibilities supposedly open to them as brilliant girls.

Jaye Taylor's family embodies privilege and possibility. Being successful professionals (doctor father, writer mother, lawyer sister, and academic brother), they are horrified by her job and by the fact that she lives in that ultimate signifier of downward mobility, a trailer. At twenty-four, she represents the farther end of the protracted adolescence mentioned earlier. As her sister points out: "Troubled teen is no longer flattering on you" (*Wonderfalls* 1.1.). Unlike George, however, Jaye leaves the parental home through choice; her decision to do so is strongly reminiscent of Kathleen Noble's description of the beginning of her own "hero's journey" in *The Sound of a Silver Horn: Reclaiming the Heroism in Contemporary Women's Lives* (1994). Noble describes how she knew she would incur her family's "wrath, rejection, and estrangement" and also lose their financial support. But she describes the necessity of following her own path for the sake of her "sanity, hopes, and dreams."[20] Leaving both the comforts and the pressures of the family constellation can be a necessary survival strategy for the gifted girl; the importance of this strategy for Jaye's self-respect is underlined when she complains that her elder brother, Aaron, "is considered more successful than I am but is still living at home"(*Wonderfalls* 1.2). Both the validity of her choice and the financial insecurity it entails are underscored by Aaron, who lives at home because he is pursuing his doctorate. Here we have both a sly sideswipe at her brother for not being independent, and an acknowledgment that independence can be hard to achieve for the aspiring academic.

While there are many similarities with George's dilemma, Jaye's own analysis and response seem more deliberately gendered, and one can find resonance with contemporary feminist analysis. McRobbie identifies the ways in which increasingly independent and financially self-supporting young women have become "disembedded" from communities where gender identities were fixed and class structures stable; these young women are called upon increasingly to "invent their own structures . . . both internally and individualistically, so that self-monitoring practices (the diary, the life plan, the career pathway) replace reliance on set ways and structured pathways. . . . As the over-whelming force of structure fades, so does the capacity for agency increase." She states,

"Individuals must now choose the kind of life they want to live. Girls must have a life plan," and she links such accounts of "reflexive modernization" to the dilemmas facing such popular culture heroines as Bridget Jones.[21] While McRobbie chooses Bridget Jones as her illustrative example, Rachel Mosely and Jacinda Read view in *Ally McBeal* a dramatization of the frustrations of the "utopian project" of the bright young woman's life.[22] They draw our attention to this speech of Ally's in the show: "I had a plan. . . . Big home life, big professional life, and instead, I am going to bed with an inflatable doll, and I represent clients who suck toes. This was not the plan."[23]

While it is true that *Ally McBeal* does not reject the aims or premise of Ally's "Big Plan," the show does support postfeminist analysis such as McRobbie's in that, as in *Bridget Jones*, the apparent culture of choice and flexibility is in fact constrained and compels the individual to be the person who can make the successful choices. For women especially, the choices are loaded with risk, and an awareness of this fact can be paralyzing. I would argue that this awareness is a factor in Jaye Taylor's stasis. Here we have a further insight into the slacker girl's dilemma, one that reflects the particular constraints and conditions created for the smart girl by her gender. The postfeminist heroine has not the advantages of her Second-Wave forebears, because the nature of individualization itself makes a collective response/resistance, with its attendant community identities and securities, impossible by its very nature. Where is she then to look for security, fulfillment, community, and guidance?

Jaye is intriguing because she resists not only traditionally inscribed roles and pathways for women, but also the culture of female individualization, the illusion of choice, which has superseded them.

The *Wonderfalls* pilot opens, as does *Dead Like Me*'s, with a variation on the voice-over. It is interesting that both shows should choose this technique, which allows the demonstration of the heroine's metacognitive awareness (a distinguishing feature of the gifted individual[24]) of her own dilemma, an understanding of and ability to analyze her plight (even though she lacks energy), and resources or strategies to resolve it—hence the need for supernatural intervention.

Central to the introductory episode of *Wonderfalls* is the "Maid of the Mist" myth, which becomes a central motif for Jaye's own plight. The Maid is a Native American princess. In terms of her combined talent and privilege, one could argue that Jaye is the twenty-first-century version of the princess, the highest status attainable by a young woman, with the brightest future. Joan is introduced narrating the story for the edification of tourists visiting the falls. The use of the myth establishes Jaye's analysis of her plight as more overtly gendered than George's from the outset. The Maid is put in a boat and sent over the falls as a sacrifice to the god of the falls whose fancy she has caught. She does not protest; "I surrender to destiny" are her last words. But she is eventually saved, to live with the god in his cave beneath the falls because, as Jaye puts it, "she was hot." The modern manifestation of the myth is presented immediately after the opening sequence, when a high school contemporary of Jaye's comes into the shop. This young woman shows off her expensive ring and announces that she has adopted her husband's religion and culture "for love." She has become the Maid, who is saved because she is "hot" but gives up her life and community in the process. So here then is a young woman's fate: throw yourself into the rushing river of life and hope a man will save you. However, this will only happen if you are "hot," and you will lose yourself anyway. No wonder Jaye would rather waste her days selling tourist tat at the river's edge.

Jaye's response to the myth, her slacker stance, is clearly her refusal to undertake the Maid's sacrificial role. This is underlined later in the episode when she turns a video show of the story in the shop into her own Rocky Horror-style audience participation event, telling the princess, "Don't get in the boat!" and then calling her "Dumbass!" when she does. To emphasize the metaphor at work, she is shown watching the story three times in the pilot alone, and it is referred to in later episodes too. From the outset, we find that the underachieving behaviors that Jaye adopts are a sort of protective coloring, one that will stop her from getting appropriated and negated by a god or sacrificed by her community. She later instructs a trainee: "A combination of body language and 'tude can create a kind of invisible protective barrier" (*Wonderfalls* 1.2).

However, while Jaye rejects a traditional role, she seems incapable of taking advantage of or unwilling to access other possibilities. In refusing to be an Ally McBeal—achieving much yet obsessing over her career, partner choices, biological clock, and appearance— she is also refusing to "invent her own structures" in the way described above by McRobbie; Jaye thus embodies aspects of the postfeminist as well as postmodern dilemma.

Part of this dilemma is Jaye's understanding that identity, especially for women, is inherently unstable; the very first episode confronts her with three instances. There is the notion that she has outgrown her well-worn rebellious teenager armor and must choose another "self" to be; she is brought face-to-face with an old classmate who has adopted a new cultural persona as if born to it, and in the same opening episode her sister changes her sexual identity, apparently done in an instant. (Jaye: So you're a lesbian now? Sharon: Just now.) These instances show Jaye that identity is not fixed. The passing of time, what she does, and the person with whom she chooses to be will change who she is.

This is especially true for adolescents, and especially girls. Adolescence itself is defined by what it is not. Unlike the states of teenhood or puberty, there is no temporal or biological end point; the state is that of transition between two periods of culturally defined stability: childhood and adulthood. For girls, adolescence is com- plicated further by what Judith Butler has revealed to be the performative nature of girlhood and femininity.[25] In her study, *Girls: An Analysis of Feminine Adolescence in Popular Culture* (2002), Catherine Driscoll shows how this performative nature becomes particularly acute in adolescence; for clever girls, the situation is even more acute, in that cleverness frequently becomes something that they need to disguise to achieve popularity.[26] While both Jaye and *Dead Like Me*'s Georgia are anxious to avoid creating expectation through their abilities, it is refreshing to see that neither masks her sharpness of either observation or expression.

The difficulty of distinguishing between performance and identity is illustrated in episode 2 of *Wonderfalls*. Jaye has to deal with a strange stalking journalist, Bianca, who steals her identity and "becomes" her. The fact that this is made possible by a change of dress and hairstyle, and by the picking up of some mannerisms, speech patterns, and a little attitude, draws our attention to the surface nature of identity.

As well as providing an illustration of this superficiality, Bianca gives a pithy analysis of the slacker state. She calls Jaye "the prototypical Gen-Y-er. You represent a generation of young people who've been blessed with education and opportunity and who don't just fall through the cracks, but jump though." She recognizes Jaye's intelligence but comments that it is only revealed though her "Ivy League irony." Bianca's analysis emphasizes the will, the agency involved in slacking, and defines it as an act of refusal, a choice in itself for the young woman confronted by too many choices.

Jaye demonstrates that, for the contemporary gifted girl, the adolescent identity crisis is particularly complex. First, she must move on to a state of apparent stability and choose who she is going to be for the rest of her life. Jaye recognizes that the apparently fixed identities from which she is choosing are performances. This awareness is written into the show, for example, when Bianca tells Jaye that her choice to live in a trailer is "the crowning achievement in the performance art that is your life." The resultant combination of pressure to choose and pressure to maintain performance results in both stress and a loss of sense of self and gives us, in effect, the slacker girl's dilemma. Again, this awareness is made clear through the dialogue when Bianca points out that Jaye's trailer is a metaphor for her life: full of the potential to go some-where but never moving—but never breaking down, either. She tells Jaye, "You've really managed to create a stressless, expectation-free zone for yourself"(*Wonderfalls* 1.2).

The resolution offered by *Wonderfalls* is the same as that offered by *Dead Like Me:* self-actualization via connectedness and service to others. The medium by which it is achieved in *Wonderfalls* is less dramatic—nobody has to die—but nonetheless super-natural. This resolution suggests not only that it is by authoritative intervention that the slacker girl can be shaken out of her paralysis, but also perhaps that women's roles and abilities are ordained to lie within certain spheres.

Jaye, like Georgia, is shown to be disconnected from others, as much unwilling to please as deficient in the art of pleasing. In fact, we discover in episode 2 that this unwillingness is her motivation for working in a tourist outlet. Tourists are merely passing through, and hence, as she says in episode 2, "You're never in any real danger of developing a rapport with them." She takes this unwillingness to its furthest limit and does not feel obliged to extend even politeness. In refusing to be "a people person," she refuses to perform femininity in the same way that George does. This behavior is interesting because it constitutes another layer to her rejection of the roles and identities that are on offer to bright young women. Both George and Jaye seem to share the suspicion of Carol Tavris in her *Mismeasurement of Women: Why Women are Not the Better Sex, the Inferior Sex or the Opposite Sex* (1992).[27] Tavris rejects what she describes as "cultural feminism" and its "appealing theories that women have a natural ability to be connected, attached, loving and peaceful," arguing that such a philosophy, while seeking to affirm women's self-esteem, keeps them focused on supposedly innate personality traits. It is refreshing therefore that Jaye, though lowest in the pecking order at work and at home, nonetheless continually locks horns with those in power; she calls her boss "Mouth Breather," she challenges customers, and she continually questions her parents. She may be slacking off, but she refuses to adopt subordinate behaviors in doing so.

It is interesting that both Jaye and George have women in their immediate families who have power in their professional roles: George's mother Joy and both Jaye's mother

Karen and sister Sharon (the rhyming of the names is not accidental—brother Aaron and father Darrin complete the set, serving to underscore her distance and difference from them) display these qualities. The fact that these highly achieving career women are presented either unsympathetically or as conflicted and unhappy is disturbing; part of the slacker girl's plight is that nowhere can she find a role model embodying identities or possibilities she can relate to or embrace.

Jaye gets the message to connect with others by the end of the first episode; after being instructed to give aid by a toy bear, she tells a customer, "I think I'm supposed to help you." Both ambivalence and compulsion are suggested by her choice of words, "I think" and "I'm supposed to," but given the absence of any other direction, help she does. Like George, Jaye is no easy mark; she continues in some ways to resist the message as well as the strange medium. Bianca's article encapsulates her plight at the end of episode 2:

> Like the Falls of Niagara which rage at the center of her little town, some powerful force threatens to sweep (Jaye) into the roiling chaos. It is a force against which she struggles, a power she cannot name. . . . Whether it is the undertow of contemporary life or something more ancient, . . . (Jaye) will continue to struggle.

This observation illustrates the dual nature of the dilemma of the contemporary gifted girl; she cannot see her way across the "rapids" of contemporary social and economic conditions, or the "undertow" of more deeply inscribed and culturally powerful notions of womanhood.

Why Joan Girardi Will Not Take a Shower

It is these culturally powerful notions that trouble my third and youngest super slacker. Joan Girardi, the most clearly adolescent of the three, is still in high school and is struggling in an environment where effective performance of girlhood is central to social survival. School is also the environment where intellect is most clearly on display and where the appearance (or not) of ability is inextricably bound up with social identity.

Like George and Jaye, Joan is in a state of transition. Her family has recently moved to the town of Arcadia, where her father has been made chief of police. In the seemingly closely knit and communicative family, there are nonetheless rifts and instabilities that contribute toward Joan's state of precariousness. The family has moved to start again after a road accident that left their eldest son, Kevin, formerly a popular athlete looking forward to an athletic scholarship, unable to walk. This accident demonstrates from the outset the instability not only of apparently secure social identities such as his as "jock," for adjusting to the loss of identity takes him longer and is far more complex than adjusting to the loss of mobility, but also of the Girardis as a stable, happy, lucky family. As in *Dead Like Me*, the show opens with the notion that nothing is certain.

It is into this mix of uncertainty that the voice of God is inserted, and God speaks to Joan. The formula broadly follows the same pattern each week: she is given a task by God, a task of which she can rarely see the point until she is confronted with the outcome. Through undertaking these duties, she is becoming better acquainted with the way the universe works and, like George and Jaye, learning the necessity for trust and connection between people. Joan's narrative arc finds her continually bumping against the socially inscribed definitions and constraints of girlhood: popularity, appearance, and sexual identity. The positions and identities she must assume in taking on the tasks are frequently uncomfortable for her but lead her to a better understanding of the adult she wants to become.

Expanding on the states of transition and instability that the first two shows displayed, *Joan of Arcadia* has added to the mix a direct addressing of the concepts of talent and giftedness, what they mean individually and culturally. What I find particularly interesting about this show is its dramatization of some of the gendered issues surrounding talent and genius within Western cultural history.

In her groundbreaking *Gender and Genius: Towards a Feminist Aesthetic* (1989), Christine Battersby explores the ways in which aptitudes and attitudes ascribed to the gifted are culturally and historically constructed around a presumption of male gender; genius in women, if acknowledged at all, is inherently problematic.[28] Through Joan, her mother, and her friends, one can observe some of the central tensions in constructions of gender and giftedness played out.

Talent and ability abound in Joan's family: her father, Will, is a successful policeman, highly effective in deductive reasoning; her mother, Helen, teaches art and is a talented painter in her own right. Kevin was a star athlete but now, wheelchair bound, discovers a talent for writing; Luke, the youngest child, is a scientific genius. At different points, Joan herself displays a range of talents, some of which are disconcerting to her parents and peers.

From the outset, we can see some clear divisions in the gendering of talent; the men are scientific, logical, and objective; the women are intuitive, creative, and connected. This reflects traditional gendered assigning of abilities—the privileged, quantifiable model identified as male, and the subordinate, instinctive/qualitative as female. However, in *Joan of Arcadia* these boundaries and binaries are disturbed in several ways. Kevin, as mentioned, turns his energies to writing when he loses his sporting abilities. This talent was previously unsuspected and may have remained dormant had he remained contained within his secure and privileged athletic identity. The same principle holds true for Joan. When she is forced, albeit unwillingly, to break the restrictions surrounding girls' behavior and achievements, she discovers hidden abilities.

It seems at first as if the tasks God gives her are designed to do just this. He makes her join the AP Chemistry class and then the chess club. He requires that she build a boat and take part in a competitive debate. All of these things compromise Joan's status and identity as "girl," just as she is engaged in negotiating her place within the social hierarchy at her new school. The issue for the intelligent female high school student we see highlighted here is this: to be smart is to be considered defective in girlhood. This phenomenon is well documented by educationalists and psychologists writing in the field of gender and giftedness; for example, Kerr observes of the able girl: "Her peers are caught up in symbols and rituals of adolescence. . . . Her acceptance into this world requires knowledge of the symbols and gracefulness in the rituals. And the culture is a quickly closed one: if she doesn't join in when she gets the chance, she may face ongoing social rejection."[29] This constitutes a recurring theme in *Joan of Arcadia*; the start of the pilot finds her anxiously trying on different outfits and hairstyles for school, indicating lack of security in her image and identity.

By the second episode, God shows concern about Joan's underachievement and instructs her to "stop squandering the potential" he gave her. She duly signs up for AP classes and finds that the only vacancy is in chemistry; the other girls distinguished in the class are Grace, who refuses to conform to any institutional expectations including those regarding gender-differentiated dress code, and Glynis, who is portrayed as the stereotypical girl version of the science geek, skinny, bespectacled, and enthusiastic about learning—matching bookend to Luke's boy science geek. However, Luke's growing attraction to Grace, and Glynis's growing discomfort with the constraints of her identity and her experimentation with alternate performances of femininity, form interesting developments later in the series, developments that challenge the straight-jacket of teen identities. For Joan, though, this AP class and her next task, joining the chess club, are enough to guarantee her social exclusion from the central popular coterie. Through defending Grace, Joan makes a moral choice regarding her friendship group but recognizes that this places her in the social category of "sub-defective." The choice of terminology is interesting—it is not that she has tried and failed to participate in the rituals of girlhood, as described above by Kerr (i.e., been "defective"), but that she rejects them as unworthy of investment. She is therefore beyond defective, a "sub-defective." She is branded, along with Grace and a collection of other opters-out of mainstream identity, as one who will not play the game.

As in *Wonderfalls*, the performed nature of girlhood is debated within the show. In episode 21, Joan is instructed by God to take a cosmetics class. She is quickly disheartened by what she sees as "the media's ideals of feminine beauty" and states that "caring about your appearance is a soulless expression of vanity." She takes this to extremes and refuses to shower or change her clothes. But she is then surprised by how hurt she is when her boyfriend Adam appears not to notice either her disheveled state or the fact that previously she was a walking cosmetics ad. She realizes that aspects of the performance are attractive to her—as does Glynis, who discovers the power of her own allure for the first time. The confluence of appearance with reality, of seeming with being, for girls is highlighted in this exchange:

Joan: Glynis has certainly become a different person.
God: It appears that way, doesn't it?

Through this episode, Joan comes to realize that all identity is to a degree performed, even Adam's too-cool-for-the-mall stance, and Joan is more forgiving of herself and of others for their pleasure in surfaces. Notwithstanding this quasi-acceptance, she remains anxious that she and Adam should achieve some sort of authenticity with each other.

Joan recognizes and comes to some sort of accommodation with her need for personal authenticity and surface/preformed aspects of girlhood. However, the fundamentally gendered nature of her talents and the ways in which they are realized also reveal some interesting tensions. Repeatedly, her abilities are positioned as intuitive and female and in opposition to the objective logic of the constraining and limiting, largely male, forces abounding in her world. Representing these forces is Mr. Price, the cynical and unsympathetic vice-principal, the defender of "Premise, argument, conclusion. The correctness of reasoning"(*Joan of Arcadia* 1.2), and also Joan's sympathetic father, who is deeply suspicious of alternative medicine, psychics, and all things religious.

When in episode 3 Joan wins a chess match, faculty and family find it hard to believe: she does not know the rules; she plays by chaos and intuition, which God tells her are "impossible to guard against" through logic. Observers can only categorize her triumph as genius, because they cannot understand it in any other way. In another episode, she, Grace, and Adam manage to solve a chemical equation though working backward and combining their peculiar talents, which include Joan's lateral thinking and Adam's photographic memory. Joan's science whiz-kid brother Luke's comment underscores the scientific rejection of reasoning that is not logical and linear: "It's like watching three monkeys build a particle accelerator using tinfoil and a B-B gun"(*Joan of Arcadia* 1.2). Regarding Joan's success at chess, he speculates, "You see four moves ahead, it's empirical. You see five moves ahead, it's still grounded in science. . . . Now maybe if you see twelve moves ahead, maybe you're crossing over into psychic phenomena" (*Joan of Arcadia* 1.3). He attempts to find a rational scientific explanation.

The centrality of intuition, and its forays into traditionally male fields of expertise, is again demonstrated in episode 4 when God orders Joan (who has no carpentry skills) to build a boat. She is at first understandably reluctant; her astounded "Build a boat? Why couldn't you ask me to get a boyfriend?" shows where her priorities lie. Once started, she throws away the blueprint and builds it intuitively. Miraculously, it fits together, and she is on a roll of commitment and enthusiasm, until Mr. Price convinces her that she cannot build a boat at all. At this point, her intuition and creative energy desert her; the pieces no longer seem to fit and she abandons the project altogether. The message here regarding the impact of others' beliefs on girls' abilities is clear, as is that regarding the relative value of intuition and inspiration as opposed to logic and reason.[30]

This dichotomy is deeply ingrained into Western constructions of genius, and it is Battersby who points out the double bind for women: a legacy of the Romantic period is the conception of genius as a quality divinely inspired or derived, intuitive, passionate, and beyond reason.[31] Yet, as Jenny Boyce-Tilman affirms in her analysis of prevailing knowledge systems in the West, these are the very same qualities that culturally define women's thinking as opposed to, and subordinate to, the rationality of the male model.[32] The roots of this belief, Battersby finds, reach back to Aristotelian traditions of femininity as "deficient in judgment, wit, reason, skill, and talent."[33] The definition of genius is, therefore, of a man who also possesses the traditionally female qualities of intuition, irrationality, imagination, and passion. A woman displaying these qualities is not a genius—she is simply a woman. Battersby quotes Edmond de Goncourt's epigram to summarize such perspectives: "There are no women of genius; the women of genius are men."[34]

In *Joan of Arcadia*, as in *Dead Like Me* and *Wonderfalls*, not only is connectedness and engagement with others consistently maintained as imperative for the brilliant girl, but, in Joan particularly, the inherently gendered nature of her very smartness makes her peculiarly fitted for such work. Her very intelligence is characterized by intuition, connectedness, and empathy.

The Super Slackers: Challenging Postmodernists or Chastened Postfeminists?

A study undertaken by Kathleen Noble, et al., at the turn of the millennium would seem to support the forms of cultural feminism as dramatized through the super slacker girls.[35] It found that, typically but not exclusively, for women and girls from minority groups and developing countries, talents are made manifest within the available sphere of influence, so that for many women this manifestation means the home, family, and immediate community. Perhaps the reallocation of the super slacker's exercising of their abilities to these same spheres in the face of uncertainty is a sign of anxiety regarding economic recession among the middle classes.

The super slacker girl represents a critical, and in some respects feminist, response to an increasingly insecure, competitive, and materially driven cultural climate. If her education no longer delivers security and prosperity, as is the case with Georgia, she will drop out. If the realities of professional life do not live up to the postfeminist promise of "having it all," as with Jaye, she will not engage with it. If she feels increasingly the pressure to consume and conform in her identity and appearance, like Joan, she will not play the game. As such, the slacker phenomenon could be seen as a positive development, one that supersedes the anxious femininity of *Ally McBeal* and the neurotic consumption of *Sex and the City*, because it exposes the false promise of the postfeminist turn in popular culture and creates a new model for bright young women, a model in which fulfillment is defined not in terms of material or romantic success, but in terms of self-actualization through community engagement.

However, it is equally and more disturbingly possible to read the super slackers as the latest manifestation of a tradition that allots women spheres of influence within the personal rather than the professional, a tradition that characterizes their best abilities as lying within intuition and nurturing. For Georgia, Jaye, and Joan, an external voice continually directs their energies toward the service of others. This voice engages them in actions and situations where it is required that they take the benefits on trust and where the sole reward is personal growth and understanding. The girls learn to perform their allotted tasks accepting that society rather than they themselves will benefit. In *Chosen Ones: Reading the Contemporary Teen Heroine* (2004), Jenny Bavidge shows how *Buffy the Vampire Slayer* works as a contemporary model of the American heroine, a construct that characterizes girls as figures of social redemption and salvation.[36] For the gifted girl, this construct gains extra resonance; as her powers are greater, so is her potential to disrupt as well as to redeem. The supernatural element of the super slacker show—whether it speaks via an undead patriarch, a stuffed toy, or the personification of God—becomes the voice of cultural anxiety, the speaking of the need to control and contain the powers of gifted young women. Ultimately, the response to the slacker girls' dilemma illustrated in these dramas is a reaffirmation of the old adage "Be good, sweet maid, and let who will be clever."

Notes

1. See for example, Linda Morton, "Targeting Generation X," *Public Relations Quarterly* 48.4 (2003): 43–45; and Robert Miklititsch, "Gen-X TV: Political-Lividinal Structures of Feeling in *Melrose Place*," *Journal of Film and Video* 55.1 (2003). 16–30.

2. Laurie Ouliette, "Victims No More: Postfeminism, Television and *Ally McBeal*," *Communication Review* 5 (2002): 315–335.

3. Rachel Mosely, "The Teen Series," in *The Television Genre Book*, ed. G. Creeber (London: BFI, 2005), cited in Glyn Davies and Kay Dickinson, eds., *Teen TV: Genre, Consumption and Identity* (London: BFI, 2004), 7.

4. Leonie Rutherford, "Teen Futures: Discourses of Alienation, the Social and Technology in Australian Science Fiction Television Series," in *Teen TV*, Davies and Dickinson, 29.

5. Carol. S. Dweck, *Self Theories: Their Role in Motivation, Personality and Development*, (Philadelphia: Psychology Press Taylor & Francis, 2000), cited in C. J. Cimister, "Bright Girls Who Fail: The Limitations of the Active Passive Learner," *Gifted Education International* 20.1 (2005): 88–97.

6. Barbara Kerr, *Smart Girls: A New Psychology of Girls, Women and Giftedness* (Scottsdale, AZ: Gifted Psychology Press, 1997), 170.

7. Sally M. Reis, "Internal Barriers, Personal Issues, and Decisions Faced by Gifted and Talented Females," *Gifted Child Today* 1.1 (2002): 2.

8. Douglass Kellner, "*Buffy the Vampire Slayer* as Spectacular Allegory: A Diagnostic Critique" in *Kinderculture: The Corporate Construction of Childhood*, ed. S. Steinberg and J. Kincheloe (Cambridge, MA: Westview Press, 2004), 49.

9. Rhonda Wilcox, *Why Buffy Matters: The Art of Buffy the Vampire Slayer* (London: I. B. Tauris, 2005).

10. Kellner, 50.

11. This aspect of gifted girlhood is discussed in Mary Pipher, *Reviving Ophelia: Saving the Selves of Adolescent Girls* (New York: Ballantine Books, 1994).

12. Henry Giroux, "Slacking Off: Border Youth and Postmodern Education," *JAC: Journal of American Composition* 14.2 (1994): 7.

13. Andrew Kopkind, "Slacking toward Bethlehem," *Grand Street Magazine*, Issue 10 (1992): 87.

14. Cited in Steve Best and Douglass Kellner, "Contemporary Youth and the Postmodern Adventure," http://www.gseis.ucla.edu/faculty/kellner/papers/youth.htm (accessed 12 September 2005). No source given.

15. Pipher, 11.

16. Barbara Kerr, Michael Gottfried, Corissa Chopp, and Sanford Cohn, "The Happy Family Studies: Exploring the Origins of Creative Lives," http://courses.ed.asu.edu/ kerr/ happy_family.rtf (accessed 22 September 2005).

17. Angela McRobbie, "Post-feminism and Popular Culture," *Feminist Media Studies* 4.3 (Philadelphia: Taylor & Francis, 2004), 259.

18. Elyce Rae Helford, "Tank Girl: Postfeminist Media Manifesto," www.electronicbookreview. com/thread/writingpostfeminism/solo (accessed 13 November 2005).

19. Ouliette, 316.

20. Kathleen Noble, *The Sound of a Silver Horn: Reclaiming the Heroism in Contemporary Women's Lives* (New York: Ballantine Books, 1994), 18.

21. McRobbie, 260.

22. Rachel Mosely and Jacinda Read, "Having it *Ally*: Popular Television (Post-) Feminism," *Feminist Media Studies* 2.2 (2002): 247.

23. Quoted in Mosely and Read, 247.

24. Metacognition and giftedness was the focus of much research in the field of Gifted Education in the 1990s, and this work continues to inform development of programs internationally. For a discussion of the correlative relationship see, for example, Pui-wan Cheng, "Metacognition and Giftedness: The State of the Relationship," *Gifted Child Quarterly* 37.3 (1993): 105–112; L. K. Chan, "Motivational Orientations and Metacognitive Abilities of Intellectually Gifted Students," *Gifted Child Quarterly* 40.4 (1996): 184–193; and Norbert Jausovec, "Are Gifted Individuals Less Chaotic thinkers?" *Personality and Individual Differences* 25.2 (1998): 253.

25. Judith Butler, *Gender Trouble: Feminisation and the Subversion of Identity* (New York: Routledge, 1990).

26. Catherine Driscoll, *Girls: An Analysis of Feminine Adolescence in Popular Culture* (New York: Columbia University Press, 2002).

27. Carol Tavris, *Mismeasurement of Women: Why Women Are Not the Better Sex, the Inferior Sex or the Opposite Sex* (New York: Simon & Schuster, 1992), 324, cited in Kerr, *Smart Girls*.

28. Christine Battersby, *Gender and Genius: Towards a Feminist Aesthetics* (London: Women's Press, 1989).

29. Kerr, 126.

30. For discussion of gendered perceptions of abilities in schools and the effects of female students see, for example, B. Francis, "The Gendered Subject: Students' Subject Preferences and Discussions of Gender and Subject Ability," *Oxford Review of Education* 26.1 (2000) 35–48.

31. Battersby, 10.

32. June Boyce-Tilman, "Unconventional Wisdom—Theologising the Margins" *Feminist Theology* 13.3 (2005): 317–341.

33. Battersby, 12.

34. Edmond de Goncourt, originally quoted in Cesare Lombrose, *The Man of Genius* (London: Scott, 1891), cited in Battersby, 5.

35. Kathleen Noble, "To Thine Own Self Be True: A New Model of Female Talent Development," *Gifted Child Quarterly* 43.4 (1999):140–149.

36. Jenny Bavidge, "Chosen Ones: Reading the Contemporary Teen Heroine," in *Teen TV*, Davies and Dickinson, 43.

CHAPTER 6

Back to the Future: The Brilliant Witches in *Bewitched*

Linda Baughman, Allison Burr-Miller,
and Linda Manning

Witches are better than you and I. Well, popular culture witches, anyway. The "real" ones, the ones at local county fairs who are too thin with the inevitable red hair, and the ones in cities with their own tarot reading studio are, admittedly, a bit mystifying. But the television witches and the movie witches are amazing. When we are not busy being more than a little afraid of these powerful women—after all, who wishes to cross the Wicked Witch of the West in Oz, or the Blair Witch?—we want to be like them. Who would not want to control flying monkeys, command armies, terrify campers, alter time and space, materialize needed objects from thin air, and fly?

We like to dream it could happen; a woman could wake up one morning to discover she is a witch. After all, Michael J. Fox woke up one day to discover he was a werewolf. But that was in the movie *Teen Wolf* (1985). None of us will actually wake to discover we are witches. Nevertheless, witches are important; they are a central part of our national as well as our media history. Few place names resonate more than Salem, Massachusetts, for its association with the seventeenth-century witch trials. As children in modern America, we were raised on Disney's wicked witches in *Snow White* (1937), *Sleeping Beauty* (1959), and *The Little Mermaid* (1989). We cut our teeth on the *Wizard of Oz*'s Wicked Witch of the West and Glenda the Good Witch (1939). The recent film *Chronicles of Narnia* (2005) depends on the actions of the evil White Witch. Contemporary movies even feature teenager witches; Harry Potter's pal Hermione Granger is the best example.

Popular culture witches are more than powerful—they are brilliant. They do not simply have the power to turn us into candlesticks, feed us poisonous apples, or set flying monkeys on us. Witches use their heads. They pay attention to their surroundings and make the best of them, as when the White Witch in *Narnia* uses Edmund, who foolishly crosses her path, to destroy her enemy. They also find novel solutions to difficult puzzles, as when Hermione solves a difficult riddle in *Harry Potter and the Sorcerer's Stone* (2001). In short, witches are smart, successful women—not simply powerful ones—who help to create a space for strong, intelligent women.

Depictions of witches are a way by which our culture thinks about and grapples with the idea of brilliant women. After all, at some points in our history, intelligent women were thought to be as unlikely (and as potentially dangerous) as witches.[1] In a blatant pairing of intelligence and witchcraft, the Harry Potter series presents Hogwarts School of Witchcraft and Wizardry, where wise Professor McGonagall tutors Harry, and his female cohort demonstrates their mastery of spells, potions, and magic. Current media witches owe much to *Bewitched*; it was the series that reimagined witches, domesticating them. *Bewitched* created a space for the modern witch; it is a space that today's media witches continue to occupy—the home. Both Samantha of the television series and the recent Isabel of the movie *Bewitched* (2005) want nothing more than to settle down into a nice, calm, mortal suburb.

In earlier popular culture renderings, witches were smart, even wily, but rarely beautiful. They had warts, big teeth, dark straight hair, and green skin. The witches from *Macbeth*, the witches crafted by the brothers Grimm, and the aforementioned Disney witches support the tradition of physically ugly old women who are often feared as demons or witches. There were rare exceptions to this historical rule of hag, such as *I Married a Witch* (1942), in which the blonde Veronica Lake, a woman perhaps more beautiful and covertly naughty than any actress before or since, plays Jennifer, a witch out to avenge herself against the descendents of a man who persecuted her.[2] Instead, she falls for her mark, a hapless mortal. Romance, recklessness, and humor ensue, until all is resolved with a typical romantic happy ending. Although hags are suspected of being witches, witches need not always be hags. Another beautiful blonde witch appears in *Bell, Book, and Candle* (1958). In this film, the alluring Kim Novak plays the jaded and thin-skinned Gillian Holroyd, a witch who falls for Jimmy Stewart's Shep Henderson. After first toying with Shep, Gillian eventually falls in love with him and loses her power. Veronica Lake and Kim Novak were traffic-stopping beauties. Both were blonde sex symbols of their time. Both played clever, vengeful, knowing witches. Lake's Jennifer craftily messed up an important political marriage to satisfy her need for revenge. And while the New York beatnik scene pulsed in the film's background, Novak's powerless Gillian used her good sense, set to a bongo beat, to support herself, mortal-style, and win back Shep's love. In sum, these two exceptions are significant because they open up the shifting perception of witches at a cultural moment when women are beginning to assert themselves in ways that threaten the status quo.

Film witches are not our only representations of brilliant women wrapped in black magic. We also have stunning and smart television witches who come by their beauty and brilliance from their genealogy via Novak's and Lake's witches.[3] Witches are magical women who embody the intellectual, psychological, and emotional attributes (and charms) associated with powerful women. Elizabeth Montgomery's Samantha Stephens of the *Bewitched* television series (1964–1972) is the most important witch in American popular culture, after the green Wicked Witch of the West.[4]

At 350 years of age, Samantha is a Renaissance woman. The well-traveled Samantha can fit in anywhere. She vacations in exotic places: the Riviera and the moon. She was present at famous historic moments such as the Salem witch trials. She is informed and speaks Italian and Colonial English. Like Doctor Dolittle, she can speak to animals, including the Loch Ness Monster. She appears well-versed in the legal system and defends Ben Franklin from charges of theft in modern America and, more notably, Darrin from charges of witchcraft in old Salem. Moreover, she seamlessly performs an array of everyday tasks: cooking, cleaning, vacuuming, laundry, even mending broken objects. In short, Samantha is not just an amazing witch; she is an amazing woman.

Samantha has excellent television company, starting with her own family of witches: sarcastic mother Endora, hip cousin Serena, forgetful Aunt Clara, and the rest of her matriarchal world of witchcraft. There is also Jeannie from *I Dream of Jeannie* (1965–1970): while she is not really a witch, her power amounts to the same thing.[5] There are young television powerhouses—Alex Mac, Sabrina, and even Raven on Nickelodeon have power.[6] Finally, we cannot forget the cool contemporary witches of television, including the sweet lesbian witches of *Buffy the Vampire Slayer* (1997–2003) and the lovely sisters of *Charmed* (1998 to present).

Witches are interesting vehicles by which to explore the production of women inside popular culture. These women are smart, even mind-bogglingly clever. Our media landscape is troubled by intelligent women; it is littered with the debris of smart women who were not so smart after all and a mountain of truly embarrassingly dumb women: Corky Sherwood, Ally McBeal, Jeannie, Mary-Ann, and Ginger, and most female characters in Lifetime Channel movies. But witches are different; when we portray women as magical, and a little mean, they suddenly also become really smart—five-day winners on *Jeopardy* smart. This smartness makes witches worth contemplating, and Elizabeth Montgomery's Samantha provides a key to the media universe of magical women. As a transitional figure of the 1960s, she stands between the brilliant but mostly ugly and single-minded witches of the past and newer incarnations of witches—still brilliant, but pretty and with problems of an everyday sort.

Samantha's importance in the canon of our popular culture witches cannot be over-estimated. When we watch *That's So Raven* (2003 to present), *Sabrina, the Teenage Witch* (1996–2003), *Charmed*, and *Buffy the Vampire Slayer*, we measure these shows' stars against Samantha. Are they as clever and as smart? We remember her cleverness as she kept the bald Ben Franklin from getting frustrated and going to jail[7] and as she switched places with her more hip and less grounded "twin" cousin Serena, foiled her brilliant mother, and sparred with her hapless husband.[8] When we watch newer media witches on television or in film, we see them via Samantha's twinkling example; she is our lens for recognizing brilliance in the magical world of popular culture.

The modern American pop culture witch lives in the real world: a world of laundry, broken cars, empty bank accounts, and a little magic. The modern witch is domestic and smart, even while saving the world from demons or mean ex-boyfriends. The modern witch is street-smart. She can fix her car and kickbox and go to college or earn a living in a coffee house or working as an art dealer. This brand of witch starts with Samantha; she is the difference that makes the difference. Before her, witches were touchy, mostly mean-spirited, and ready to turn us into a variety of slimy amphibians at a moment's notice. Since Samantha, witches have often worked to help humans. They like us and, believe it or not, they want to be like us.

The women of the original television series *Bewitched* haunt us, both through our own media histories and through their reappearance in Nicole Kidman and Will Farrell's movie remake of the program. The Asher/Montgomery television series is a high-water mark for representations of smart women. Although the television series set the bar high, the respected media giants, the Ephron sisters, took up the challenge of presenting a contemporary read on how smart women can be articulated inside the home through the witch.[9] Most recent television series that focus on witchcraft (*Buffy the Vampire Slayer; Sabrina, the Teenage Witch;* and *Charmed*) understand witches as smart women located in the home. We are interested in how the witch offers a space for the representation of intelligent women inside the home. Specifically, we compare the standards of intelligent television witches, Samantha and Endora, with their contemporary film counterparts, Isabel and Iris.

We begin with the assumption that the television series *Bewitched*, as a part of our media history, is implicated in our cultural imagination. Using the notion of inter-textuality, we examine how *Bewitched* operates as a part of our cultural capital. Then we consider Samantha's place as the keystone on the bridge from the evil, spell-casting witches of the past to the powerful, mortal-loving witches in the present. Drawing on characters from the sitcom and the film, we address the media's production of domesticated intelligent witches. Finally, we ask, What is the importance of the witch as a vehicle for smart women?

Haunted by Witches

Samantha haunts us as the archetype of the modern witch. Her show was produced from the mid-1960s to the early 1970s, the same time we were carving out a space for the modern woman via the likes of the *Mary Tyler Moore Show* (1970–1977). Elizabeth Montgomery's beautiful blonde frame and Mary Tyler Moore's long legs linger with us, though neither program has produced a new episode since President Gerald Ford stumbled out of the White House. Though *Bewitched* went off prime time in 1972, it is—even without the Nicole Kidman remake—part of our modern media history. Samantha, Endora, Tabitha, and Serena are not trapped playing bridge and having tea parties in the 1960s and the 1970s on Morning Glory Circle; they are a part of our larger television experience. Originally, we watched them in prime time after a dinner of meat loaf and StoveTop stuffing; we later watched them in reruns along with Jeannie, Jethro Bodine, and Morticia and Gomez Addams after school with Oreos and milk. Recent generations of viewers wake up in the morning, eat cold pizza or cereal, and watch the brilliant women of *Bewitched* along with *Diff 'rent Strokes* (1978–1986) and *Fresh Prince of Bel Air* (1990–1996) on TV Land. The smart witches of *Bewitched* are a part of what the cultural studies scholar Lawrence Grossberg calls our media history.[10] Witches create a space in our media memory for women in the home who do not look like Elly May Clampett or Faith Fairfield.[11]

How do we remember our media? How do we come to know and understand "Beam me up, Scotty," Travolta's *Boy in the Plastic Bubble* (1976), *The L-Word* (2004 to present), and the mystical number eight via *Schoolhouse Rock* (1973–1985), especially now with cable and satellite and TiVo introducing new layers to our television viewing practices and experiences and the relationships between media texts?[12] Grossberg suggests that in this landscape of complicated media, television programs influence us without our having ever seen them.[13] The idea that Samantha only affected loyal fans of the show is incorrect. We all live in the shadow of this magical intelligent woman, because, as he argues, "television creates its own history and its own reality within which programs and characters increasingly refer to each other. . . . This is an intertextuality that requires no elite knowledge or even actual viewing history."[14] We use television to understand who we are and how we relate to one another. In short, given the focus of this chapter, television helps us understand what it means to be a smart woman.[15]

Bewitched is a part of our television present. It operates as a part of current cultural capital—when a woman wants to insult the new goofy guy her best friend is dating, she calls him Durwood. Our use and understanding of the characters, story lines, catchphrases, and even music of *Bewitched* live on through what Julia Kristeva calls intertextuality. It is "a way of making history go down in us."[16] The term hints at the fact that texts pay little attention to pesky things like the time-space continuum. Media events connect inside our collective media history, a history that aligns characters and concepts across medium, content, genre, and audience.[17] When we watch *Buffy the Vampire Slayer*, we compare both Buffy and her friendly witches to Samantha because of our media history.[18] When we watch Sabrina the teenage witch's life, we find the aunts and Sabrina's antics reminiscent of Samantha's hectic life. There is logic to the *Charmed* sisters' life sending demons back to hell, while also worrying if they will make it home in time for their dinner date, because we see them in the company of other intelligent domesticated witches, including Samantha, Endora, and Serena.[19] The witches of our recent media history are connected together via intertextuality and through their post-*Bewitched* heritage. Modern witches can be intelligent beauties because of *Bewitched*; its heritage allows modern witches to refuse earlier less complicated, and more evil, versions of the witch. We have gone from brilliant witches who fatten us up for dinner to clever witches who invite us over for pizza bites and lingerie parties (see figure 6.1).

Alive in our media landscape, the post-*Bewitched* witch is intelligent, like all witches of her past, but she is also recognizable as a desirable woman, rather than as a repulsive hag. This is a new element to the media understanding of intelligent women. Before *Bewitched*, it was easy to dismiss witches as powerful and nothing more. After *Bewitched*, we are able to understand that witches are not just magical; they are thinkers and beautiful women. *Bewitched* opened a space for the possibility of intelligent domestic women, who happened to be magical.

Media critics overlook the importance of the series as an arena for smart women and, instead, place the importance of *Bewitched* in other locales. Culturally speaking, the show has fingers in every pie—from the gender wars to nontraditional marriages. First, Susan Douglas argues that *Bewitched* is on the front lines of the "battle of the sexes." She suggests, in short, that in response to the feminist movement of the 1960s, puzzled men asked, "We gave them the vote, what else do they want?" The solution to the baffling nature of women's continued demands was to produce popular culture programming that curtailed the power of amazing women, like Samantha, by making them fall in love with simple men, like Darrin, who tried

Figure 6.1　Endora teaches Tabitha the finer points of flying. Credit: "Bewitched" © 1964, 2006 CPT Holdings, courtesy Sony Pictures Television.

to control them.[20] Douglas argues that *Bewitched* reflects the cultural anxiety of women's power awoken at that moment in American social history. David Marc adds to Douglas's reading of *Bewitched* as a show lingering in the world of male-dominated America. Focusing on Darrin's attempts to keep Samantha in line, Marc writes, "Darrin Stephens, however, is the most ideological committed sexist of them all. In episode after episode, he expects Samantha to entertain his advertising accounts at home, yet he forbids her from using her magical powers to do so . . . for no other reason than to satisfy his incorrigibly puritanical vision of what a marriage ought to be."[21]

There is more to this story of the witch who would be queen.[22] Scholars also read *Bewitched* as questioning this nostalgic view of family life. Disagreeing with Douglas and Marc, David Allan Case argues that *Bewitched* does not support conservative notions of the family but that it critiques them.[23] He finds that *Bewitched*'s production of the family as unreal and romantic undercuts "The American Father Who Had Once Known Best" (in this case, Darrin).[24] Finally, Dana Heller reads *Bewitched* as a program about the difficulties of a secret, mixed marriage: "As the civil rights and women's movements worked to shift the axis of legible identity from cultural 'consensus' to cultural 'difference,' the social anxieties that surfaced found a sort of displaced representation in family sitcoms such as *Bewitched*."[25] Heller argues that the show's eight-year run was about hiding the mixed nature of the Stephens' marriage (one mortal, one witch). When most media critics read *Bewitched*, they focus on it as a family sitcom. While this is interesting, they are brushing up against something fascinating—the intelligence of these domesticated witches—only to pass it by.

As with any cultural text, *Bewitched* can be, and was, many things to many viewers; it has enormous potential in our media history via intertextuality. But rather than focus, like other scholars, on its successes or failures in the battle of the sexes, we are interested in its place in our struggle concerning intelligent women in the home as they garner power from supernatural sources. Is it a coincidence that *Bewitched*'s reign on prime time happened simultaneously with the emergence of the Second Wave of the women's movement? At the very least, Samantha's continued ability to upstage her husband implicates the series in the struggle over how we define women as "smart and successful." Alice Jardine's work suggests that *Bewitched* does not have to be overtly feminist to be a part of the cultural conversation about intelligent women.[26] *Bewitched* arrived in our living rooms at a time when women were buying mirrors to view their naughty bits, finding that they needed to work twice as long to earn what men did, and reading *Cosmopolitan*. At the same moment, women were reconceptualizing their roles in society, a process mapped onto *Bewitched*'s landscape. In one sense, Samantha fits the traditional image of the successful woman: she settles down with a man with a good job, who buys her that charming little colonial in the suburbs. But there is more to her than that.

Why do we care whether media witches are smart or stupid any more than we care if they ride broomsticks or vacuum cleaners, and cook in cauldrons or Crock-Pots? Turning on the television or watching the latest movies tells us a great deal about how we view the world.[27] Using *Bewitched* and other television shows that have followed in its footsteps, we imagine smart women and the damage they can do through the image of the witch. By examining *Bewitched*, we can discover how smart women rate. This is not to say that the only smart women in our media history are witches, but the idea of the witch itself has us under a spell. Popular culture, from Samantha to Pru, tells us that witches are powerful because they are brilliant. There is a complex "war of position" being fought around our understanding of smart women, and popular culture is the battlefield.[28]

There are futures available to the women of *Bewitched* beyond a Danish Modern dinette set and a bone china gravy boat. The gap between the life Samantha leads and her mother's way of being allows many possibilities for smart women in the media. While Samantha lives in a nice house with a man, Endora does not. Inside the narrative of the series, we are not forced to choose one as smart and the other as a sad outcast. Instead, both are terribly clever and in control. Looking back from this side of history, it is easier to side with Endora because she does not flee the matriarchal world of witches and willingly cease using her powers to shack up with a man. But even if Samantha's lifestyle is not the one that we currently expect all smart women to choose, we still know she has a brain in her head—much like Isabel and Iris of the 2005 movie. The rest of this chapter examines how smart women reenter the home, but as witches, rather than as normal spouses—first through the television series *Bewitched*, then through the film *Bewitched*.

Bewitching, Brilliant, and Beautiful

The television series *Bewitched* is set in a suburb of New York City. Samantha, Darrin, and their two children, Tabitha and Adam, reside on 1164 Morning Glory Circle. Gladys Kravitz, the quintessential nosy neighbor, carefully scrutinizes the mortal and magical comings and goings from across the street. Samantha's mother, Endora, plays a vital role in the show. Her single-minded goal is to disrupt her daughter's embarrassing marriage to a mortal and whisk her back to where she belongs—preferably on Cloud Nine sipping ambrosia with a twist.

In the *Bewitched* series, we see the beginnings of modern media witches' understanding of life and love. For Samantha, love is not about casting a spell on your object of affection. She leaves love potions to her mother and opts for a more honest approach to love and the "happily ever after" life that follows. For example, in "If They Never Met," Endora bullies Samantha into visiting a world where she and Darrin have never married.[29] This happens because Endora's magical mischief causes Darrin to be fired again, and he rails that he would have been better off without his witchy spouse and her interfering family.[30] Suddenly, he disappears: Endora overhears his rant and, altering the time-space continuum, creates a reality where Darrin has not met her lovely daughter.

In this Samantha-free universe, Darrin is nothing like his usual boorish self; in fact, he comes dangerously close to cool. He is more successful at work, vacations in sunny spots, and is about to marry the wealthy Sheila. At one point, Samantha seems ready to hand her husband over to her sneaky nemesis. In the nick of time, Samantha sees him ditch his engagement party and head to Al's bar. She listens in as Darrin laments that something is missing in his life. Given a glimmer of hope, she zaps herself into the bar. He gazes at her with a "red-blooded" longing unbefitting a man on the eve of his nuptials. He resists buying her a drink and says he cannot stay. Here Endora almost gets rid of her son-in-law. Suddenly, he comes to his senses and says, "That was very rude of me. Not to mention stupid. This might be my last chance to buy a drink for a beautiful girl." Samantha and the audience know that she has won. By using her wits, patience, and wiles, for better or worse, Darrin is hers to keep. Samantha is an example of the intelligent domestic witch. Rather than disappearing into the night, she keeps her home and her family by using her head. She plays it cool and wins the day.

Having achieved the suburban utopia that seems to be her destiny, Samantha is never challenged by the quotidian—unless her mother is tormenting her. Like any good witch, Samantha is in charge of everyday life. She is a witch, but a domestic one, and knows how to live in the world of mortals. She accomplishes tasks from the mundane to the almost impossible with grace and wit. In her spare time, she reigns supreme over the entire magical community and occasionally helps the mortal world sort itself out. With a twitch of the nose, she accomplishes an array of everyday tasks: cooking, cleaning, vacuuming, laundry, even mending seemingly irreparably broken objects. If things look as if they might get a bit difficult, she dons her black cape and haute couture evening wear before she solves the world's problems. Life for Samantha is not a series of obstacles, but opportunities for fun and genius. With little effort, she manages to keep Darrin and occasionally the entire historical timeline out of harm's way, as evidenced by her saving Thanksgiving and Darrin in a memorable episode of the series.

In "Samantha's Thanksgiving to Remember," audiences see why Samantha is the linchpin between the old mean-spirited media witches and the new universe of domestic beauties. In this episode, Samantha exemplifies the brilliant and domestic witch.[31] Eccentric Aunt Clara, whose inept use of power is easily more dangerous than a pyromaniac with a blowtorch, has transported the family to seventeenth-century Plymouth. Knowing that witches were burned in this era, Darrin becomes a basket case and Samantha, wisely, a more cautious witch. The locals quickly discover that they have a witch on their hands, but they accuse the mortal husband, not any of the actual witches present.

The mistake begins with typical sitcom fare. Darrin uses a match to light a fire, never thinking that it will not be invented until the Industrial Age. A local oaf witnesses the frightful event and calls him a witch. This is not a huge surprise as Darrin, unable to shed his "1960s advertising executive" persona, strikes an awkward pose even before he strikes the fateful match. His lovely magical spouse manages to "pass" as a local and a mortal in an age where everyone is suspected of being a witch. She walks like a pilgrim, talks like a pilgrim, and even curtsies. Samantha uses her head to save her husband's skin, rather than jumping on her broom and carrying him off into the night. To rescue him, she implies that the gentleman crying witch is looking for excuses to cover his own ineptitude—he drops a turkey and blames Darrin, and forgets to say grace and blames him. Samantha shows the trial judges that the accuser is using Darrin as his own whipping boy.

Unlike Samantha, Endora does not use magic and brains to make life easy for others; she uses them to make life difficult. She is a quixotic blend of old-school witch and modern woman. Her primary goal is to make Darrin miserable and save her daughter from boredom among mortals. As a representative of smart women, Endora is easy to miss. We see her as the archetype mother-in-law, but she is also a brilliant woman. She sees Darrin for what he is, "a middle-class man striving to comply with bureaucratic dictates," and she works hard to remove him from her daughter's life.[32] Her every action with regard to her son-in-law comes with meddlesome meanness. For example, in the episode "A Nice Little Dinner Party," Endora comes to dinner to meet Darrin's parents; fearing the worst, he makes her promise to behave.[33] She goes further, promising to be charming. Endora proceeds to flirt mercilessly with Darrin's

Figure 6.2 Three generations of witches relax on Danish Modern. Credit: "Bewitched" © 1964, 2006 CPT Holdings, courtesy Sony Pictures Television.

father. Cranky, but no fool, the senior Mrs. Stevens sees right through Endora. A fight ensues between Darrin and Samantha. Endora pretends to try to make Darrin happy, while working very hard to make him miserable—she does not need magic to make Darrin unhappy, though she enjoys using it. She makes him unhappy by using her very good mind (see figure 6.2).

Although Endora has a single-minded and seemingly hopeless goal of ending Samantha and Darrin's marriage, she is immanently resourceful in her strategies. Her technique of choice is to magically alter the offending object of misplaced affection. Since Samantha seems to love Darrin as a werewolf,[34] a young boy,[35] an old man,[36] or a statue,[37] Endora tries to introduce third parties into the romantic equation. For example, in "The Crone of Cawdor," she spies on Darrin and his beautiful client Terry, an old hag in disguise who steals the youth from mortals she kisses.[38] Endora gleefully reports back to her daughter that he took this client to Samantha's favorite restaurant and that he had an evening rendezvous planned at Terry's apartment. Unbeknownst to Darrin, Terry is using him to break a spell cast on her, to his peril. Fortunately for Darrin, his wife foils this magical scheme. When all else fails, as it inevitably does, Endora tries to tempt her daughter with charming, eligible warlocks.[39] Endora is persistent. Rather than give up and revel in her life of bohemian luxury, she seems to thrive on the challenges presented by Samantha and Darrin's marriage. She is determined to succeed using the many spells in her repertoire in conjunction with the vast experience and profound knowledge she has gained over her centuries of well-lived life. Endora has a hard-won intelligence available to women in the domestic sphere—the intelligence born from experience. Endora is not just smart; she is a woman who has used her experience to become smarter. She learns from her mistakes, using her past to create action in the present. Endora exemplifies the type of intelligent woman rarely found in the home—the older smart woman. By the time women hit fifty, they all but disappear from media representations of the home. Granted, older women return to the home in the form of the grandmother, but this subject position does not offer room for anything but the most down-home type of intelligence. Endora, while a grandmother, is not the cookie-baking, contest-entering grandma that audiences are used to seeing. She offers us a different kind of older woman in the home—an older woman to be feared and respected. She has the experience and the brains to do harm to the most powerful of foes. Those who underestimate her do so at their peril. However, audiences do not often see Endora's brilliance; caught up in her power, they pass by her cleverness.

Media witches are an excellent place to hide brilliant women; viewers are so busy wondering at their magic that they do not notice their great minds. This is typical of *Bewitched* audiences. Though Samantha relies more on wit than witchcraft to resolve problems, audiences usually remember her flipping pancakes with magic and not the logic she uses to endlessly save Darrin's job. In love or doing laundry, she is the best example of the modern domesticated brilliant witch. Endora's intelligence is also obscured by her magical ability. We see a witch so powerful that we miss the fact that she and her daughter are smarter than most other people on the television series.

What Makes You So Smart?

Smart women are important not only in the television series, but the film version of *Bewitched* also offers an entirely new set of intelligent women, who happen to have a little magic up their sleeves. Set in Hollywood, the film follows Nicole Kidman's Isabel Bigalow as she descends from Cloud Nine to embrace mortal life and love, much to her father Nigel's chagrin. With the impeccable timing that is only manifest in films and theoretical physics, magical Isabel lands on the scene at the precise moment that Hollywood begins auditioning for a remake of the television series *Bewitched*. The only element missing is someone to play Samantha. Blessed with the uncanny ability to twitch her nose in a method very reminiscent of Sam, Isabel is quickly spotted by her future love interest, Will Ferrell's Jack Wyatt, who is cast as Darrin in the remake. *Bewitched* would be incomplete without the meddling mother-in-law; Endora is played by Shirley MacLaine's Iris. This Ephron-delivered romantic comedy is the backdrop for understanding how *Bewitched* offers a space for smart women in our media history and contemporary popular culture.

The film premiered on the forty-year anniversary of the television show. In the four decades between these media events, we find that the more things change, the more they stay the same. This is true of fashion—Samantha and Isabel both sport cute capri pants—and this is true of the media's representation of smart women as witches. Although some feminists might take issue with Isabel, she manages to be a new incarnation of a Second Wave feminist woman, complete with brain and lipstick. Iris offers a more obvious sense of the smart woman; she is a delightful new-millennium version of the witches of yesteryear.

One of the running themes of the movie *Bewitched* is that everyday mortal life is a trial for Isabel: she tries, but it is difficult for her to live without magic. On the surface, she is constructed as a witch out of her element. At first, this seems to have dire consequences for the representation of witches as smart women. While waiting for her lack-wit mortal à la Darrin to arrive and marry her, Isabel conquers mundane obstacles and practices being normal. A twenty-first-century witch, she has to contend with nanotechnology, computer-driven coffee machines, and automatic air fresheners. While audiences may find delight, or horror, in the simple pleasure she discovers in manually working dimmer switches and opening soda-pop cans, they envy her ability to tug her ear and solve things magically when life gets out of hand. Audiences are happy when Isabel finally gives up trying to install the cable on her own, and, wiggling her ear, sets her magic free. Suddenly, not only does she have cable, she has the television programmed, and the DVD player's clock working as well. Here Isabel shows the good sense, like Samantha, to turn to magic when she realizes that getting the job done is more important than maintaining a mortal lifestyle. This is the mark of a smart woman, who knows when to follow the rules and when to bend them to get things done. Although audiences are often frustrated with Isabel, she continues the historical line of smart women disguised as witches—in this case a naïve witch, but an intelligent one nonetheless. Isabel seems overemotional and rash, acting first and thinking later. In this way, she seems to resemble the lovely Samantha very little. However, there is another witch, an interesting witch, hiding just below Isabel's surface, Endora. Isabel is smart, like Endora. The young strawberry blonde witch lives her emotional life; she does not check it at the door to please a man. With her "take no prisoners" approach to her emotional life, she lives life with an intelligence that is much closer to Endora's than Samantha's. Isabel has figured out how to have her cake and eat it, too. Like Samantha, Isabel yearns for a life in which she is loved for who she is, not for who others imagine her to be. She wants love, she wants a man who needs her, and she wants to argue over things such as what color to paint the bathroom. She uses the specter of smart witches before her to help her achieve her goals. When faced with a difficult decision, Isabel often invokes Samantha by asking, "What would Samantha do?" though more often than not, she then proceeds to do what Endora would do. By following both of these witches, Isabel offers us a new kind of smart woman disguised as a witch: one who thinks and feels. Isabel is a new domestic witch. She is not willing to settle for half of the pie; she wants the entire deal. She wants to use her head, live her emotions, get her man, and live happily ever after.

By following Endora's brilliant lead, Isabel uses her magic and responds to situations in ways that feel good. She does not ignore her more complicated emotional impulses; she embraces them. This approach is a new venue for creative thinking for women in the home. Isabel offers audiences an image of the thinking, emotionally expressive woman in the home. For example, when angry at the annoying Jack, she conjures up a foul wind that threatens to destroy the sound stage, which she must then recall. So, unlike Samantha, Isabel uses magic to express her emotional life, which is more Endora's cup of tea. But, like Samantha, Isabel has the sense to know that she cannot simply leave in place the destruction she has wrought. Where Endora is happy to wreak havoc and go, Isabel must clean up after herself. For instance, in a rash moment, Isabel manages to murder her rival for Jack's affection, his ex-wife. She quickly realizes that this should not stand, and rewinds time to reconsider her better options. This moment unfolds when Jack's ex-wife arrives on the set of the *Bewitched* remake. While cast members, stagehands, agent, and director are milling around a central location, the voracious ex-wife flounces in, telling Jack that she wants him back. Isabel eyes the ex with the jealousy and loathing of one of Cinderella's stepsisters. The ex embodies what Isabel hates—people loving others for who they could be rather than for who they are. As the scene unfolds, Isabel, pushed beyond her patience, makes an industrial light crash down on the ex—flattening her like a pancake. We can almost hear Isabel saying, "Damn that felt good." And then, smart woman that she is, she recognizes that violence is not the answer. Instead, she has the ex gleefully state that she will sign the divorce papers and dance out of Jack's life. This is a media representation of a new kind of magical woman—one who is in control, but still lives her emotional life. Our media witches have moved beyond the hypervigilant women who fear being found out and, as a result, have very little fun. But with Isabel, we are offered a new means to consider smart domestic women—they can be smart, still have fun, and maybe even be a little mean like the witches of the past.

Isabel is not the only witch in the film worth watching. Shirley MacLaine's redheaded Iris is the most flamboyant character she has tried since *Sweet Charity* (1969). She offers another view of the intelligent woman via the witch. While both older *Bewitched* witches are redheaded, biting, over the top, and mean, Iris also has a bit of fun to her, something Endora never could manage. MacLaine's redhead is better at finding success in the mortal world. Iris's intelligence is based, in part, on her ability to manage a social situation. This is a skill often attributed to women by the media, but Iris brings it to a level of brilliance. She has the ability to see the entire chessboard, and she plays beautifully. Iris is a witch who can pass as mortal, for decades it seems. Even Samantha could not pull that off. Iris has the gift of veiling her abilities—both her magic and her intelligence. She is the subtler version of Endora. Iris's skill at passing as a mortal is so seamless that not even Isabel's warlock father, Nigel, figures out she is a witch.

Unlike Isabel, Iris takes well the fact that she has become a movie star in the mortal world. Throughout the course of the film, the only moments when Iris needs to use magic are when she is foiling Nigel's attempts to date younger women. She does not use elaborate love spells, like Isabel; instead, all Iris needs is a bit of clear thinking and, of course, good timing. Her method of clearing the romantic field is comic and genius. Whenever she notices Nigel's eye wandering to young voluptuous women half his age, she bewitches them into saying such outlandish things that he rejects them and returns to her. For example, as Iris notices him eyeing a young brunette, Iris puts the follow-ing in her mouth: "Yes. I will sleep with you because I have a thing for father figures . . . , but in the morning I will not get ninety percent of your jokes and I'll go on and on about opening an aerobics center." In another moment, Iris has a beautiful blonde mannequin gleefully report to Nigel, "Hey there, I have hepatitis C."

Iris uses her social intelligence not just to win a man but to put Jack in his place. At the filming of the pilot she humiliates Jack. She does this for more than good fun, though that may be reason enough. Iris sees Jack treating Isabel poorly; she uses her social skill to offer up a little well-earned revenge. Aware of Jack's desire to be the star of the new *Bewitched* series, Iris uses her renowned status as an actor to trounce him. She comes out of character and breaks the fourth wall, to the dismay of the producers, to thank the live audience for their applause during the show. In a flashy display of her social brilliance, Iris upstages Jack without using magic. Much to Jack's dismay, this was not the first time she had managed to make him look bad in public. During a press conference to unveil the remake of *Bewitched*, Jack introduces his costars Isabel and Iris. While Isabel meekly follows Jack's lead, Iris has her own agenda. In an amusing game of cat and mouse, Jack looks to the left of the stage and Iris appears right. When Jack looks to the right, Iris arrives at the left. Jack finally disappears behind the curtain in search of Iris, and she appears flamboyantly to wild applause and laughter. Here again we see the clever witch using her wits to work a situation to her advantage. But the intelligence of these moves is easy to dismiss as clever play, as audiences are overtaken with funny moves and do not see intelligence at work. Many female comedic actors find themselves in this dilemma: when men are brilliant at comedy, critics say they are comic geniuses; when women are brilliant at comedy, critics say they have good timing, or they are pretty, and hence miss the cleverness required to make humor happen. Again, the witch becomes a useful trope to both display and investigate this form of intelligent social performance.

Though Iris might not seem like the perfect role model for intelligent women, after all, she employs her power and thinking in the traditional direction of passion and love and does so with intelligence. She uses her ability to read the social situation, an intelligence the media often locates in women to win love. Here is another example of a smart woman hiding in plain sight. Iris seems to speak for the Ephrons in the film, as Endora spoke for feminists in the television series. In the end, Iris is aware of her aesthetic shortcomings—that she is Nigel's age, rather than a decade or so younger—and uses a witty bit of magic to compensate and win her man. She is not dependent on power but is smart enough to recognize when its use is beneficial. In the end, Iris uses her intelligence to make the rules and beats Nigel at his own game. But the intelligence of these moves is easy to dismiss as clever play, as audiences are overtaken with the comedy and do not see intelligence at work.

Current incarnations of media witches prove to be intriguing sites for representing smart women in the domestic sphere. Viewers pause for the special effects, but neglect to pause for the intelligence exhibited by Isabel and Iris. In a reversal of roles, Isabel seems to embody Endora's "do-magic-first-ask-questions-later" approach to life. Distracted by her beauty and naïveté, we might first assume that she is nothing more than a pretty frame for the latest fashions. But she is a kind and savvy woman, who when pushed too far will think of ways to make people regret their folly. She creates a space for smart women to cross the line of appropriate behavior and play endlessly with alternate endings. In contrast, Iris seems to be a middle-aged Samantha and channels the wit and wisdom displayed by the main character of the television series. Iris, a successful and closeted presence in the mortal world, points to her shining ability to exist effectively regardless of context. The witches of the film live up to the promise of witches of the past, though forms of intelligence sometimes differ from the earlier witches. Samantha and Endora lived their own way in the world of magic and brilliance, formed, in part, on the earlier abilities of the more scary, less domestic witches of film. Iris and Isabel are more modern witches using magic through the lens of Second Wave feminism.

Back to Smart Witches

An examination of *Bewitched* gives a glimpse into both our media history and the modern media production of intelligent women in the home, veiled in the guise of the witch. The world has changed since the green Wicked Witch of the West laid waste to Oz, while Kim Novak and Veronica Lake won love and lost a bit of themselves. Witches are no longer living half lives—lives with power or lives with love. The modern witch can have it all. But a witch is not representative of just any woman, but is a model for women who do not fold under pressure. In her previous incarnations the witch was evil, powerful, and very inventive in ways of punishment and revenge. The modern image of the witch does not lose this touch of devilishness. Therefore, in her modern form, the witch is a bit of a quandary for some. She is usually breathtakingly beautiful, domestic, always intelligent, in control, and up for a bit of fun. These elements have not always worked together in modern media portrayals of women in general. If women are beautiful, they generally exhibit the intelligence and good sense of the average Labrador Retriever. Domestic women are usually not time-stopping beautiful. Furthermore, their forms of intelligence seem to revolve around the best ways to keep their children from having sex before prom. Women in the media are rarely, in themselves, fun; instead, they are usually the punch lines to jokes. Finally, control is rarely granted to domestic or beautiful women. They are usually controlled, not in control. The modern media witch offers a space for the grand slam—a woman who is beautiful, smart, in control, and fun.

The modern witch has become everything women want to be. Yet, the witch also comforts those who see these traits as unlikely or dangerous in women; after all, witches do not exist, so it is equally as easy to dismiss their other positive qualities, should audiences choose. Unfortunately, audiences can, and do, happily see around the intelligence of these modern magical beings. They usually perceive modern witches as powerful but miss their intelligence. This chapter works to point out the various types of knowledge found in the home via the witch. Not only are witches book smart, but their brilliance runs to more interesting types of knowing—operating in complicated social situations, being true to their own sense of right and wrong, getting what they need without exposing all of their best assets, and, of course, using traditional intelligence. Witches have all this and more.

The notion of witches allow intelligent women a return to the home. As Susan Faludi notes, our media makers do not effectively produce images of the smart wife and mother, so the solution was to simply remove these pesky women from the domestic scene.[40] But smart women have resurfaced in the home remade, as witches. On television, there are domestic witches of all ages—we have adult witches in *Charmed* and *Buffy the Vampire Slayer*; with Sabrina, we have a teen witch; and with Raven, we have an adolescent woman of power. In film, we have Hermione Granger and her other witch cohorts from the Harry Potter series; Sally and Gillian Owens from *Practical Magic* (1998); and Sarah Bailey and Nancy Downs from *The Craft* (1996).[41]

Intelligent women have reentered the home at all stages of life, slipping through the backdoor as witches. In *Bewitched*, Samantha is essential to the witch's evolution in popular culture. Endora, as the requisite resident harpy, shows the first of many smart alternatives to the model presented by Samantha. The 2005 movie remake of *Bewitched* offers contemporary twists on smart witches through Isabel and Iris.

As well, the film illuminates the first domestic, brilliant witch—Samantha. She continues to twitch her nose on TV Land, influencing new audiences every day. She haunts and, in some way, inhabits most images of the modern domestic witch. Therefore, our media history will never lose sight of the first real "house-haunting, broomstick-flying, cauldron-stirring" brilliant woman—Samantha Stephens.

Notes

Many thanks to Bill Atwill, Kathleen Byars, Libby Forrester, Sonja Foss, and David Gosser for their comments on this chapter.

1. See Lana Thompson's book *The Wandering Womb: A Cultural History of Outrageous Beliefs about Women* (Amherst, MA: Prometheus Books, 1999), for a full discussion of the imaginative ways our culture dismissed intelligence in women.
2. Lake was a beautiful blonde. A popular pinup during World War II, she did not achieve the longevity of some of her peers.
3. Lynn Spigel argues that beautiful supernatural women like Samantha and Jeannie (and the witches of *I Married a Witch* and *Bell, Book and Candle*) are not just feminine but hyperfeminine. They have amazing beauty and powers unknowable to men. Yet, they chose the domestic life over adventure. They settle in the home, the space of the feminine. Lynn Spigel, *Welcome to the Dream House: Popular Media and Postwar Suburbs* (Durham, NC: Duke University Press, 2001), 128.
4. A statue of Elizabeth Montgomery, as Samantha Stevens, stands in Salem, Massachusetts, indicting her current power as a cultural icon.
5. The 1960s mark the beginning of television's full intrusion into virtually every household. It is fascinating that two of the most memorable shows of the three-network era are *Bewitched* and *I Dream of Jeannie*.
6. These young and powerful television women appeared on *The Secret World of Alex Mac* (1994–1998), *Sabrina, the Teenage Witch*, which was both live action (1996–2003) and animated (1999–2001), and *That's So Raven* (2003 to present).
7. This is a two-part episode: "My Friend Ben," *Bewitched*, ABC, 8 December 1966, and "Samantha for the Defense," *Bewitched*, ABC, 15 December 1966.
8. "It's So Nice to Have a Spouse around the House," *Bewitched*, ABC, 24 October 1968.
9. Nora Ephron directed the 2005 film version of *Bewitched*. She cowrote the script with her sister Delia. Independently, the sisters have worked on a variety of "girl power" or "woman power" projects such as *You've Got Mail* (1998), *The Sisterhood of the Traveling Pants* (2005), and *Sleepless in Seattle* (1993).
10. Lawrence Grossberg, *Dancing in Spite of Myself: Essays on Popular Culture* (New York: Routledge, 1997), 130.
11. Faith Fairfield is the foolish sister on the sitcom *Hope and Faith* (2003 to present).
12. For an extended discussion of television viewing habits see Waller's argument about audience flow versus the reading of media genre. Gregory Waller, "Flow, Genre, and the Television Text," *Journal of Popular Film and Television* 16.1 (Spring 1988): 9.
13. Grossberg, 130.
14. Grossberg, 131.
15. For further discussion of how media texts enter into conversation with one another, see also Horace Newcomb, "On the Dialogic Aspects of Mass Communication," *Critical Studies in Mass Communication* 1 (1984): 34–50.

16. Julia Kristeva, " '*Nous Deux*' or A (Hi)story of Intertextuality," *Romantic Review* 93.1 (2002): 7–14.

17. Other authors have seen the connection between *Bewitched*, its place in our media history, and more contemporary representations of magical women. See, for example, Rachel Moseley, "Glamorous Witchcraft: Gender and Magic in Teen Film and Television," *Screen* 43.4 (2002): 403–422.

18. Lorna Jowett discusses the *Buffy the Vampire Slayer* episode "Bewitched, Bothered, and Bewildered," which comes complete with a bumbling man—Xander, in this episode. *Sex and the Slayer: A Gender Studies Primer for the Buffy Fan* (Middletown, CT: Wesleyan University Press, 2005), 155.

19. Samantha's daughter Tabitha had her own spin-off series. William Asher directed this sitcom. It ran from 1977 to 1978.

20. Douglas, 127.

21. David Marc, *Comic Visions: Television Comedy and American Culture* (Boston: Unwin Hyman, 1989), 135–136.

22. "Long Live the Queen," *Bewitched*, ABC, 7 September 1967.

23. David Allen Case, "Domesticating the Enemy: *Bewitched* and the Seventies Sitcom," in *The Seventies: The Age of Glitter in Popular Culture*, ed. Shelton Waldrep (New York: Routledge, 2000) 196.

24. Case, 197.

25. Dana Heller, *Family Plots: The De-Oedipalization of Popular Culture* (Philadelphia: University of Pennsylvania Press, 1995), 54.

26. Alice Jardine, *Gynesis: Configurations of Women and Modernity* (Ithaca, NY: Cornell University Press, 1988), 26.

27. Hall, 28.

28. See Stuart Hall, "Problem of Ideology: Marxism without Guarantees," in *Stuart Hall: Critical Dialogues in Cultural Studies*, ed. David Morley and Kuan-Hsing Chen (London: Routledge, 1996), 42.

29. "If They Never Met," *Bewitched*, ABC, 25 January 1968.

30. Being fired is not as bad as it might seem, as Darrin is fired and rehired regularly according to Larry Tate's whims and Endora's spells. Authors of *Prime Time* call this "the blundering sitcom management style." S. Robert Lichter, Linda S. Lichter, and Stanley Rothman, *Prime Time: How TV Portrays American Culture* (Washington, DC: Regnery Publishing, 1994), 222.

31. "Samantha's Thanksgiving to Remember," *Bewitched*, ABC, 23 November 1967.

32. Spigel, 130.

33. "A Nice Little Dinner Party," *Bewitched*, ABC, 28 January 1965.

34. "Trick-or-Treat," Bewitched, ABC, 28 October 1965.

35. "Out of the Mouths of Babes," Bewitched, ABC, 25 March 1971.

36. "Samantha's Old Man," Bewitched, ABC, 3 December 1970.

37. "Darrin on a Pedestal," *Bewitched*, ABC, 22 October 1970.

38. "The Crone of Cawdor," *Bewitched*, ABC, 16 March 1967.

39. "George the Warlock," *Bewitched*, ABC, 22 April 1965; "Samantha's Bad Day in Salem," *Bewitched*, ABC, 5 November 1970; and "The Warlock in the Gray Flannel Suit," *Bewitched*, ABC, 1 December 1971 are but three examples.

40. See Faludi for a full discussion of this argument.

41. Sally and Gillian are sisters in the film *Practical Magic* (1998). Nicole Kidman plays Gillian.

CHAPTER 7

Dangerous Minds: The Woman Professor on Television

Leigh H. Edwards

"My mom's insane. Certifiable," complains Jack McCallister on *Jack and Bobby* (2004–2005). "She's the most popular professor on campus and the weirdest mom on the earth." In his view, a mother who is also a feminist professor is the height of embarrassment, and on this prime-time drama, his mother mortifies him on a daily basis. Grace McCallister, played by Christine Lahti, is a history professor at a small college in the Midwest—Plains State University in the fictional Hart, Missouri. Described as an "eccentric single mother," she is raising two teenage sons, one of whom we are told eventually becomes the President of the United States. It is her intellectual acumen that earns her accolades and academic success at work, but that continually lands her in trouble at home. She becomes the too-cerebral, too-principled, nerdy mom her sons think broke up their family because she is too difficult to handle. Feminist theory works splendidly in the college classroom, but its precepts can get your adolescent son beaten up in school. Grace is an exemplar of the academic woman trying to balance her professional and personal life.

This chapter analyzes the depiction of female professors on contemporary television. What does it mean to have brilliant women academics on prime-time series? Why women eggheads, and why now? Are they trailblazers who use their smarts to rewrite the cultural scripts of traditional gender roles? Or are they exceptions who do not change the fact that their fellow female characters ultimately submit to male intellectual authority? How do they speak to the status of real women in academia—the professors these shows seek to portray?

Recent television portraits of women professors offer a complex commentary on the status of women in academia and, by extension, on changing ideas of gender in society. I focus my discussion on the two recent prime-time drama series about academia: *Jack and Bobby* (2004–2005) and *The Education of Max Bickford* (2001–2002). While women faculty have appeared on other prime-time drama series, these two shows are the only recent dramas that focus on the workplace setting of academia and that feature women professors as lead characters. In both series, we see women historians who are celebrated for their intelligence and career success yet condemned for how they depart from traditional gender roles in their private lives. For every great lecture she delivers on campus, a woman professor is bemoaned as an embarrassing geek or an inept mother at home. For every exciting intellectual discovery that brings her perks and prestige, she embarks on a failed attempt to fix her private life that brings her shame and dishonor (such as having an affair with a student).

Tracing the successes and failures of these women, the series fashion the figure of the female professor in popular culture into a measure of how able smart and talented women are to rewrite the cultural scripts of traditional gender role expectations today. The conclusion the programs imply? Female agency is still limited by some tenacious, residual norms. Both programs present their women professors as frustrated characters because they cannot fully reconcile their public and private gendered roles. The series support their characters' feminist critiques of gendered expectations and inequitable social institutions. Yet the shows' depiction of women professors' family and personal life reinscribes some of those gendered social norms and stereotypes, often by showing that their career success undercut their ability to replicate a modern nuclear family unit. For both characters, their career potential and the idea that strong, smart women academics could change role models for women is diminished by supposed failures in their personal life. Both had affairs with male academic mentors when they were younger. Both have broken family units, which the series represent as the root of their troubles. Both series portray this dynamic as a private-life problem that mitigates public-life successes.

Like the heady but flawed Grace on *Jack and Bobby*, the leading female professor character on *The Education of Max Bickford* finds that personal drama detracts from her glowing career. The series locates the source of her problems in her decision to not marry or have a family so that she could devote herself to her career, a decision about which she retains some ambivalence. Andrea Haskell (played by Marcia Gay Harden) is an American studies professor at Chadwick College, a small New England women's liberal arts college loosely modeled on Smith. A former student of Max Bickford's, with whom she also had an affair when she was his student, Andrea returns to Chadwick after a stint at Harvard to take an endowed chair that Max (played by Richard Dreyfuss) coveted. He decries her promotion over him as reverse discrimination, and the series sets out to reeducate him away from his old liberal views and toward a more updated (though highly reductive) liberal pluralism. Max learns to accept difference, like feminist and transgender colleagues, but his model of pluralism still privileges white patriarchy. Max is a caricature of an academic curmudgeon, and thus his extreme critiques are discredited. Yet that does not mean the show supports Andrea's position in its narrative point of view. She is lauded for her genius but portrayed as problematic and inept in her private life, particularly when she begins looking to Max for support. Her social status also sometimes threatens her academic status, as when she gets into trouble for having loose boundaries with her students, which leads to a visiting male student making an unwanted pass at her.

Both series celebrate their female professors' intelligence and career successes yet also reinforce the tensions attributed to these women's departures from traditional female gender roles. Both thus mark gender role issues specific to an early twenty-first-century historical moment—notably the generational conflict between Second Wave and Third Wave feminists, and the sometimes fraught integration of the women's movement with academic feminism. As feminist professors, Grace and Andrea are role models for their young women students, yet those students disdain the professors' seeming inability to "have it all," career and intact family. The series suggest that brilliant career women still need to replicate more traditional female roles at home—that they should be able to do both. The shows articulate a critique that some Third Wave or even postfeminist students have made of the life trajectories of some Second Wave feminist career women who did not have families. Witness the recent trend of more women college graduates jumping off their career track to be stay-at-home mothers. Scholar Laura Wexler sees this trend as a symptom of a structural problem. While Second Wave feminism gained women access to career opportunities, social changes in gendered family patterns have not developed as quickly. Citing the fact that working women do 70 percent of household labor duties today, author Judith Warner argues that "the gender caste system is still alive and well in most of our households" and that it will require national policies on childcare and parental leave to change that dynamic.[1] Wexler notes that many of the young graduates who may have begun turning to part-time or suspended careers in order to meet the still-gendered demands of family mistakenly understand this transition as an individual rather than a structural issue: "They are still thinking of this as a private issue; they're accepting it. Women have been given full-time working career opportunities and encouragement with no social changes to support it. I really believed twenty-five years ago this would be solved by now."[2] As many scholars have noted, feminist theory continues to struggle with the quandary of how to achieve autonomy for women through both workforce advances and through revisions of inequitable patriarchal family and domestic labor structures.[3] If young women like those Wexler studies fail to see this effort as a group issue, feminism (in both theory and movement) suffers. Likewise, when these television series present the private-role problems that women professors face as personal rather than structural problems, they obscure the underlying institutional issues that need to be addressed.

Postfeminism is another relevant sociohistorical framework for these television images. Routinely, in both series, we encounter student characters who believe that the goals of the women's movement have been achieved, that feminism is "over," or that they are not feminists—yet they want to benefit from the gains the women's movement has won in areas such as public life, wages, and access to leadership positions. Some of the promotional press for *Jack and Bobby* explicitly pinpoints this postfeminist context. In an interview plugging the program, actress Lahti argues of her character: "She's a strong, strong feminist, and you don't see a lot of those on TV. You look around at the young girls today, and you feel like they forgot that we went through all that for them."[4] The series stages the status of women as a topic of ongoing debate.

Many feminist critics would argue that popular culture texts represent fantasy resolutions to or meditations on the real contradictions in women's lives.[5] Representations of brilliant women professors on television are important because they speak to ongoing tensions and issues that women experience in contemporary U.S. society (particularly efforts to juggle career and family). If these highly trained, academic women experience deep frustration over friction between their public and private roles, such fantasy television depictions are implying that these problems have yet to find satisfactory resolution for many women in general. *Max Bickford* producer David Black has suggested that one reason such shows keep portraying smart career women who experience problems maintaining their private or family lives is that the myth that the career woman cannot "have it all" still circulates in Hollywood (both in popular culture representations, on film and television, and in common entertainment industry beliefs and labor practices).[6] When television shows foregrounding these problems garner enough production and reception interest to make it to the air, there is public interest in these issues. *Max Bickford*'s audience averaged 12 million viewers for CBS, while *Jack and Bobby* hovered around 2 to 3 million for the smaller WB network.[7]

These programs speak to the current status of the smart, single career woman, just as a series like *The Mary Tyler Moore Show* did in the 1970s. As critic Bonnie Dow has argued, reading that paradigmatic show in its historical context of Second Wave feminism's emergence, the show's feminist message was qualified because it "blended discourses of the 'new woman' with traditional messages about the need for women to continue fulfilling traditional female roles as caretakers and nurturers in the . . . 'family' of the workplace."[8] These recent shows exhibit a related but slightly different dynamic, in which women must excel in their career but replicate the nurturer-caregiver role at home, part and parcel of an effort to "have it all."

My focus is on the cultural politics of this textual representation. In feminist television studies, scholars such as Julie D'Acci have advocated an "integrated approach" to analysis, which attempts to account for four interrelated spheres: television production, reception, programming, and the sociohistorical context.[9] While a full account of production and reception dynamics lies beyond the scope of this chapter, I do address important aspects of these programs' sociohistorical contexts as well as the texts themselves. In addition to the contexts of tension between Second and Third Wave feminists, and of conflict between career and private life for women academics, these series also speak to two other key historical frameworks: ongoing academic debates about intelligence and gender, and continuing structural inequities for women in higher education. As the shows both question and reinscribe conventional gender role norms in relation to these cultural and historical contexts, they represent complex moments of negotiation in which we can read traces of both resistance and denial.

Smarty Pants: Definitions

How is intelligence constructed for these "smart women" on television? They tap into larger social tensions about not only women's advancement within academe but also debates about the tools of the scholarly trade. Both series reflect how critics continue to question what constitutes intelligence, which academic disciplines are seen as most valuable, and how gender informs these dynamics.

Both programs reflect on ongoing academic squabbles about intelligence and gender (the old canard that women are better at humanities, men at math). Those debates have enough legs to spark controversies, even though theories of gendered intelligences have largely been discredited. The fact that Harvard president Lawrence Summers could have made his infamous 2005 comment about men perhaps having an "innate" advantage over women in scientific aptitude illustrates the continuing impact of those ideas.[10] Both programs also note the ongoing structural inequities for women in higher education. Men still dominate in senior and administrative positions and in math and science positions. On the issue of gender inequity in academia, studies done by the American Association of University Professors show that women faculty still only earn 80 percent of what men do, they make up only 38 percent of the faculty nationally, and they constitute only 23 percent of full professors.[11] The ramifications of these battles are evident in the portrayal of our television professors. As feminist historians, they are seen as passionate but less important than some of their male colleagues, and their work as less central than math and science labor. They are sharp, but their work is perceived as fluffy. Their job is to inspire their students, but there are limits to the practical effectiveness of their feminist theories, which are often seen as excessive. As sociologist Michael Kimmel notes, while the academic debate over whether men and women have different intelligences is an outmoded one, it still sparks discussion and press attention because of persistent structural inequities. And, as Kimmel would argue, it is the structural inequities that produce (and construct) gender difference, not the other way around.[12]

The ramifications of these kinds of debates about gender and intelligence are evident in these television depictions of female professors. In both shows, the women present a hearty critique of emphasized femininity, specifically via academic feminism. Yet, each cannot escape the ongoing impact of traditional gender roles. In that sense the shows speak directly to their postfeminist context, involving precisely the way in which people assume that the goals of the women's movement have already been reached, even while women remain marginalized. This ongoing problem presents a dilemma for our television professors that they never fully solve.

The series' focus on the life struggles of brilliant women illuminates how performing "intelligence" is a key aspect of gender performance more generally. Kimmel's discussion of gender stereotypes is useful here, because he notes the importance of education and intelligence in these schemas. Citing sociologist R. W. Connell, Kimmel analyzes traditional gender role norms, what Connell terms "hegemonic masculinity" and "emphasized femininity." Here, masculinity involves what Erving Goffman describes as a virtually unreachable ideal fantasy: "a young, married, white, urban, northern, heterosexual, Protestant, father, of college education, fully employed, of good complexion, weight, and height, and a recent record in sports."[13] Emphasized femininity describes an ideal in which women comply with male desires, privilege social over technical skills and downplay their intelligence, and capitulate to gender inequality and a patriarchal social sphere and labor organization.[14] The masculine exhibition of education (and its link to good employment) is as important as the feminine belittling of self-intelligence.

While our television women professors do not comply with emphasized femininity in the sense that they actively showcase their intelligence rather than hide it, they nevertheless perform their intelligence in a way that is explicitly gendered and devalued. On *Jack and Bobby*, Grace's academic intelligence is gendered in the sense that the work she does on women's history is seen as not fully applicable to real-world issues or serious endeavors such as serving in political office. She is a staunch feminist, doing historical scholarship on women's history and fighting to revise the school's sexual harassment policy. When her sons go on to successful political careers, they do not carry her academic pretensions with them. They refuse to be in "gifted" classes in high school, and both reject what they see as the impracticality of her intellectual life.

The series sets up a tension between different gendered academic intelligences, but also between scholarly knowledge versus more practical intelligences, such as political astuteness. Indeed, *Jack and Bobby* is distinctive for how extensively it addresses the gendered power relationships of both education and government in its plot and themes. It is somewhat critical but mostly idealistic about these two key arenas. Importantly, on her faculty, Grace is one of very few full professors who are women; the television series thus questions academia's gender hierarchy. The show's primary focus is on her raising the future president during a formative "year in the life" (marked as the "present time" on the program) when her sons are aged thirteen and sixteen (grappling with standard high school and family problems). It intercuts interviews from a future 2049 documentary about Bobby's life after he is elected president in 2040 and serves two terms.

The fact that Grace's "greatest success" comes not through her own life but via her son's further illustrates the limits of her own agency. She becomes more important as a maternal influence on a "great man of history." Indeed, her son Bobby, as a political leader later in his life, is shown to be much more successful at reconciling private and public gender role expectations for men. Yet *Jack and Bobby* also frames her battle itself as momentous. After all, she raises a future president in the crucible of her struggles. As the network's description for the series argues, "Her personality is a force of nature destined to shape both these young men's lives and secure one a place in the history books," since her younger son Bobby will become "the mid-century's greatest presidential leader."[15]

However, the feminist professor can only raise a president, not be one herself. One reason is that her brilliance is in the area of feminist history, which the series presents as separate from rigorous science or public policy. She is often reduced to delivering emotional appeals to her students, urging them to see college as a "renaissance" journey to adulthood and exhorting them into incipient adult subjectivity almost like a mother hen: "You have the front row seats to your own transformation and in transforming yourself you might even transform the world. And it will be electric. I promise you it'll be terrifying, but embrace that. Embrace the new person you're becoming."[16] When the feminist historian has the chance to perform her brilliance publicly, to put her feminist insights on display, she merely offers trite platitudes, literally telling her listeners to take the "road less traveled." Thus, her intellectual labor is not taken seriously on the show.

We see a similar depiction of feminist scholarship as marginal on *Max Bickford*. Here, our woman professor has undisputed career success, but her work is viewed as trivial, distinctly set apart from serious scholarship. The gendered tension between Andrea and Max is a focal point for the program. She works in popular culture, and he, as a political historian, sees her work as trite and ephemeral. The series places them in sharp contrast: her radical, cutting-edge cultural studies work as opposed to his stuffy, conservative brand of history, in which he disengages from recent scholarship, rejects the influence of cultural theory, and only addresses older models of what he calls "dead white guy" history.[17] The series means to coax him out of his stultified corner, but it implies that she is equally, on the other end of the academic spectrum, also an extremist in need of a corrective, in need of more substance.

As he attacks her work, the series' narrative point of view does not side with him, but it also does not fully support her claims for the importance of her scholarship. Swooping in to win the endowed chair he wanted, she, in addition to having taught at Harvard, has already published three books, all feminist critiques of popular culture, including *Class and Gender in the Music of Bruce Springsteen* and *Sexual Violence in American Culture*. Meanwhile, he is disaffected, suffers from a midlife crisis, and has been teaching the same three courses for the past twenty years ("Historiography," "The Civil War," and "Paranoid Style in American Politics"). He has taken to writing a novel about his disaffection, a thinly veiled autobiography, and the series uses his voice-over of passages from that novel to frame many of the episodes from his narrative point of view. Chagrined to find a former student (and former lover) promoted above him, he attacks both her career advancement and her subject area. He claims that he lost the endowed chair because of "sexism" and "ageism." He attacks her work by calling her an "academic sellout" and a "cheap popularizer." She defends her scholarship by saying, "Popular culture reflects the values of a people." But he insists, "It's not history, it's current events."[18]

The academic politics here are aggressively gendered. The series both critiques and reinscribes a gendered high culture versus mass culture divide. The program treats Andrea's subject matter as equal parts vital cultural history and less-than-weighty passing fancy. In one lecture, as she shows them slides, Andrea uses 1950s television to teach her students about gender history:

> *Andrea*: Take 1950s television. Dad was usually portrayed as a doofus. And Mom as a robot homemaker. Why?
> (The students giggle.)
> *Student*: Because Dad just got back from World War II.
> *Andrea*: Right. And what he was doing in the war was scary. It was so scary that he had to seem ineffectual. Why did Mom have to seem a robot homemaker? Because otherwise she would have had a sex life. Which at that time of course was even more threatening than the war.[19]

While the episode takes her arguments seriously, the lecture ends with her slide of a pinup girl from the '50s as the students giggle again, and the entire exercise has remained on a superficial level. The class as depicted reads like a trivialized pop culture detour from the seriousness of other classes taking place, like Max's heated debate over the Vietnam War and conscientious objectors, whether or not the United States should have dropped the bomb, and whether or not people should be willing to die for their country. Andrea's work remains a supplement to the masculinized intellectual wars raging elsewhere.

The series also uses ideas of gendered intelligence to explain the gendered subject matter. It scripts her interest in her subject matter in terms of familial relationships, because she studies popular culture to feel closer to her absent mother, a Broadway showgirl. Meanwhile, he engages with the great leaders and great events of history from the point of view of individualism and individual achievement, a stereotypically masculinized stance. He states of his own teaching philosophy, "When you know history, you can take your place in it. . . . When you know history, all the problems of your life are placed in a larger context."[20] His liberal humanism draws on intellectual history to further individualism, while her scholarship is about defining the self in relation to family or in terms of gendered roles like daughter or mother.

Angel in the Classroom, Harpy in the House

Both *Jack and Bobby* and *Max Bickford* suggest that intelligence is good for their snappy doyennes at work but bad at home. For Grace, her sons reject her model of academic intelligence and, while they admire her laudable career, insist that her ideas put her out of step with mainstream society and cause her inability to adjust and have a happy home life. They think it is her eggheadedness and uncomfortable ideological purity and intellectual rigor that drove their father away just two years into the marriage and that often alienates her sons. For Andrea, her academic work on the history of popular culture becomes a way for her to work through her own family's past. Her mother, the Broadway singer and dancer, sent her away to live with her military father so the mother could have a career. Andrea has always resented the woman for being "a bad mother," and instead of replicating that dynamic herself, she throws herself into her scholarship and shuns a family life of her own. But the show insists that her academic work is in fact her attempt to "know" her mother and be a part of her mother's world—an intellectual working out of her familial problems and her own unease with a mother who focuses on career over her children. The series cannot imagine a sustainable model of motherhood and career for either her or her mother, and thus, for all its support of her feminist media studies, its message is regressive concerning career and family.

These series are not unique in their depiction of a woman laboring to reconcile her intellectual or career aspirations with her gendered role as mother or daughter. Often in such popular culture images, as critics such as Tania Modleski and Sherrie A.Inness have shown, such accomplished women can be depicted as the exception that reinforces norms, as these popular culture texts both challenge and reaffirm traditional values.[21] These series exemplify that pattern, since our two professors are highly successful in their careers, but the potential threat to traditional norms they pose is partially recontained by the way the series portray their private life.

Jack and Bobby's treatment of Grace centers on plotlines that establish the tension between her work and home life. In academia, she is a prolific researcher and popular teacher. Her intellectual weapons are prodigious. She levels a stinging critique of the corporatization of the academy, calling the new president, Benedict, an MBA hired to cut budgets and fundraise, a "money-grubbing whore whose sole talent is for streamlining and revenue increase."[22] Admiring such cutting arguments from her as well as his genial rebuttals, the series presents both as intellectual equals eventually granting mutual respect for each other. But part of their evolving détente has to do with his flirtation with her; sexual politics trumps her convictions, to a certain degree (the series ends by implying that they will begin dating).

Grace is everywhere characterized by her academic intelligence. The first time we meet her, in the pilot episode, she comes out swinging. She always leads with her head. Taking son Bobby to an electronics store to buy him a television set for his birthday, she whips out her critical thinking skills to lambaste television. She lectures him: "Of course the idea that we're stupid just because we sit around watching TV all the time is just as simplistic as the idea that kids shoot other kids because they witness violence in the media. But what *is* clear is that the majority of television caters to the majority of Americans and is, as a result, garbage."[23] In one fell swoop, she executes a critique of the mass culture industry and a defense of her ideas of quality in popular culture. While one could easily fault her elitism (if masses water down quality, does that mean too much mass democracy is also problematic?), her argument is relatively complex, especially for television writing.

However, the point of the episode is that while she might excel at cultural critique, she fails as a parent. She forces her ideologies on Bobby rather than nurturing his own individual desires and beliefs. She wants him to be a great man so as to live vicariously through him. She defines him as special, different, superlative. Instead of buying the television set, she gets Bobby a Casio keyboard because, she tells him, he could "be a grand master by the time you're thirty." Jack later tells Bobby, "You could learn to twirl a baton by the time you're thirty . . . who cares. The point is it's not what you wanted, it's what *she* told you you wanted. And you agreed like you always do." "Not always," Bobby replies, torn between two role models.[24]

The show does, of course, recuperate her rhetoric, in the sense that it exalts Bobby, an odd, sensitive kid formed by her intellectual ideals. Her drive makes him aspire to lofty heights. When Bobby worries that he will be a social pariah in high school, she exhorts him: "All the best people were geeks. George Bernard Shaw, Bertrand Russell, Kafka, yours truly."[25] Yet the series also critiques her—because it explicitly insists that without Jack's pragmatism and human empathy, Bobby would not have matured into a leader. Her intellectual idealism is presented as flawed. Doctorate-level knowledge only translates into parenting or political leadership in limited ways. As Grace tells Bobby that concerns about friends are "beneath him," Jack grimaces in horror (and the series does so along with him). She is all head, no heart.

Significantly, as the source of her unreasonable and irrational behavior, she herself identifies the tension between her career and her status as a single mom. She tells Jack why she often smokes pot to cope: "My work is stressful, and raising two sons on your own, well, I try not to let it show but sometimes it can be a little difficult. Sometimes, I need some kind of escape." Taking on a paternal role, Jack insists they must both give up their escapes to care for Bobby "so maybe one day he can escape. For real."[26] It is Jack who must remind Grace of her maternal call to self-sacrifice, and it is Grace who, painting her structural situation as dire and unmanageable, insists that it is hard for her to function as a single mother and academic without the help of drugs. Tellingly, Jack attributes her alienation from mainstream society to her loneliness. He tells girlfriend Courtney that if his father had not left, his mother would not be so unmanageable. Courtney, the smart and sensitive daughter of the college president, tries to separate Grace's identity as professional from that of abandoned wife: "Well, personally, I think your mom would be intense even if your dad hadn't left." Jack insists, "But maybe she'd be happier. And if she was happier, it'd all be different.

Everything would have been different."[27] He imagines that if she had been a mother in an intact family, she would have been more satisfied with her sense of identity because she would fit in with more traditional gender role expectations.

Not only does Jack ascribe her dysfunctionality to her failed efforts to embody emphasized femininity, he also identifies her academic pretensions as the source of what he perceives to be her disconnect from reality. In a particularly cutting exchange, Jack asks why she refuses to let Bobby be normal, and she replies that "normal is overrated." Jack rebuts: "Normal is what you have to be if you don't want to spend every day of high school getting beat up." He then observes: "You just wanted someone to control and agree with you and keep you from feeling lonely all the time." Against her protestations about the sacrifices she has made for them, he levels his harshest assessment: "You're just a lonely, pathetic, middle-aged woman hiding behind your books and your words and your freak of a teenaged son." As Jack excoriates her for making Bobby live a "fantasy life" with her, the series supports his sense that she has been smothering Bobby, shutting him up in her ivory tower because she cannot handle her life, and that her intellectual pretensions cover up a deep dysfunctionality that she unloads on her sons.[28]

In contrast to Grace, Bobby's later personal-life snafus enter his public life but do not, apparently, create problems for him. His wife, Courtney, remains with him even after he has an affair with his female vice president. His masculinized role as father figure and provider for his family and for the nation allows him this latitude without substantial stigma, and he merges public and private roles effectively, as the faux documentary host (Gore Vidal) notes while enshrining his history. As for the two women in the next generation after Grace, while they have both public and private roles of significance (vice president and First Lady), they are each ultimately defined by their sexual or marital relationship with the male authority figure. As for Grace, she enters the documentary record, as it were, only insofar as she leaves a legacy in President McCallister. The show portrays her as an evolving, flawed, but nonetheless admirable character, yet she continually rejects a maternal, nurturer-caregiver role and remains the ideologue always ready for a fight.

This kind of gendered difficulty in integrating an academic career with a family life is also evident in *Max Bickford*. When Andrea's mother, Elaine Haskell, shows up on her doorstep and wants to live with her because she can no longer afford her own apartment in New York City, Andrea attacks her mother by saying that she "wasn't there" for her or the father. They argue in Andrea's house, which is scattered with mid-century pop culture artifacts of events that her mother actually lived through and experienced firsthand, from Broadway playbills to magazines of celebrity photos from the '40s through the '60s. As the episode intercuts image of these texts with the two women, we are made to realize Andrea's internal motivation before she does. She does pop culture scholarship in order to get closer to her mother's life and to her mother, since she has always been shut out of a meaningful relationship with her.

The episode lends credence to both women's points of view (the daughter felt abandoned, the mother wanted to follow her own dreams), but it does not allow them to find an equilibrium. Neither do they know how to balance career and family, nor do they know how to sustain a relationship with each other. Moreover, the episode supports the mother's view that the daughter's work is merely a pale reflection of real life, an artificial endeavor meant to access the actual living that is taking place elsewhere. Andrea's academic work can lend Elaine's life legitimacy, but it cannot exist on its own. As the mother shows her daughter a pinup picture of herself while discussing a magazine she has brought, Andrea is interested in the photo academically, whereas Elaine wants her daughter to appreciate something about her glory days. The pinup girl in Andrea's earlier lecture is not just an academic footnote; she is someone with a real life and real dreams, captured in still photos. Noting that the shot was taken by a famous photographer she studies, she asks her mother for details and fails to get them: "You worked with one of the great photographers of the 1950s and you don't remember?" Elaine replies, "I get it, you teach him, he's *your* history." When Andrea insists that the photographer is not just her history, Elaine asks, "Where do I fit in? I'm the lousy mother. And I come up here, and you're the lousy daughter." Andrea responds, "Because you were a lousy mother. You never taught me how to cook, you never taught me how to wash, you never taught me how to fix anything for that matter." Their shared but different interest in the photo occasions an excavation of female gender roles in families.

Even given her feminist scholarship, our professor excoriates her mother for not teaching her the rituals of traditional female gender role performance and for not being in the home with her. Her attempts to value popular history appear misplaced because she has only focused on that history in order to displace angst about her relationship with her mother. Speaking of the photographer, she insists, "He's important. An important cultural figure of our era. I mean, you're important too." Neither woman knows how to value the other's labor. The mother whips out a copy of one of the daughter's books, *Johnny Mercer, Julie Stein: The Three Martini Lunch*. Surprised that her mother has read it, Andrea asks what she thought of it. Elaine passionately explains, "What you write honey, that's *my* world. You say I didn't teach you anything, I taught you this. I gave you what I have to give. I lived the life you write and teach. Don't say I was never there for you. This is proof I was there. You're the proof I was there."[29] They perpetuate each other's life work and history without understanding each other.

This psychological explanation for the feminist scholar's own work exists in a profound tension with the work itself. Her yearning for an intact nuclear family is apparently what drove her into feminist scholarship, and this scholarship, by implication, exists as a poor substitute for that family. The two women later try to reconcile, but only succeed partially. The mother tells the daughter that she was always on her mind, that she always carries a note her child wrote her in youth that says "I love Mommy." As the mother flashes the wrinkled note, scrawled in crayon, the daughter replies, "That's not enough. It's got nothing to do with *me*, Mom. It's not the same as growing up together, Mom." She gives her mother money to live somewhere else, and she later finds that her mother left a signed copy of a magazine for her, an artifact of the mother's life, the daughter's work, and their failed relationship.

Hearts and Minds

Such moments of disconnect between public and private life are cruxes for thinking about gender and the limits of these women's agency as smart professionals. Nowhere are those limits more evident than in story lines about their sexuality.

On *Jack and Bobby*, Grace's problem of career values in tension with traditional feminine roles is evident in her family life. But it becomes most evident in the show's portrayal of her sexuality, the place where the series' cultural politics become the most complex and problematic. This nexus of issues is strikingly apparent in one particular university plotline: her disastrous affair with her male teaching assistant. When she has this steamy affair with her graduate student, her sexuality threatens to destabilize her professional position. Her personal concerns enter her work world and undermine it. The show presents her search for a fulfilling relationship in this context as inappropriate, and it examines her comeuppance, her sense of humiliation and public shame. On *Max Bickford*, Andrea almost finds herself in the same boat when her chumminess with students leads to a visiting male undergraduate student, Theo, making an unwanted pass at her.[30] Max was at first jealous when Theo chose her over him as a thesis advisor, but instead of the student choosing her for her academic excellence, the scenario turns out to be about sexual politics. The series blames her for her lack of appropriate boundaries with students.

Meanwhile, on one level, *Jack and Bobby* delivers a knockout punch to gendered double standards in terms of academic affairs of the heart, or issues of sexual harassment by men, because many of the men who criticize Grace's behavior have themselves had affairs with their female students. When a male faculty member, Roger Hennessy, reports Grace for having an affair with her teaching assistant, Tom, she exposes his hypocrisy: "Spare the holier-than-thou for someone who doesn't remember you married your TA."[31] The series indicates that the gendered politics between the two colleagues is sexual: the male professor tried to hire her to "become his wife," and he remains angry at being spurned. The series sides with her narrative point of view when she similarly criticizes another colleague's double standard. When her former mentor, Julius Edelman, visits to deliver a superstar lecture, he slams her behavior even though he had had an affair with her when she was his student. Making her affair a metonymy for her academic career, he says that she must be all washed up as an academic if she is resorting to affairs with her students.[32] Arguing that she should be publishing more books in order to reach her full potential, he slams her for her romantic, feminized weakness. He sees her behavior as the irrational hysteria of female sexuality and his as accepted male sexual prerogative.

But while the series supports Grace when she rails against the double standard, pointing out all the male faculty married to their former graduate students who have never faced any public outcry or social opprobrium, it also condemns her. It is her need for a male partner that represents her undoing, and everyone in her private and public communities disapproves.[33] Her behavior undermines her professional stature. She wrote the ethics committee bylaws that she then bends, and she is embarrassed and discredited when the committee condemns her affair with Tom and removes him as her graduate assistant. She horrifies herself when she breaks her own moral code as an academic when she offers to write Tom's work for him.[34] But it is only when she realizes that she is a female version of a cuckold that she halts the affair. She discovers that he, well into his involvement with Grace, has been sleeping with a young female student.

In this scenario, the series brings traditional gender role ideas from the private sphere into Grace's public sphere identity and implies that she brings ruin upon herself if she does not comply with the conventional roles involving heterosexual romance. When she struggles with her relationships with male colleagues, they respond to her intellectual authority by exerting sexual authority over her. She is awkward and nervous around Tom, and he exerts sexual authority over her; at one point, when she expounds on an intellectual topic, he silences her by kissing her and saying, "Grace, be quiet," while she laughs, "Why does everyone always tell me to be quiet?"[35] The college president protects her during the scandal, but only because he wants to date her. At a college reception, he silences Grace's attempts at academic debate with him by telling her that she should not continue harboring feelings for her student, then declares his own feelings for her by commenting on her appearance. He surveys her ball gown and observes, "I may dance like a geezer, but I still know a good-looking woman when I see one." As Grace sputters, he says, "What? You didn't know I was looking? Yes, you did. And I was looking all along."[36] His commentary frames her in his male gaze. The program identifies him as the more appropriate mate for her. In its treatment of their relationship, while it establishes them as equals, it nevertheless undercuts her. While she can one-up him in their academic debates, he can assert a male power to judge her appearance; in previous discussions with her, he flusters her, deflecting her scholarly points by asking her to dinner or telling her she looks nice. His protection of her during the affair scandal also becomes suspect.

These problems of power and sexual politics remain unresolved, but the feminist professor certainly emerges having suffered harsh critiques from the series' narrative point of view. The series here foregrounds the historical context of tensions between Second and Third Wave feminists, particularly when women of the next generation react to her with disdain. An undergraduate student on the ethics panel expresses her grave disappointment; while she formerly saw Grace as a role model, she says she will no longer do so.[37] Another female student notices the affair early on and tries to blackmail Grace for a better grade, which Grace resists, but the student is eager to play on stereotypes about female sexuality and the professor as a middle-aged woman.[38] Notably, in another plotline, Jack's pregnant ex-girlfriend, Missy, had previously dismissed Grace as a radical freak, but she immediately turns to Grace for feminist solidarity when she needs someone to take her for an abortion.[39]

"Normal Is Overrated": Smart Cookies, Dysfunctional Families

Our professors' tribulations are emblematic of larger trends. Their quarrels with family structures are particularly important, both for the series' commentary on gender and the family and because of television's investment in the family. Television focuses very frequently on the family because it is a domestic medium and addresses the family grouping inside the home. As Cecelia Tichi has shown, television is historically the "electronic hearth" around which the family gathers.[40] As Lynn Spigel has detailed, the white, suburban, middle-class nuclear family unit has historically been television's favored topic and target audience, as television's expansion into national markets in the post–World War II era corresponded with white families moving in large numbers to the suburbs.[41] These series register the tensions involved in reconciling women's roles with family norms.

Depictions of brilliant women fighting with family roles speak to a still ongoing struggle between what sociologists term the "modern family," an older nuclear model emerging from industrialization that became a culturally idealized form in the Victorian period and peaked in the 1950s, and a diversity of "postmodern family" forms emerging in the second half of the twentieth century.[42] Blended, single-mother, postdivorce, and gay and lesbian families have emerged, prompted by higher divorce rates, more single-parent households, women's entrance into the labor force in large numbers after 1960, the decline of the "family wage," and the pressures on labor caused by postindustrialism and by globalization.[43] Such demographic changes spurred a political backlash beginning in the 1970s. The "family values" media debates have intensified since the 1990s. One high-water mark was Dan Quayle's attack on the sitcom character Murphy Brown as a symbol for unwed motherhood in his comments during the 1992 presidential election campaign. *Jack and Bobby* and *Max Bickford* each capture society's changing ideas about family forms and the role of women in our current epoch, especially through their focus on accomplished women who have postmodern family arrangements.

Grace fails to replicate the nuclear family unit of her parents' generation, just as she is unable even to replicate television's new, modified norm of a modern nuclear family unit (rather than the traditional stay-at-home wife, we see a widespread television norm of a two-parent family with both parents working). Grace's family failure and Andrea's family dissatisfaction are part of a newer televisual trend, as more television shows depict nontraditional families and move away from a long-standing emphasis on intact nuclear families. Even though Grace and Andrea are part of a demographic trend, the series blame them for the supposedly subpar state of their families—yet another stance that reinforces gender stereotypes.

Jack and Bobby and *Max Bickford* thus question conventional ideas of gender even as they reinforce them in new, complex ways in a postfeminist world. Both of our women professors buck the system by achieving career success. But they are constrained, because they do not replicate the family unit, do not perform maternal or daughterly roles fully, and do not control their own sexuality. These characters illuminate their cultural and historical contexts, in which some key ongoing gender problems remain unresolved, including generational tensions in the women's movement, public-private life conflicts for women professionals, academic debates about gendered intelligence, and persistent gendered structural inequities in institutions like academia. As they draw out these themes, both *Jack and Bobby* and *The Education of Max Bickford* offer a commentary on the role of women in higher education and in public life—and on the role of television in both reflecting and producing some of these ongoing gender norms.

Notes

1. Judith Warner, "The Parent Trap," *New York Times*, 8 February 2005, http://www.ngtimes.com/2006/02/08/opinion/08warner.html?th&emc=th(accessed 8 February 2006).
2. Quoted in Louise Story, "Many Women at Elite Colleges Set Career Path to Motherhood," *New York Times*, 30 September 2005, http://select.nytimes.com/search/restricted/article?res=F10A13FF38540C738EDDA00894DD404482&emc=eta1(accessed 30 September 2005).

Though this trend has been debated in the press, some scholars do argue that these numbers are increasing.

3. Alice Kessler-Harris, *In Pursuit of Equity: Women, Men, and the Quest for Economic Citizenship in 20th-Century America* (New York: Oxford University Press, 2001). Nancy Folbre, *The Invisible Heart: Economics and Family Values* (New York: New Press, 2001).

4. "Lahti Says Strong Feminista Rare Breed on TV Today," *Chattanooga Times Free Press*, 23 April 2005, E7.

5. For classic examples of this approach, see Tania Modleski, *Loving with a Vengeance: Mass Produced Fantasies for Women* (Hamden, CT: Archon Books, 1982), 14. Rosalind Coward, *Female Desire: Women's Sexuality Today* (London: Paladin, 1984), 14. For a recent example, see Linda Mizejewski, *Hardboiled and High Heeled: The Woman Detective in Popular Culture* (New York: Routledge, 2004).

6. David Black, personal interview, 10 November 2005.

7. " 'Agency,' 'Max Bickford' Get Extensions," *Jam! Television*, 1 November 2001, http://jam.canoe.ca/Television/TV_Shows/E/Education_of_Max_Bickford/2001/11/01/734384.html (accessed 27 October 2005); *TV.com*, http://www.tv.com/jack-and-bobby/show/21658/episode_guide.html.

8. Bonnie Dow, *Prime-Time Feminism: Television, Media Culture, and the Women's Movement Since 1970* (Philadelphia: University of Pennsylvania Press, 1996), 25.

9. Julie D'Acci, "Gender, Representation and Television," in *Television Studies*, ed. Toby Miller (London: British Film Institute, 2002), 91–94.

10. Summers made the remark at a January 2005 Harvard conference on "Diversifying the Science and Engineering Work Force." James Atlas, "The Battle Behind the Battle at Harvard," *New York Times*, 27 February 2005, http://www.nytimes.com/2005/02/27/weekinreview/27atlas.html?8br (accessed 27 February 2005); Stanley Fish, "Clueless in Academe," *Chronicle of Higher Education*, http://chronicle.com/temp/email.php?id=2mhd2zsvar2h4k1szawyz5icd413ktmo (accessed 23 February 2005).

11. Roger W. Bowen, "Gender Inequity," *Academe* March/April 2005.

12. Michael S. Kimmel, *The Gendered Society* (New York: Oxford University Press, 2000), 31–33. On the gendered inequities in education, see Janice Petrovich and Amy Stuart Wells, eds., *Bringing Equity Back: Research for a New Era in American Educational Policy* (New York: Teachers College Press, 2005). For classic studies see Myra Sadker and David Sadker, *Failing at Fairness: How Schools Shortchange Girls* (New York: Simon & Schuster, 1994). See also American Association of University Women, *How Schools Shortchange Girls: A Study of Major Findings on Girls and Education* (Washington, DC: American Association of University Women, 1992). On the question of debates over gendered intelligence, see Mary Wyer et al., *Women, Science, and Technology: A Reader in Feminist Science Studies* (New York: Routledge, 2001); and Sarah Milledge Nelson and Myriam Rosen-Ayalon, *In Pursuit of Gender: Worldwide Archaeological Approaches* (Walnut Creek, CA: Alta Mira Press, 2002). For classic accounts of the sociobiology debates over gendered intelligence, see Jo Durden-Smith and Diane deSimone, *Sex and the Brain* (New York: Warner Books, 1983), 171; and Ruth Bleier, *Science and Gender: A Critique of Biology and Its Theory on Women* (New York: Pantheon, 1984).

13. Michael S. Kimmel, *The Gendered Society* (New York: Oxford University Press, 2000), 11.

14. Kimmel, 11.

15. "Jack and Bobby," WB Homepage, http://www.thewb.com/Shows/Special/0,11116,171889%7C%7C,00.html (accessed 9 September 2005).

16. "Better Days," *Jack and Bobby*, WB, 19 September 2004.

17. "Pilot," *The Education of Max Bickford*, CBS, 23 September 2001.

18. "Pilot," *Max Bickford*.

19. "Genesis," *The Education of Max Bickford*, CBS, 3 March 2002.
20. "Pilot," *Max Bickford*.
21. Tania Modleski, *Feminism Without Women: Culture and Criticism in a "Postfeminist" Age* (New York: Routledge, 1991), 7–9, Sherrie A. Inness, *Tough Girls* (Philadelphia: University of Pennsylvania Press, 1999), 178–179.
22. "Pilot," *Jack and Bobby*, WB, 9 September 2004.
23. "Pilot," *Jack and Bobby*.
24. "Pilot," *Jack and Bobby*.
25. "Pilot," *Max Bickford*.
26. "Pilot," *Max Bickford*.
27. "Legacy."
28. "Legacy."
29. "Genesis."
30. "Hearts and Minds," *The Education of Max Bickford*, CBS, 21 October 2005; "In the Details," *The Education of Max Bickford*, CBS, 28 October 2005.
31. "And Justice for All," *Jack and Bobby*, WB, 23 February 2005.
32. "Friends with Benefits," *Jack and Bobby*, WB, 13 April 2005.
33. "Into the Woods," *Jack and Bobby*, WB, 9 February 2005.
34. "Querida Grace," *Jack and Bobby*, WB, 2 March 2005.
35. "Chess Lessons."
36. "Legacy."
37. "And Justice for All."
38. "Running Scared," *Jack and Bobby*, WB, 26 January 2005.
39. "A Child of God," *Jack and Bobby*, WB, 20 April 2005.
40. Cecelia Tichi, *Electronic Hearth: Creating an American Television Culture* (New York: Oxford University Press, 1991).
41. Lynn Spigel, *Make Room for TV: Television and the Family Ideal in Postwar America* (Chicago: University of Chicago Press, 1992).
42. Stephanie Coontz, *The Way We Never Were: American Families and the Nostalgia Trap* (New York: Basic Books, 1992), 12. See also Coontz, *Marriage, A History: From Obedience to Intimacy, or How Love Conquered Marriage* (New York, Viking, 2005). The modern nuclear family was naturalized as universal but was never the reality for a majority of people, even though it was upheld as a dominant cultural ideal. Two-parent households were the majority only from the 1920s to 1970s, and the modern nuclear family represented only a minority of those households. William H. Frey, Bill Abresch, and Jonathan Yeasting, *America by the Numbers: A Field Guide to the U.S. Population* (New York: New Press, 2001), 123–124.
43. Edward Shorter coined the term "postmodern family" in the 1970s and Judith Stacey has expanded on its usage since then, taking it to mean "after" the modern family, in a postmodern, late capitalist epoch and also considering the idea of "the contested, ambivalent, and undecided character of our contemporary family cultures," in keeping with philosophical definitions of postmodernism as involving uncertainty and doubt. Shorter, *The Making of the Modern Family* (New York: Basic Books, 1975). Stacey, *In the Name of the Family: Rethinking Family Values in the Postmodern Age* (Boston: Beacon Press, 1996), 7–8. See Stacey, *Brave New Families: Stories of Domestic Upheaval in Late Twentieth Century America* (Berkeley: University of California Press, 1998), 3–19. See also Deborah Chambers, *Representing the Family* (London: Sage, 2001); and Nancy F. Cott, *Public Vows: A History of Marriage and the Nation* (Cambridge, MA: Harvard University Press, 2000).

CHAPTER 8

Raising the Bar: Brilliant Women Lawyers from Ann Kelsey to Miranda Hobbes

Sharon Sutherland and Sarah Swan

If you see a beautiful young woman in a snappy business suit on your television set, chances are she is a lawyer. Since *L.A. Law*'s debut in 1986, countless shows—both with legal themes and otherwise—have featured women lawyers as significant characters, with more arriving every season. This trend is not new; popular culture has long been fascinated with the image of the female attorney. From Shakespeare's Portia to the 2006 midseason premiere of *Courting Alex*, the female lawyer has appeared in countless films, plays, novels, and television series.[1] Academics and critics interested in popular culture have noticed her and devoted many articles and even books to her.[2] With this chapter, we add to this lively discussion a study of brilliance in television's women lawyers. Intelligence in these characters echoes society's understanding of "smartness" in real women lawyers. However, the intelligence of television's female lawyers occurs amid many unrealistic contextual factors and gives a distorted image of women in the profession. Television shows us beautiful, brainy female lawyers who can display their smartness by practicing in any area they like and in any manner they like, but whose intelligence is undercut by an inability to have successful personal relationships. Real women attorneys often do not have beauty to accompany their brilliance, have been traditionally relegated to showing their intellectual abilities in particular areas and through particular methods of lawyering, and are sometimes married and have children. The disparity between the popular culture picture of female attorneys and real women lawyers suggests much about how U.S. society conceptualizes brilliance.

The issue of intelligence in women lawyers is not purely academic. One of the tenets of law and popular culture scholarship is that there is an interaction between what popular culture portrays, what the audience accepts and reproduces, and what the legal profession actually does. Much of what the public thinks about law and lawyers is influenced by popular culture, while at the same time popular culture reflects, often in exaggerated forms, what society thinks about law and lawyers.[3] Since television is a particularly pervasive and powerful medium, the image of female lawyers on television is of great significance: their image will reflect society's understandings and misconceptions of real women attorneys. By considering how female lawyers are portrayed in popular culture, we can learn much about the place of women in the legal profession. The relatively short history of female television lawyers limits this exploration to the past twenty years, but the plethora of shows featuring women attorneys provides plenty of fodder for this exploration. This chapter focuses primarily on the most influential and intriguing series of this period, including *L.A. Law*, *Ally McBeal*, *The Practice*, *Judging Amy*, and *Sex and the City*.

The twenty-year period of dramatized female lawyers coincides with a dramatic increase in the number of female lawyers in practice, allowing us to explore a rapidly shifting legal culture and the role of women within it. Until the 1970s, women constituted a tiny minority of the legal profession. By 1975, only 3 percent of all U.S. lawyers were women.[4] The sexism facing women who dared to participate in the profession during this period was palpable and pervasive. At law school, in a class of fifty men, there would often be only one or two women. These women who chose law as a profession struggled against systemic and personal challenges that did not necessarily afflict other fields to the same degree. Law was a true "old boys' club": hundreds of studies conducted over the past thirty years in the United States, Canada, and elsewhere "have consistently identified and documented the existence of bias and discrimination against women in the legal profession."[5]

Despite these challenges, women still wanted to practice law: there was a swift increase in the number of women entering law school from the 1970s on. By the time *L.A. Law* appeared on America's television sets in 1986, women made up at least half of most incoming classes.[6] Unfortunately, the dramatic change in the numbers of women entering the profession only swelled the number of junior women lawyers. By 1995, only 16 percent of all lawyers were women, and most of these were necessarily quite new members of the bar.[7] In that same year, 40 percent of associates in private practice were women, but only one in seven law firm partners was female.[8] Similarly, the small number of senior women lawyers translated into relatively few female judges and few others with high profiles and prestige within the legal community.[9] Eighty percent of the law professors—those first exemplars of legal study for most students—were male.[10] Now, the number of women in more senior positions in law is naturally changing as more women enter the legal profession and advance within it, but the rate of change is slower than might be anticipated.[11] The reason for this slow growth is that twice as many women as men leave the legal profession.[12] Women are entering the legal profession in equal numbers with men, but many are not staying. Nonetheless, the female lawyer is profoundly impacting the legal profession and the television screen.

Beauty and Brains

On television, female lawyers are smart by definition. The simple fact that they are lawyers signals that they are intelligent. Being a lawyer is shorthand for being brilliant. Drawing on recent examples, intelligent female lawyers show up on comedies (Alex on *Courting Alex* and Kate Fox on *Miss Match*), on dramas (*Medium's* law-student-turned-psychic-investigator Allison Dubois and Lilah Morgan on *Angel*), and on daytime television soap operas (Jessica Griffin Harris on *As the World Turns* and Christine Blair on *The Young and the Restless*). We do not often see these women work as lawyers or display their vocational brilliance, but we automatically accept that they are intelligent because we know that they are lawyers. Television's women lawyers are able to draw from the traditions and assumptions of intelligence that have grown around male lawyers and evoke the same response. Carol Shapiro explains how the female lawyer becomes brilliant by definition:

> Women as lawyers need to have facility in analysis, logic and language—areas traditionally considered masculine. . . . When women become lawyers, they show by definition that they have both the aptitude and the training to do what has traditionally been a man's job. In other words, they have shown that they are equal in an area that has previously been an exclusively male preserve.

> That women in law have finely honed reasoning and analytical abilities is disorienting to some, given traditional myths about women as highly emotional creatures, incapable of thought or logic. . . . The female attorney by definition stands on its head the idea that women's intellectual faculties are defective.[13]

In 1986, the first prime-time television series to celebrate this brilliance, and feature women lawyers in leading roles, debuted. *L.A. Law* broke new ground in its portrayal of female lawyers, and its success was no small reason for the multitude of law shows and female lawyer characters that followed. The series set a pattern for female lawyers that continues to this day. It armed its female lawyers battling traditional gender roles and social norms with the weapon of physical beauty.

Television's images tell us that successful female lawyers must combine brilliance with beauty. In television land, only attractive, slim, and fashionable women become successful lawyers: brains alone are not sufficient. A lineup of women lawyers from *L.A. Law* to *Boston Legal* would accurately reflect the changing images of beauty in American fashion magazines over the past twenty years, but would woefully misrepresent the average female lawyer. The beauty of television's women lawyers soothed society. During the uncomfortable adjustment that male and female lawyers had to make as the profession diversified, beautiful women lawyers on television provided comfort that not everything had changed—women lawyers were still women in all the most obvious physical ways.

Oddly, it was precisely this conformity to beauty norms that incited virulent attacks on two law shows in the late 1990s. In a striking example of the often disproportionately intense public scrutiny of women lawyer characters, two actresses playing lawyers on hit television dramas, Calista Flockhart as Ally McBeal on the eponymous show and Lara Flynn Boyle as Helen Gamble on *The Practice*, faced incessant, vitriolic criticisms for their extremely thin frames.[14] Their thinness, however, was entirely consistent with the current image of beauty perpetuated in Western popular culture generally—thin was in. Both actresses were maligned for presumed eating disorders and censured for their failure to present healthier role models for young women.

After all, their roles reflected the potential for success that women could achieve through brains. The sheer number of women lawyers on television marked a significant degree of success in breaking down gender barriers, but the degree to which these representatives of success outwardly catered to an even more pervasive stereotype of physical beauty showed that society was still uncomfortable with the idea of unadorned brilliance in women.

A few exceptions exist to the rule that beauty must accompany brains. For example, Dorothy Wyler (Nancy Vawter), a middle-aged associate who was returning to practice at a junior level after many years at home raising children, joined the firm on *L.A. Law* in season three. She was admired by many as a break from the typical television practice of casting only attractive women. Dorothy, however, did not get much opportunity to develop before she was usurped by the bevy of beautiful women lawyers vying for screen time.

More notable is Ellenor Frutt (Camryn Manheim) of *The Practice*. While Flockhart and Boyle were receiving attention for their extreme thinness, Manheim was gaining attention for her body weight, though this time at the other end of the scale, since she was significantly overweight. Her presence as a central character on the show challenged television's stereotype of the woman lawyer, evidencing the emergence of a world in which beauty is no longer necessary and where intellect and legal ability matter more. Unfortunately, since Manheim left the air at the conclusion of *The Practice*, no evident heirs have appeared on the scene. The new women lawyers replacing her on the spin-off *Boston Legal*—Shirley Schmidt (Candace Bergen), Denise Bauer (Julie Bowen), and Sara Holt (Ryan Michelle Bathe)—are all attractive and thin.

Sara Holt represents more than just another standard beautiful woman lawyer. She demonstrates that women lawyers from cultural and ethnic minorities are welcome on the airways, provided they meet the criteria of being slim and attractive. But while African American female lawyers are cast in many shows, few have strong story lines or roles that extend beyond "diversifying" the cast. Rebecca Washington (Lisa Gay Hamilton) of *The Practice* is an exception. She had a relatively central role, which grew as she developed from an assistant to a full member of the legal team. Rebecca aside, most African American female lawyers—and most minority characters generally—are minor characters. Even their conformity to the beauty norm does not catapult them on to center stage. The message that diversity is good (so long as everyone is attractive) is undercut by the pattern that nonwhite, nonheterosexual females are less successful and less central than their white sisters.

One man who has attempted to open up representations of brilliance to include members of minorities is David E. Kelley. Getting his own start in law television as a writer and then coproducer on *L.A. Law*, Kelley has carried the zeal for diversity in casting that was so much a core part of that program into his own law shows *Ally McBeal*, *The Practice*, and now *Boston Legal*.[15] Speaking of *L.A. Law*, Stephen Gillers (1989) wrote of the casting philosophy:

> With a nearly subversive zeal, the writers and producer have populated the show's legal terrain with a rainbow coalition of characters. Women, blacks, Latinos, Asian-Americans, and individuals of various sexual orientations are shown as lawyers, judges and other persons of achievement. . . . And recently it employed an older

woman associate, whose presence challenges popular assumptions about age with the same visual bluntness that other characters challenge assumptions about gender, sexual orientation, and race. The inhabitants of *L.A. Law* are demographically improbable—for law in L.A. and elsewhere—which is what makes them so valuable on prime time television.[16]

Diversifying the cast of female lawyers with representations of brilliant minority women attorneys started a bit slower than diversifying the cast in general, perhaps for the simple reason that casting a female as a lawyer in the 1980s was itself considered diversifying. *L.A. Law* had a "rainbow" of lawyers, but the women were universally white. Only two female lawyers carried any extra differences into the *L.A. Law* world.

As noted above, Dorothy Wyler was a short-lived, underutilized exception to the rule that all female lawyers are young and beautiful, while C. J. Lamb (Amanda Donohoe) was added in the fourth season as a lawyer more notable for her bisexuality than for her celebrated, but rarely viewed, skills as a litigator. But again, physically, C.J. was most certainly young and beautiful.

Since those days of near stunt casting on *L.A. Law*, Kelley has been bringing to the screen not just the overweight Ellenor Frutt and the African American Rebecca Washington, but also Ally McBeal's African American roommate, Renee Radick (Lisa Nicole Carson); the brilliant, aggressive, and sexually predatory Ling Woo (Lucy Liu); and the African American Coretta Lipp (Regina Hall), a minor part on *Ally McBeal*. All these women, however, have remained minor characters who demonstrate diversity in the workforce, but do so attractively and in small doses. This same casting philosophy—women lawyers may now add to being female a maximum of one other difference—is reflected in many of the shows that have been influenced by Kelley's successes. These shows tend to be short-lived. A show that places a brilliant, attractive female lawyer in a leading role but asks us to accept a second category of lawyerly "otherness" in addition to femininity is apparently doomed from the start. For example, Tess Kaufman (Marlee Matlin) provided us with an example of a smart, attractive, deaf female lawyer in *Reasonable Doubts*, which survived two seasons of low ratings (1991–1993). Interestingly, this show was structured such that the lead female was usually heard to speak through a male sign language interpreter. Her presence was arguably diluted by reliance on the continuous translation of her views through her male interpreter and her male costar. Nonetheless, the show did attempt to cast a more diverse representation of the brilliant female lawyer. Unfortunately, it was not successful in its attempt to nuance the beauty norm.

While female lawyers must maintain a high standard of beauty, male lawyers need not be so easy on the eyes. Leading male lawyers have been old, racially diverse, overweight, balding, and any combination thereof.[17] A common pattern, perhaps best exemplified by *Ally McBeal*'s highly eccentric senior partners Richard Fish (Greg Germann) and John Cage (Peter MacNicol), is the smart but odd-looking male lawyer. Certainly, there are leading roles filled by attractive males, starting with Harry Hamlin's Michael Kuzak on *L.A. Law*, but the same rules do not apply. The linkage between brilliance and beauty that television insists upon for female lawyers is clearly a gendered predisposition. By being less than beautiful, these male lawyers often make us focus on their brilliance: there are no physical distractions to take our minds off their legal maneuvers. Women, though, must be beautiful in order to infiltrate the legal world and must sneak in their intelligence beneath their good looks. Beauty provides these women with access to the profession and allows them to be brilliant within it, because the distraction of their pretty faces makes the new role they are taking on seem less threatening.

Although television's women lawyers must be beautiful, being sexy is altogether a different matter. When Ally McBeal showed up for work in her hyperfeminine ultra-miniskirt, vigorous argument erupted over the length of her hemline and over the extent to which a woman could be both brilliant and sexy. The show addressed the issue head-on. In one episode, the stunning and intelligent Nelle Porter (Portia de Rossi) began her association with Cage & Fish by arguing against a contempt order that would put Ally in prison for insisting on wearing short skirts to court. In response to the judge's allegation that it disrespects him and undermines the credibility of the courtroom, Nelle retorted:

> Why should it? That very assumption endorses the myth that a sexually attractive woman can't have credibility. That's a prejudice. It's bad enough the legal profession is still an old boy's club. Why should we come in here looking like old boys? . . . Every billboard and magazine cover tells us we should look like models. All the while, we have to fight the mindset if she's beautiful, she must be stupid. . . . What's most disappointing here? You saw this woman perform in court. You heard her argue. She won her case. And you're still judging her on hemlines? What do we have to do?[18]

Nelle's words were aimed as much at critics of the show who filled pages with the argument that Ally's hemlines detracted from her credibility as a lawyer. Short skirts and other "sexy" attire, those critics argued, lacked credibility and turned their wearer from an intelligent lawyer into a sex object.[19] As Nelle pointed out in her address to the judge, the very idea that brilliant and sexy are mutually exclusive is sexist. *Ally McBeal* required us to consider whether we are comfortable with this dichotomy.

The skirt dispute is not the only instance of intense debate over the wardrobe choices of television's women lawyers.[20] In the early 1990s, gender anxiety became frenzied over a traditionally male sartorial choice: the pantsuit. The short-lived series *The Trials of Rosie O'Neill* launched a cacophony of criticism over the appropriateness of professional women wearing pants when it showed its title character wearing a pantsuit in court. As a statement of equality in dress between male and female lawyers, the pantsuit was clearly controversial.[21] One reason for its significance can be extrapolated from a modern fashion consultant's advice to professional women on dressing for success: women who work in male-dominated environments prefer not to "stand out." It is "easier for them to be taken seriously when they are dressed similar to the men they work with."[22] As a statement about the brilliance of the women lawyers wearing it, the pantsuit's message was clear: women lawyers were claiming professional parity with male lawyers and demanding that their brilliance receive the same recognition. Television embraced this image of equality—at least for the women who were slim and attractive enough to wear the pants well.

Lawyering Like a Woman

Although the pantsuit represented parity in dress, there was little parity in practice areas when women entered the legal profession. Women tended to congregate in specific areas, the so-called pink ghettos of law. This observation is consistent with an identified phenomenon:

> When an occupation becomes gender-integrated as a whole, stratification by gender still frequently exists within the occupation, with women typically holding lower status positions. The legal field conforms to this pattern. Women's successful access to the law profession over the past several decades has not been accompanied by equal success in their progression within the profession.[23]

In law, gender integration has occurred in the sense that women are now in the profession, but this integration is limited. The stratification is obvious when one considers that practice areas are often divisible by gender. Traditionally, women have been slotted (or have slotted themselves) into lower-status areas of law. Studies have demonstrated that female lawyers are overrepresented in public interest law, academia, government, and judicial clerkships—all positions that are statistically lower paying than private practice and are often viewed as "alternative legal careers" that lack the rigors of private practice.[24] Similarly, female lawyers are overrepresented in areas of practice such as family law, wills and estates, poverty law, human rights, pay equity, and residential tenancies but are rarely seen in many other more "male" practice areas, such as criminal defense, securities, and commercial law.[25]

Not surprisingly, television's reflection of and reaction to the real gender divides present in the legal profession is complicated. *L.A. Law*, for example, took diabolical delight in placing women in traditional male areas as part of its overall zeal for unusual casting. Of particular note is that the show featured many criminal trials conducted by female lawyers. Whereas women in the real world significantly underpopulated the criminal defense bar, on *L.A. Law* and its contemporaries, female lawyers were frequently criminal defense lawyers. In fact, shows that featured women lawyers practicing typically female areas of law, such as *Civil Wars*, were often unsuccessful. No doubt the choice to put women in criminal court largely reflects the dramatic possibilities of the criminal trial compared with tax law, but it also creates a television legal profession where women take on more diverse roles than in the real legal profession. The practice restrictions that push on real female lawyers do not confine television's female lawyers; the fictional versions of women attorneys are free to show their brilliance in whatever area the writers choose.

The women, however, competed successfully in these male areas only when they competed in the same ways that men competed. Just as there are "male" and "female" practice areas, there are also modes of practicing that have been categorized as "male" and "female." The possibility of gendered lawyering has been discussed by many feminist legal scholars, often with reference to Carol Gilligan, who introduced the theoretical distinction between lawyering from an ethic of care (which emphasizes nurturing, connections with others, and contextual thinking) and lawyering from an ethic of justice (which emphasizes individualism, the use of rules to resolve moral dilemmas, and equality).[26] Traditional legal practice privileges the notions embedded in the ethic of justice and has been identified with a male lawyer style:

> Experiential and clinical evidence indicates that profiles of successful professionals conflict with profiles of normal or ideal women. The aggressiveness, competitiveness, dedication, and emotional detachment traditionally presumed necessary for advancement in the most prestigious and well-paid occupations are incompatible with traits commonly viewed as attractive in women: cooperativeness, deference, sensitivity, and self-sacrifice.[27]

Television's women lawyers are successful when they adopt male traits. On *L.A. Law*, Grace Van Owen (Susan Dey) was every bit as ruthless in court as Michael and possibly a better litigator because her demeanor was chilly and calculating while his was occasionally marred by heat and emotion, and Ann Kelsey (Jill Eikenberry) was more tough-minded and adversarial than her foil and spouse, the kindly Stuart. Abby Perkins (Michele Green), however, was criticized for her more "female" approach to law: she was deemed incompetent when she sought out conciliatory options rather than seeking to inflict the greatest damage on the opposite party.

Following the 1980s presentation of aggressive female litigators, the early 1990s opened the doors to women lawyers practicing "female" areas of law, in "female" ways, with pride.[28] Shows like *Civil Wars*, and later *Family Law* and *Judging Amy*, assured us that practice area is a question of personal preference; women did not choose "female" areas of law because they were not brilliant enough to practice in "male" areas, but they chose areas where the issues were important to them. "Female" and "male" areas both became options for women lawyers. Ally McBeal, for instance, maintained a general civil litigation caseload made up of files involving sex, love, marriage, or any combination of the three. She represented a Jewish woman wanting a rabbi to grant her spiritual release from her marriage to a comatose husband, a jilted spouse who wanted to sue a senator for "interfering with happy marital relations," and a woman accused of having sex with a minor. Ally was personally preoccupied with issues of love and marriage, and this preoccupation made her naturally excel in this area. Her brilliance connected to her own ideals and values and created success for her.

Ally herself practiced law in a very "female" way, though some argue that her way had little value. Her character can be seen in one of two ways: She is either a positive trendsetter, ushering in a new era of female lawyers gaining autonomy as odd individuals with interesting personalities, or yet another example of the stereotypical neurotic woman.[29] Some critics acclaimed her as a groundbreaking, innovative character with normal human frailties like those of real professional women, and some argued that she was nothing more than a hysterical woman whose method of practicing law was a disgrace to the profession.[30] One female lawyer anxious to distance herself from Ally McBeal wrote,

> As an attorney, Ally McBeal's character embodies virtually every stereotype of female attorneys which my friends and I have attempted to overcome professionally since we began practicing law. . . . She seems to approach all legal issues with

virtually no legal analysis. . . . Instead of practicing law, Ally McBeal spends most of her time questioning why she has not found happiness in life and why her dream of having a successful career coupled with an adoring husband and a few children has not been fulfilled.[31]

Ally's way, though, yields results. Her relational approach to legal issues and her contextual analyses achieve success in the courtroom.

Like Ally, Judge Amy Grey (Amy Brenneman) on *Judging Amy* worked in a traditionally feminine area of law, as a judge in family court. That is not the beginning and end of her story, however. She was a graduate of Harvard Law School, an obvious and stereotypical sign of intelligence, and thus a strong candidate for any type of law she should desire to practice. She participated in many areas of law: before her foray into family law, she was a corporate lawyer; in the middle of the series, she switched from family court to regular court; and as the series closed, she entered politics and ran for Senate. In this way, the show presented her as a brilliant female lawyer and judge who was eminently capable of success in any field of law, including areas that are male dominated. Her decision to work as a family judge was consequently a clear choice of an area presenting important issues, rather than a default gender selection.

Other women lawyers also demonstrate success in many areas of law. Like Amy Grey before she took the bench, Miranda Hobbes (Cynthia Nixon) on *Sex and the City* practiced corporate law in New York. She thrived in this high-powered environment, fitting into the old boys' network with her characteristic aplomb. Additionally, in *The Practice*, the female lawyers practiced areas of law not generally associated with the feminine, criminal law, though their chosen field was often portrayed as threatening. Lindsey Dole (Kelli Williams) was victimized by stalkers, Rebecca Washington was badly injured when a bomb exploded in the firm, and Ellenor Frutt was also placed in dangerous situations. Though their jobs threatened their safety, they were able to effectively perform their duties as lawyers. Television's smart women lawyers generally shifted their approach over time from aggressive and adversarial lawyering in male-dominated practice areas to more relational and context-based lawyering in areas that matched their own personal interests. Whereas the women of *L.A. Law* succeeded by virtue of performing in male-dominated areas in masculine ways, Ally, Miranda, Amy, and the women of *The Practice* exemplify mobility within practice areas in accordance with personal interests. These more contemporary women can be successful, brilliant lawyers while practicing family law or while mediating estate disputes; they do not need to be aggressive commercial or criminal litigators to be successful. While the choices these women make about practice areas are not an accurate reflection of the gender breakdown in real legal practice, television's portrayal of brilliant female lawyers arguably influences both public perception of the roles women play in the law and the next generation of legal professionals in ways that may actually increase the likelihood of greater gender integration in the future.

Weak Points: Smart Women Lawyers' Flaws

Unfortunately, television giveth, and television taketh away. Women may be smart enough to practice law on television, but they are often given some sort of feminine failing.[32] Lindsey Dole illustrates this point. Although she was portrayed as an excellent litigator and her intelligence was unquestionable, her mental health status was not so reliable. Her capabilities as a lawyer were impressive. She was able to cite cases from memory,[33] and in her first major civil jury trial she delivers such a powerful opening that the other side offered the largest settlement in the history of the area of law involved.[34] But, as the series progressed, she was repeatedly victimized until finally, as a result of her client's continual abusive behavior toward her, she ended up shooting a man and standing trial for first-degree murder. Her defense was that the abuse caused her to have battered women's syndrome. At this point in the series, her mental health was shaky, suggesting that she was mentally ill-equipped for the rigors of law. Like *L.A.Law*'s Abby Perkins (who also was forced to shoot a client), Lindsey became unable to focus at work because of personal issues. She reflects a phenomenon that Carole Shapiro (1998) identified in the context of women lawyers in film, that of the "less than" woman. The "less than" woman pays a price for success. She is unable to do things that other women can: "The films gave us lawyers who were smart enough, but who were 'less than' women. They couldn't cook, couldn't dance, were bad at sex, had no social life or friends, or were workaholics."[35]

Judge Amy Grey is a prime example of a "less than" woman. We learn about Amy's lack of friends from a scene in which she asks her brother, Vincent (Dan Futterman), about the appropriate lingerie attire for her to wear when she begins dating after her divorce, and he asks her why she cannot talk to her friends about it. She responds that the only close female friend she has is battling cancer and is therefore not a good candidate for that kind of frivolous conversation. In addition, when Amy has a date in her house, she cannot cook:

> *Amy:* David's coming over. I'm cooking.
> *Maxine:* You don't cook.
> *Amy:* Just because I don't doesn't mean I can't.
> *Maxine:* Means you shouldn't.[36]

In Amy we find a highly competent, skilled judge, and a caring mother, but a woman who also has domestic shortcomings.

Amy was also unable to have a successful love relationship. The show began with her failed marriage to her husband, Michael (Richard Burgi), and throughout the series, her relationship with him remained acrimonious. The two were unable to resolve many of their conflicts concerning their daughter, Lauren (Karle Warren). They engaged in bitter custody battles that often resulted in both of them retaining high-powered lawyers to fight it out. We also saw Amy make a questionable judgment call when she had one last fling with Michael on the day their divorce became final. Amy's post-Michael dating relationships invariably ended badly.

Other women lawyers fit this pattern. Most shows portray women as unlucky in love.[37] Their legal brilliance is undermined by a lack of smartness in another category: Despite their ability to effectively manage a legal case, most of the women are unable to manage a significant other. These brilliant women lawyers find that maintaining a successful legal career and a positive personal relationship are mutually exclusive propositions. *L.A Law*'s Ann Kelsey and Stuart Markovitz were exceptions to the rule, as were Leon Robinovitch (Eric Peterson) and Alanna Newman (Julie Kahner) in later seasons of *Street Legal*, but these were the only happily married couples among all of television's lawyers in the 1980s, and they were happily married to other lawyers who shared their career goals. *L.A. Law*'s Dorothy and Abby were divorced; Grace was single and moved through a series of unstable relationships. Shorter-term employees of the firm, such as Rosalind (Diana Muldaur) and C.J., were single as well. The evidence of television lawyers was that legal careers and relationships could not be combined.

The relationship status of television's women lawyers differs from reality. While singlehood remains an overarching theme throughout shows featuring women lawyers from *L.A. Law* on, the real-life statistics form a different picture. The marriage rates of real women lawyers are on par with the national average, but television's women lawyers marry at a much lower rate.[38] The number of divorces and breakups on television, however, remains statistically accurate. This combination of numbers presents a picture in which the single lawyer has a predominance that does not correspond to reality.[39]

One explanation for this single status is that it provides a plot opportunity. Another is that it is simply a reflection of the time and commitment demands of a successful professional career. More likely, though, the single status of these women is meant as a cautionary tale, telling women that while we may be brilliant enough to become lawyers, even lawyers in traditionally male areas, we cannot have it all, and if we want to be brilliant, we may be alone.[40]

In addition to not being able to sustain healthy long-term relationships with significant others, women lawyers pay another price for choosing to work in the profession:

> The women long for and need certain things as women, but being lawyers greatly complicates their quest for gender fulfillment. The women have chosen to live through their minds, which places them at odds with their bodies. "Mind/body stories generally show that a woman cannot cross the line into the world of men without relinquishing something of her womanhood, and suffering for it."[41]

By choosing to live through their minds, and to live this way in a male profession, women lawyers on television have to sacrifice the joys of motherhood. On *L.A. Law*, Ann and Stuart struggled with the adoption of a child, only to lose him to his biological mother. They then had their own child who interrupted Ann's career and caused considerable challenges for both Ann and Stuart—but especially for Ann, who took on the role of primary caregiver. Abby was a single mother, but beyond the fact that she was criticized for being unable to complete her work because of her family life, we saw little of the impact of this challenge on her career. Her son was not obviously a part of her life as she became better as a lawyer. Women fit in during this period by joining the boys' club, which meant accepting the rules of practice that called for demanding hours, not by challenging the way in which law firms operated and the need for one-hundred-hour work weeks.

Even in the later shows, motherhood is incompatible with being a brilliant woman lawyer. When Ally McBeal was united with the ten-year-old daughter she never knew she had (she donated an egg while in college), she soon learned that mother-hood has its price and that the price would be her career. When her daughter, Maddie (Hayden Panettiere), began to experience problems adjusting to life in Boston, she decided that, in the best interests of her child, she must leave the state. Although she was offered partnership in the firm at which she has spent years working, Ally decided to resign and move to Maddie's hometown of New York City.

On *The Practice*, Ellenor Frutt made a similar sacrifice. By the time the series ended, she had decided to take a break from the practice of law in order to raise her daughter. This decision, like Ally McBeal's choice to resign and leave Boston, high-lights the difficulties women face in balancing childrearing with lawyering. These women feel that they must leave the practice of law as they know it and physically remove themselves from the firm in order to be successful mothers. In other words, their mind-body conflict persists, and they switch their focus from the mind to the body, but being unable to reconcile the two. The difficulty in reconciling the desires of the mind with those of the body is a reason that many real women lawyers leave private practice or leave the profession altogether. The attrition rate for women lawyers is much higher than that for men, with some studies noting that women leave the profession 60 percent more quickly than men.[42] The message from these two shows, that a life devoted to the pursuits of the mind and intellectual fulfillment is incompatible with a life that involves the pursuits of the body, can be seen embodied in these real-life decisions.

Even *Sex and the City*'s Miranda Hobbes, who provides the best vision of a woman lawyer successfully balancing work with family, must make a sacrifice. Through careful timing, she was able to be a partner, wife, and mother. She delayed mother-hood, and marriage, until after achieving partner at her firm. (In fact, her pregnancy was accidental, but she explicitly refused to become pregnant during the time she was trying to make partner.)[43] At one point in the series, it appeared that Miranda, like Ally, Lindsay, and Amy, would be unable to juggle all three roles. The hours and stress of trying to make partner contribute to her relationship breakdown with her then boyfriend Steve (David Eigenberg). Their relationship failed on the eve of the day she made partner, prompting Carrie Bradshaw, the lead character, to narrate it: "That night, Miranda lost her partner. The next day, she got a new one—fifteen of them."[44] As the series continued, however, she had a son, Bradey, and married Steve. In order to achieve this balance, though, Miranda had to pay the price that Ally had to pay: she had to move. But unlike Ally Miranda's move did not require her to sacrifice her career. Instead, she simply had to leave behind her beloved Manhattan and move her family to Brooklyn. The conflict between the life of the mind, represented by New York, and the new body/family focus, represented by Brooklyn, is present, but it is sur-mountable in a way that was not an option for Ally. Miranda stands as a rare exam-ple of the brilliant, beautiful woman who is able to have a family and a career.

Closing Argument

Ally McBeal famously declared, "If women really wanted to change society, they could do it. I plan to change it. I just want to get married first."[45] And she is right. In her position as a lawyer, she is particularly well poised to change society. This power is one of the reasons that the woman lawyer is such a significant figure in popular culture:

> In the land where law is sovereign, the lawyer is king. He is seen to have the keys to the kingdom by virtue of skill, training and perhaps some mystical quality that can spring the kingdom door wide open or keep it closed tighter than a drum. . . .
>
> As women have increasingly entered the legal profession, they have begun to acquire a modicum of the power that male lawyers previously monopolized.[46]

The female lawyer symbolizes brilliance. Television provides the perfect forum for society to consider what this brilliance means. The link between beauty and brains shows us the pervasiveness of the beauty standard and suggests that although we as a society are at a point where we accept that women can be intelligent professionals, beauty is still the most precious female commodity. Recently, characters like Ellenor Frutt suggest that the beauty mold can be broken, but that unattractiveness is used mostly as a diversification tool, as a surprising addition to the usual lineup. Women belonging to minority groups can diversify many casts; however, they too must meet the beauty standard. Beauty must accompany brilliance. Unattractive women lawyers have little part in television.

While the physical appearance of television's women lawyers has generally mirrored societal stereotypes, the practice areas that television's women lawyers engage in differ from those that real women practice. The traditionally female areas of practice, the "pink ghettos," are less likely to be seen on television; instead, television's women lawyers appear as leading litigators in both criminal and civil law. Practice barriers do not exist on television: women lawyers have uninhibited mobility. Television's women lawyers can still practice "female" areas of law if they want to, but they are free to display their brilliance in any area they choose. Women on television can also practice in any manner they choose, including ways labeled "female." Ally McBeal, for instance, can trumpet her brilliance by practicing "love law" and incorporating her own anecdotes and understanding of relationships into her arguments. The options are much wider than real-life statistics suggest.

In other ways, however, television's women lawyers are limited in their options. Motherhood and marriage are presented as incompatible with brilliance. In another instance of nonconformity with reality, television's women lawyers rarely marry and rarely have children. When women do marry or bear children, the shows tend to focus on the difficulties inherent in the situation and exaggerate all the usual pitfalls associated with balancing a career and family. It seems that television is determined to deny women families by cautioning against the lonely life that professional women can lead and showing a duality between brilliance and the home and family.

Television's female lawyers are brilliant, beautiful, capable women who are uninhibited by many realities of practice that real women lawyers confront. In this way, they show a glossy, unattainable ideal that women lawyers cannot hope to achieve. At the same time, their very presence on the screen is undeniably positive because it normalizes the idea that real women can be brilliant lawyers. In a society struggling to adjust to women in such a power position, television serves as the theater where hopes, dreams, and fears surrounding this shift can safely play out.

Television draws inspiration from the brilliance of women and shines it back to us, illuminating an endless array of possibility and potential for women lawyers in the present and in the future.

Notes

1. *Courting Alex* premiered 23 January 2006 on CBS and starred Jenna Elfman as a hardworking, smart lawyer working at her father's firm.
2. For example, see Cynthia Lucia, *Framing Female Lawyers: Women on Trial in Film* (Austin: University of Texas Press, 2005); and Stacey Caplow, "Still in the Dark: Disappointing Images of Women Lawyers in the Movies," *Women's Rights Law Reporter* 20, no. 2/3 (1999): 55.
3. Michael Asimow, "Embodiment of Evil: Law Firms in the Movies," *UCLA Law Review* 48 (2000): 1339.
4. Hannah Dugan, "Does Gender Still Matter in the Legal Profession?" *Wisconsin Lawyer* 75 (2002): 10.
5. Merrill Cooper, Joan Brockman, and Irene Hoffart, "Final Report on Equity and Diversity in Alberta's Legal Profession" Joint Committee on Equality, Equity and Diversity, 26 January 2004, http://www.lawsocietyalberta.com/files/reports/ Equity_ and_Diversity.pdf (accessed 6 October 2005).
6. Interestingly, the dramatic increase in the number of women entering law corresponds to a drastic shift in the presentation of male lawyers on film. Whereas before the 1970s lawyers are portrayed heroically, that decade marked the beginning of the reign of the "bad lawyer" on film. At least one critic theorizes that some of the resentment evident in the portrayal of the lawyer-villain could actually be resentment toward women working in a traditionally male profession. See Michael Asimow, "Bad Lawyers in the Movies," *Nova Law Review* 533 (1999): 540.
7. Dugan, 12.
8. Dugan, 12.
9. Rebecca Korzec, "Working on the 'Mommy-Track': Motherhood and Women Lawyers," *Hastings Women's Law Journal* 8 (1997): 117.
10. Carl Tobias, "Engendering Law Faculties," *University of Miami Law Review* (1990): 1143, writes that "the dearth of tenured female faculty is the most acute problem affecting women in legal education. In the period encompassing the 1980–81 and 1986–87 academic years, the number of full-time women faculty increased from 13.7% to 20%."
11. Marjorie Kornhauser, "Rooms of Their Own: An Empirical Study of Occupational Segregation by Gender among Law Professors," *University of Missouri-Kansas City Law Review* 73. 2 (2004): 293.
12. Linda Roberston, "Why Women Are Leaving the Legal Profession and What Law Firms Can Do to Stop the Exodus," outline of speech, *Law Practice Management Law Section Minutes*, Canadian Bar Association, British Columbia Branch, 26 February 2003.
13. Carole Shapiro, "Women Lawyers in Celluloid: Why Hollywood Skirts the Truth," *University of Toledo Law Review* 25 (1994): 955.
14. For a study of eating disorders in female attorneys, see Julie E. Buchwald, "Confronting a Hazard: Do Eating Disorders Plague Women in the Legal Profession?" *Southern California Review of Law and Women's Studies* 9.1 (1999): 101.
15. Kelley's extremely short-lived 2002 series, *Girl's Club*, included the racially mixed (Chinese-Filipina-American) lawyer Rhanda Clifford in a relatively minor role. Interestingly, the actress playing Rhanda, Christina Chang, has since guested as attorney Elizabeth Tyler in Kelley's much more successful *Boston Legal*.

16. Stephen Gillers, "Taking *L.A. Law* More Seriously," *Yale Law Journal* 98 (1989): 1607.

17. Examples are *Matlock*'s Ben Matlock (Andy Griffiths), *L.A. Law*'s Victor Sifuentes (Jimmy Smits), and *The Practice*'s Eugene Young (Steven Harris).

18. Episode 2:04, "It's My Party."

19. See, for example, Lisa Scottoline, "Get Off the Screen," *Nova Law Review* 24 (1999): 655.

20. Although not a source of debate, the ubiquitous power suit of the 1980s television series is significant in that the masculine shape of the blazer was often coupled with highly feminine accessories. The overall effect was a highly conflicted image that represented the confusion surrounding the role of women lawyers at that time.

21. See Ric Sheffield, "On Film: A Social History of Women Lawyers in Popular Culture, 1930–1990," *Loyola L.A. Entertainment Law Journal* 14 (1993–1994): 73–111, where he comments that women lawyers who wore pantsuits were "accused of trying to emulate men."

22. Erin, "Dress for Success: What Your Outfit Could Be Saying about You," *Happygrrl Online*, http://www.happygrrls.com/fashion/dressforsuccess.html (accessed 9 January 2006).

23. Kornhauser, 293.

24. Dugan, 12.

25. Dispute resolution has an interesting relationship to these gender issues. Whereas once it was a low-status, "female" area, its value to the business community and large corporations has catapulted it into the area of general acceptance.

26. Carol Gilligan, *In a Different Voice: Psychological Theory and Women's Development* (Boston: Harvard University Press, 1982).

27. Deborah L. Rhode, "Perspective on Professional Women," *Stanford Law Review* 40 (1988): 1163.

28. Many legal shows have included mediation scenes in the past few years. In most instances, it is a female lawyer who advocates for mediation rather than litigation. For example, Robyn Parsons of *The Associates* has to overcome the reservations of partners, other associates, and clients to advocate for mediation of a hostile family dispute in episode 1:9, "Family Values."

29. For an analysis of Ally's intelligence, see Ann Bartow, "Some Dumb Girl Syndrome: Challenging and Subverting Destructive Stereotypes of Female Attorneys," *William and Mary Journal of Women and the Law* 11 (2005): 221.

30. Naomi Mezey and Mark C. Niles, in "Screening the Law: Ideology and Law in American Popular Culture," *Columbia Journal of Law and Arts* 28 (2005): 91, opine that the series is meant to suggest that law itself is "about the performance of inner and outer controversies."

31. Lisa Friedman, "Don't Call Me Ally," *Picturing Justice: The On-Line Journal of Law and Popular Culture*, http://www.usfca.edu/pj/ally-freidman.htm (accessed 11 October 2005).

32. See Christine Alice Corcos, " 'We Don't *Want* Advantages': The Woman Lawyer Hero and Her Quest for Power in Popular Culture," *Syracuse Law Review* 53 (2003): 1225, for a study of how the female lawyer hero figure differs from the male lawyer hero figure.

33. J. G. Marek. "*The Practice* and *Ally McBeal*: A New Image for Women Lawyers on Television?" *Journal of American Culture* 22.1 (1999): 77.

34. Pilot episode.

35. Carole Shapiro, "Women Lawyers in Celluloid, Rewrapped," *Vermont Law Review* 23 (1998–1999): 304.

36. Episode 118: *Lullaby*.

37. Carolyn Lisa Miller, " 'What a Waste. Beautiful, Sexy Gal. Hell of a Lawyer.' Film and the Female Attorney," *Columbia Journal of Gender and Law* 4 (1994): 203.

38. Diane Klein, "Ally McBeal and Her Sisters: A Quantitative and Qualitative Analysis of Representations of Women Lawyers in Prime Time Television," *Loyola L.A. Entertainment Law Journal* 18 (1997–1998): 259.

39. Klein, 259.

40. See Louise Everrett Graham and Geraldine Maschio, "A False Public Sentiment: Narrative and Visual Images of Women Lawyers in Film," *Kentucky Law Journal* 84 (1995–1996): 1027, for a similar comment on the role of women attorneys in film.

41. David Papke, "Cautionary Tales: The Woman as Lawyer in Contemporary Hollywood Cinema," *University of Arkansas at Little Rock Law Review* 25.3 (2003): 485, quoting M.Harrington, "Women Lawyers: Rewriting the Rules" 7 (1994).

42. Janice Mucalov, "Women in Law," *Canadian Bar Association National*, August/September 2002, 13.

43. Episode 38, "The Big Time."

44. "The Big Time."

45. Quoted at http://en.thinkexist.com/quotes/allymcbeal (accessed 20 January 2006).

46. Shapiro, "Women Lawyers in Celluloid: Why Hollywood," 971–973.

CHAPTER 9

Savvy Women, Old Boys' School Politics, and *The West Wing*

Beth Berila

The women characters on the television show *The West Wing* are savvy, brilliant, and beautiful, and yet they constantly have to prove themselves. The story lines on the program reflect the bind in which intelligent women find themselves when they move into traditionally male-dominated fields, and the U.S. federal government is one of the most patriarchal of them all. Women in these professions need to be strong enough to go head-to-head with powerful male opponents and colleagues who consider women "aggressive" and "bitchy" if they are too assertive. If they are not direct enough, they are too "soft" and "weak." If they are attractive and see themselves as sexual beings, they are viewed as "using their sexuality to get ahead." If they are not perceived as beautiful, however, they are "threatening" and "manly." This catch-22 facing smart women is nothing new. Feminist critics have made this point regarding the Anita Hill and Clarence Thomas hearings, the high-profile actions of Eleanor Roosevelt, the criticisms of Hillary Clinton, the media coverage of Dee Dee Myers, and the tenure of Condoleezza Rice as secretary of state. The more a woman's politics support patriarchal, imperialist, and racist agendas, the more room she has to be prominent, but rocking the boat will always bring retaliation.

This chapter explores this issue in more depth as it involves representations of smart women, particularly through intersections of race and gender. How are smart women represented in popular culture, and what are the implications of those portrayals? Since much of what we know about public figures is filtered through television and print newscasts, we need to explore how representation shapes possibility. We also live in a society in which cultural production increasingly blurs the line between what is "real" and what is fiction (consider reality television shows, for instance) and in which political events are exceedingly staged. In that context, what kinds of images of smart women trickle through to the public, and what are the implications of those images?

This chapter explores these issues through the portrayals of smart women on the NBC television drama *The West Wing* for a few key reasons.[1] The vast popularity and critical acclaim of the show, particularly when Aaron Sorkin was writing it, means it deserves attention. In the United States, a minority of the population voted in recent presidential elections, and yet *The West Wing* drew an average of 15 million viewers each week in its early seasons.[2] It set the record for the number of Emmys won by a show in a single season (nine during its first season) and is tied with *Hill Street Blues* and *L.A. Law* for the most Emmy Awards won for outstanding drama series. The series is ranked eighth in number of Emmy Awards won by a series, which include awards for the all-star cast.[3] One could arguably say that some people in the United States know more about the administration of *The West Wing* than they do about actual ones. Moreover, the show accomplishes a surprising feat by making governmental, historical, and legal issues interesting, provocative, and central to the story line.

The program's influence clearly reveals that public perceptions are, on some level, regularly filtered through Hollywood, which leads me to my second reason for focusing on *The West Wing*. Despite how avidly we might read the *New York Times*, listen to National Public Radio, or watch *Oprah*, much of what the public learns about smart women in the U.S. government is shaped through fictional representation.[4] Few people work closely with such political figures. Instead, we learn about them through popular media and through their public appearances. Our knowledge of them is shaped through representation, and while the news media is, we hope, less fictionalized than Hollywood, it is nevertheless representation. Therefore, we need to consider what kinds of portrayals of smart women pervade popular culture and how those portrayals shape and limit the possibilities for women when gender, race, and brilliance intersect.

I also focus on *The West Wing* portrayals of the tensions confronting smart women in the executive branch because the show reveals the contradictions they face in provocative ways. As Tania Modleski points out, "Mass art not only contains contradictions, it also *functions* in a highly contradictory manner: while appearing to be merely escapist, such art simultaneously challenges and reaffirms traditional values, behavior, and attitudes."[5] For example, the White House Project, a national nonpartisan organization dedicated to increasing women's participation in the government, named *The West Wing* as one of the media portrayals advancing women's leadership, stating, "We honor *The West Wing* for showing millions of Americans each week women as leaders and not just 'leading ladies.'"[6] The insightful nature of *The West Wing*'s story lines, the witty dialogue, and the superb performances enable us to think about the tensions limiting smart women in ways that are often obscured by media portrayals of actual politicians. It reveals the differences between women as leaders and women as leading ladies, while also continually relegating them to the latter.

Focusing on this program, this chapter will explore the gendered and racial dynamic that occurs when intelligent women gain access to power in traditionally male-dominated spaces—in this case, presidential politics. The prominent women characters on the show are portrayed as strong, sexy, and able to directly challenge male politicians when necessary. These transgressions are often contained, however, by moments when such characters, too, are objectified or portrayed as weak, a contradiction that confronts many women who are prominent in "actual" politics as well. Moreover, while these characters are powerful and intelligent, the women characters in secretarial positions hold minor roles and are regularly the subject of demeaning dialogue or humor. The intriguing aspect of the show lies in its ability to spotlight even these moments, so that these tensions themselves become part of the insightful story line. At a time when audiences might know more about *The West Wing* story lines than they do about "actual" governmental practices, the show is worth exploring.

It is particularly valuable because, as many Cultural Studies critics point out, representation shapes what we know.[7] This is certainly true of television shows. But it is also true of much of what we know about our national politicians.[8] Campaigns are orchestrated and public statements written by speechwriters, while politicians' public personas are crafted in part by advisors and press secretaries.[9] This is not to say that officials do not take positions that they believe in or that everything is artificial, but it is to say that much of what we know about our national politicians is filtered through representations.[10]

It is worth, then, paying attention to how *The West Wing* portrays the federal government, the politics of Washington, and its smart women characters, in part because it draws explicit parallels between the show's depictions and the "actual" White House. The gendered ideologies that the show reproduces are significant, particularly because many of the plot lines echo events that happen in the "real" world, while its characters bear striking resemblance to politicians.[11] It is not hard to see a similarity between the Josiah Bartlet administration and Bill Clinton's White House. The show has dealt with issues such as whether a Supreme Court nominee believes in the right to privacy, what kind of political fallout occurs when a White House staffer insults members of the Christian right, how the State of the Union speech gets written, and whether the president should support same-sex marriage or gays in the military.[12] These are all issues that have been in public debate in recent years in the United States. Should audiences miss this parallel, the show itself invites the comparisons by featuring an episode that includes interviews with actual former presidents, such as Bill Clinton and Jimmy Carter, as well as prominent staff members, such as former Press Secretary Dee Dee Myers, who talk about their experiences while in the White House.[13] These interviews are juxtaposed with clips from episodes of *The West Wing* that directly lead viewers to compare the television show with actual administrations. Moreover, when the series is rerun on Bravo, the commercial breaks usually feature brief snippets of trivia about former presidents and their First Ladies, including John F. Kennedy and Jackie Kennedy, Richard and Pat Nixon, and Franklin and Eleanor Roosevelt. One might ask, then, whether the show is reflecting and echoing the "real" presidential administrations or whether it is also shaping our perceptions of the latter.

Either way, the portrayals of smart women reveal the contradictions of gender in a patriarchal institution.[14] As the cultural studies scholar Judith Willamson has noted in another context, the most successful films or, in this case, television shows "are those which strike on some contemporary problem or insecurity in the issues they raise, while resolving these issues in a satisfactory or unthreatening way."[15] *The West Wing* reveals a crisis of insecurity about smart women as they enter and shape patriarchal positions of power, and while the show troubles the constraints facing those women, it also ultimately reinscribes them, altering the status quo only slightly.

Smart Women, Sexuality, and Feminist Politics

One of the most notable contradictions facing smart women in old boys' school politics involves the combination of beauty, sexuality, and smarts. Brilliant women who break into traditionally male-dominated fields have long noted the demeaning treatment with which they are met, treatment that tends to question their ability and credibility. Women who are sexy are often allowed a certain degree of smarts, though their sexuality can also be used against them.[16] When feminist politics is added to the mix, the tensions become even more complex.

The West Wing reveals these issues on numerous occasions, perhaps the most notable of which involves the character of Ainsley Hayes (Emily Proctor), a Republican White House counsel who is known for her beauty and her talent for debate. Her first appearance on the show involves her besting White House Deputy Sam Seaborn (Rob Lowe) on the Washington talk show *Capital Beat*.[17] The next day, Sam returns to the office to face ongoing ridicule that he was beaten by a woman. While the president then insists on hiring Hayes for the White House counsel's office, he too cannot resist feminizing Sam because a woman bested him in debate. It is worth, then, exploring some of the contradictions in Hayes's character.

In one episode, the attractive Ainsley Hayes walks into Sam Seaborn's office in a floor-length evening gown, having been paged from a fundraiser to return to the West Wing and bring her legal expertise as a White House counselor to a speech the president will make to the United Nations.[18] As she enters the room, Sam says, "Hayes, you're enough to make a good dog break his leash." The dialogue then banters between discussing the U.S. policy at the United Nations, the legal advice he needs from her, and her sexy appearance, and culminates in his comment as she turns to leave the room, baring her full back, that he "didn't see that thing from the back." Ainsley had already been established in previous episodes as a brilliant lawyer, a Republican, and a skillful debater. She had also been established as the beautiful woman she is, and even a Republican colleague compares her to a "Gap dancer."[19] In another episode, the president tells her that while most people think she was hired because she was a "Republican sex kitten," obviously that is not the case.[20] While that might be a useful moment of naming the sexism that faces smart, attractive women, the comment is undermined by the fact that Hayes is, at that moment, dancing around in a bathrobe and drinking a frilly cocktail. The show thus problematizes the sexism while also containing smart women in positions that reinforce the stereotypes.

However, *The West Wing* is provocative precisely because it both reproduces these limiting portrayals while simultaneously troubling them. In the episode in which Sam comments on Hayes's sexuality, a temporary aide witnesses the exchange and calls Sam out, telling him that it was demeaning and sexist. When he defends his actions, saying that it was a sign of respect that is permissible because he and Ainsley are friends, the aide responds, "Isn't the point that you wouldn't have been able to find another way to show she's part of the gang if she weren't beautiful?" She points out that it is objectifying and demeaning to underestimate the intelligence of a White House counsel by making a "dog on the leash" comment about her sexual appearance.

But the program does not stop there. Sam, sensitive white guy that he is, feels guilty and confused about this accusation. He does not want to be sexist, though he does want to be able to admire that beautiful woman in a black evening gown that goes all the way down to the small of her back. So he keeps bringing it up with Ainsley, even while she tries to get him to focus on her analysis of the United Nations report. Finally, since Sam will not let it go, she challenges the aide, as the following exchange reveals:

Ainsley: "I think you think I'm made out of candy glass. . . . If someone says something that offends you, tell them, but all women don't have to think alike. . . . I like when the guys tease me. It's an inadvertent show of respect that I'm part of the team, and I don't mind it when it gets sexual. . . . I don't think whatever sexuality I have diminishes my power. I think it enhances it."

Ginger (Toby and Sam's aide): "It's called lipstick feminism. I call it Stiletto Feminism."[21]

This scene is interesting because it both reinforces the idea that sexualized comments in the workplace are acceptable and yet nuances the conversation in complex ways. Ainsley insists on defining for herself what she feels is demeaning and what is not, while saying that sexual harassment and pay inequality are very real problems facing women. She also reminds Sam that it is problematic for him to make a sexual innuendo about her in stilettos. Ainsley is claiming the right to be sexual and maintaining some control over when and where sexual comments can be made to and about her, and at the same time she is asserting her intelligence and the importance of the United Nations issues she would prefer to discuss.

But it is significant that she is allowed this control precisely because she is both beautiful and sexual. The portrayal helps produce what Michel Foucault and Sandra Lee Bartky refer to as "docile bodies" that are regulated and produced in ways that ultimately reproduce the status quo, and in this case, it allows just enough feminist politics to appease women but ultimately mitigates its resistant nature.[22] While all the actors and actresses on the show are attractive (it is Hollywood, after all), the aide who challenges Sam's sexism is portrayed in a notably "frumpier" way than is Ainsley. Viewers are positioned to side with Ainsley and see the aide as a troublemaker at the same time that we are invited to notice the problems with Sam's comments.

However, it is also significant that Sam is feminized precisely because he was bested by a woman, thereby revealing the "crisis of insecurity," to which Judith Williamson refers. Women's intelligence on the show is repeatedly positioned as threatening male power and masculinity. Sam would not have received the same kind of teasing had he lost a debate to a man, and even C. J. Cregg, the woman press secretary on the show, takes part in the teasing.[23] Of course, her role has a different tenor than that of the male members of the senior staff. Her teasing can be read as both showing that she can play as "one of the boys" in order to help her credibility as part of the team and indirectly making a feminist statement about the refreshing nature of seeing a smart woman have her say. Still, the fact that the show spotlights the feminization of a male character suggests that smart women are dangerous to male power and sexuality.

Ainsley's portrayal parallels the way *The L Word* makes lesbians more visible in productive ways and yet features beautiful, thin, middle-to upper-class lesbians, once again suggesting that visibility can only be bought by conforming to norms. The feminist scholar Rosemary Hennessey points out that queer men and women are allowed visibility as consumer objects but not as fully enfranchised subjects, and a similar observation can be made about smart women in Hollywood.[24] They can appear only in certain forms, particularly in lipstick feminist roles. Brilliant women are tolerated as long as they are beautiful or conform in some way, and while their intelligence and strength enable them to change the system in some ways, they are also limited, as *The West Wing* reveals.

Hayes is not the only smart woman who has to battle for credibility and who regularly challenges the influential male characters. One of the most notable performances on *The West Wing* emerges from Allison Janney's strong and assertive portrayal of the White House press secretary C. J. Cregg. The portrayal has won Janney two Emmys for Best Supporting Actress (2000, 2001) and two for Best Actress (2002, 2004). Cregg has input in political strategies and regularly goes head to head with Josh and Toby, which is no easy task. As the only woman member of the senior staff, she holds a large degree of power and is the public voice of the president. The role is clearly modeled after Dee Dee Myers, who has served as a consultant to the show.

While Cregg repeatedly influences government policy in the show, her positions are also consistently contained. Janney manages to highlight this balance in her portrayals, which are strong and outspoken and reveal the tensions her character faces. When the male characters on the show repeatedly raise their voices to exert their influence, C. J. is rarely daunted and often matches them. For instance, when Toby Ziegler (Richard Schiff) threatens her if the name of a Supreme Court nominee is leaked, she teases him that he's "sexy when he's like this."[25] In one episode, Josh Lyman (Bradley Whitford) participates in an Internet chat room, and she literally yells at him, threatening that she will have an intern monitor the site and will come after him if he posts on it again.[26] Though Josh points out that he outranks her, she escalates the threat until he looks clearly chastised. She goes head to head with a prominent military official who wants to bash the president on talk shows before the military official retires.[27] She is clearly annoyed when he calls her "kitten," but she stands her ground and keeps him from going on the air until the president tells her to do otherwise. In all these performances, Janney plays a strong and independent woman who garners respect for her intelligence.

She is also limited, however, as are many of the women characters on the show and, I would argue, in the actual government. Frequent comments are made about her being "freakishly tall" and not feminine enough. Though Cregg strikes a good balance around those issues, her authority is often restricted by the men in power over her. She has to bury a report about teenage sexual activity that she thinks is important and cover up the frustration with the administration felt by a father of a gay man killed in a gay-bashing incident.[28] Her press strategy about the threat of mad cow disease in U.S. beef is shot down by Toby in a power struggle between the two.[29] C. J. is uncomfortable with these constraints on her politics, but the job of a press secretary is, after all, to spin issues so that the administration looks good. That is, inherently, going to involve some compromise, as Dee Dee Myers and all other press secretaries have most likely discovered. But when combined with gender and feminist politics, such compromises highlight the limitations smart women face. In their statement explaining why *The West Wing* was honored with the award for advancing women's leadership, the White House Project includes, among their praise for the character of C. J. Cregg, her "unconditional support for her president and her country"[30]—a very telling statement about the barriers facing intelligent women in patriarchal systems. She is a brilliant and strong leader because she does not challenge the system, and when she does, she is reeled in by men who have power over her.

Like other smart women on the show, C. J. must earn the trust of her male colleagues because she is beautiful. In one episode, Toby expresses distrust in the motives of the attractive Republican Hayes working in a Democratic counsel's office. He points out that C. J. is beautiful, and no one suspected her of being ambitious or doubted her motives when she started her job. Few men are questioned in the same way. Nor is ambition in men inherently considered problematic. C. J. responds that "it took two years" for people to trust her or respect her competency.[31] Many smart women in positions such as hers face similar uphill battles of skepticism about their motives or talents.

Racial and Gendered Power Dynamics in Old Boys' School Politics

Gendered power dynamics are not the only ones that pervade patriarchal spaces, and, in fact, they never exist apart from racial dynamics. It is notable that most of the people in power in U. S. politics are white, as are most of the characters on *The West Wing*. The few exceptions are notable precisely for their rarity. When women of color advance through political ranks, they can be challenged regarding both their competency and their allegiance to a particular brand of politics. They are sometimes charged with "selling out" communities of color if the administrations for which they work do not address the concerns of marginalized groups. They also simultaneously face racism from the system in which they are working.[32] Like the smart white women characters mentioned already, intelligent women of color who advance to positions of power in the U. S. government face quandaries when the policies they are ordered to enact do violence to men and women of color around the world. *The West Wing* addresses this tension in provocative ways.

The most revealing example involves the character of Nancy McNally, the national security advisor to President Bartlet on the show. There is a clear parallel between Condoleezza Rice's roles as national security advisor and secretary of state and the introduction of Anna Deavere Smith playing McNally in *The West Wing*. McNally is another strong, brilliant female character on *The West Wing*, but she is portrayed in even more complex ways, nuanced in part by the casting of Smith in the role. She is one of the few women of color featured in an ongoing role on the show.[33] Moreover, McNally is not just in a traditionally male-dominated space, she is in one that has to deal directly with the military and with U. S. foreign and domestic defense policy—probably the social institution in the United States that is the most patriarchal and white, at least in the high-ranking positions of authority. It is a rare position for women. McNally appears in the situation room, where the president meets with his military officials to determine air strikes and other military actions, and in the Oval Office, where she advocates for her positions with the president and the Chief of Staff, arguably two of the most powerful positions in the government. One would have to be strong, intelligent, articulate, and outspoken in that position, which she is.

As McNally works directly with military policy, she often cautions against knee-jerk military offenses and argues with other high-ranking military officers about steps that should be taken. So while the nature of the position is to enforce U. S. foreign and domestic policy through military action, which ultimately means upholding the authority of the United States, McNally also illuminates some of the fissures in the construction of the nation. Notably, she is rarely depicted as speaking for the administration in public statements and press conferences, which means that she is portrayed in more contested and complex ways than is Condoleezza Rice, whom the public rarely sees disagreeing with the Bush administration.[34] There are clearly racial power dynamics for any woman of color in an administration that not only is predominantly white but also enacts many policies that do a disservice to communities of color. McNally's character reveals many of those tensions.

But one episode of *The West Wing* in particular is intriguing because of what it illuminates about racial power dynamics for smart women in high-ranking politics. The episode "Women of Qumar" begins with the president announcing to Toby that his administration will be selling weapons to Qumar (and it is impossible not to draw connections between Qumar and Afghanistan, to which the U.S. government sold arms). When C. J. learns that her boss is selling arms to a country that oppresses women, she states her opposition to that practice at every opportunity. This plotline reveals the difficult position that smart women in power may find themselves in, having to advocate for or at least support a policy with which they do not agree, particularly a policy that enacts oppression against women and other marginalized groups. As the White House press secretary, C. J. occasionally uses the podium to advance her own feminist statements, such as when she condemns the deaths of women workers in another Middle Eastern country who were unable to escape a fire because they were not "properly clothed."[35] However, C. J.'s job is to advocate for the president and spin any bad press, so that he does not lose face or political ground. This means that she has to publicly speak for positions that may require a personal compromise. Such is the case when she has to announce the sale of arms without speaking about the oppression of women that such a sale would support. Thus, though C. J. is allowed to speak out against policies and to express some of her own views on the show and often earns respect for doing so, ultimately her power is contained by her job as press secretary to ensure that the administration looks good.

This episode intrigues me for another reason as well. Near the end, there is an exchange between C. J. and Nancy McNally that reveals provocative tensions between intelligent white and black women. After several white male characters try to avoid or silence C. J.'s protests about the hypocrisy of a "liberal" administration selling arms to a government that oppresses women, they send McNally to confront Cregg. This scene highlights racial power dynamics, as women of color who are intelligent are often labeled "aggressive" and "angry," even more so than white women, particularly if they speak out against oppression.[36] In this exchange, C. J. argues that the United States actually does not need the military location in Qumar, as McNally is arguing.

The rest of the scene is worth quoting:

> *C. J.*: "The point is that apartheid was an Easthampton clambake compared [to] what we laughingly refer to as the life these women lead. And if we had sold M1 A1s to South Africa fifteen years ago, you'd have set the building on fire. Thank God we never needed to refuel in Johannesburg."
>
> *Nancy McNally*: "It's a big world CJ, and everybody has guns, and I'm doing the best I can."

The racial nuances of this scene are crucial. First, the comparison to apartheid, and the suggestion that McNally would be fighting the U. S. action if it were South Africa, reflects a very real tension as a white woman suggests that McNally is being complicit in racism in this instance, though she would have resisted in other instances, though it is partly C. J.'s white privilege that lets her take such a position. Moreover, C. J. is unusually whiny in this scene, which marks a significant shift in Janney's portrayal of the character. After this exchange, Smith as McNally looks at C. J. with an expression that illuminates the tension between the two women, and then turns and walks away without saying anything.[37] This scene is loaded with racial complexity, with the contradictions of two intelligent women caught in a policy that they did not create but are expected to carry out. Both women, to some extent, have little power to change the deal agreed upon by the president and his advisors, and yet both women will, ultimately, become complicit in the system as they defend and enact the policy.

Smart Women, Careers, and Heterosexual Relationships

Though on a very different level of intensity, one of the other threads running throughout *The West Wing* involves the difficulties smart women face as they try to juggle high-profile careers with romantic relationships, particularly when their feminist politics are seen as undermining the projects of their male partners. This issue pervades the lives of many intelligent women characters on the show, including Congresswoman Andrea Wyatt (Kathleen York), the First Lady, Abigail Bartlet (Stockard Channing), and C. J. Cregg. When romantic entanglements appear, they inevitably involve the decisions that brilliant women with active professional lives have to make between careers and relationships.

One important smart woman on *The West Wing* is Ameila "Amy" Gardner (Mary Louise Parker), the feminist leader and advocate/lobbyist of a prominent women's organization, perhaps referencing the National Organization of Women. She illustrates the tensions that intelligent women face in politics: how to be sexual beings and outspoken advocates and how to work within the system without deauthorizing their own politics. From the beginning, Gardner effectively negotiates this difficulty, but it becomes much harder for her to do so when she becomes romantically involved with Lyman. For instance, one episode depicts Gardner in the office of her organization, clearly a wealthy organization with nice office space and strong, sensual women's art on the walls.[38] Gardner argues with Josh Lyman that the Bartlet White House is weakening a provision about sex trafficking that would make it harder to prosecute prostitution rings that are exploiting young women. Lyman challenges Gardner, and the otherwise intelligent debater wavers in her certainty. The position of a very smart feminist woman is muted by her relation to men in political power. However, at the same time, when Josh argues about her logic, she troubles a long-standing feminist stereotype, saying, "I don't burn my bras, Josh. In fact, I like my bras. I ring the First Lady's bell when it's important." By doing so, she challenges his implied reduction of feminist politics.

Later in the series, after Amy and Josh are in a relationship, Parker illustrates how to be in a relationship without compromising one's issues—another potential pitfall for smart women in a society that suggests that one is worthless without a man. One episode, for instance, reveals them cooking dinner together, but then each going to their opposite sides as Amy's feminist organization disagrees with White House strategy. (My favorite part involves her tossing his cell phone into a pot of simmering stew.)[39] This character is sensual, strong, and witty and illustrates a feminist who does not sacrifice everything for her man. She in fact loses the relationship because the politics between the two cannot be entirely reconciled. The show nuances the ongoing thread of their romance by highlighting the constant barriers posed by their conflicting agendas.

In another challenge to traditional gender roles, Congresswoman Andrea Wyatt (Kathleen York), the ex-wife of Toby Ziegler (Richard Schiff), White House communications director, becomes pregnant with twins. While Toby is the father, they are unmarried at the time, and she continually resists his proposals, prioritizing her own happiness over the social expectation of marriage. One episode features a passerby challenging her for being single and pregnant, commenting that she should be a better role model for women.[40] She responds that she believes she is, and a fight ensues between this passerby and Toby and Charlie Young (Dulé Hill), personal aide to the president. While the men supposedly save the day, they also get arrested, and the episode clearly favors Wyatt as a strong congresswoman who is divorced, single, and pregnant.

These portrayals of Andrea Wyatt illustrate a brilliant woman in power advocating for her political positions without entirely conforming to traditional gender roles that linger because of her former marriage with Toby. When Toby writes a presidential speech for the United Nations in which he condemns Islamic fanaticism, Andrea comes storming into his office and a raging argument ensues about his ethnocentrism.[41] As the third-ranking member of a committee on international relations and a congresswoman, Andrea argues that his statements will offend members of the Arab world. This is a strong scene for a smart woman character, though three comments are made about Toby getting a beating from the "old lady" before she arrives. One of them is made by C. J., which illustrates C. J.'s ability to both challenge and tease her boss but simultaneously relegates Andy to a stereotypical role. In another episode, Toby is upset that Andrea is flying with the administration so late in her pregnancy, and Andrea defies him, saying that since her doctor said it was fine, she is going to go where she wants.[42] Toby comments that she is the size of a minivan and wonders how she is fitting into the airplane seats. Both Donna and Andrea look at him with disgust, and Andrea jokes, "No, no, girls, I saw him first," illustrating her refusal to be demeaned by his remarks. Since we rarely see smart women who are pregnant and beautiful on television, this portrayal is notable; but the very fact that such a comment is made also limits her power.

The conflict between smart women who have active professional careers and the roles they are relegated to in their romantic relationships is best illustrated by Abigail Bartlet, who constantly comments on the limits of her role as the First Lady. Representation here directly parallels issues in "actual" presidential administrations. Most of the public knows First Ladies only through media representation. The cultural production around the role is, therefore, telling, because it both reflects and shapes the degree to which women are allowed to be active political forces. Jacqueline Kennedy, for instance, was a cultural icon in the United States and certainly garnered her share of the press, but more for her style and charisma than for her role in public policy. The notable exception is Eleanor Roosevelt, but the extent of involvement and influence she demonstrated is rare. The role of the First Lady is in many ways to be the "proper" woman in traditional terms: to serve as a hostess, a smiling and supportive wife, and a dutiful volunteer for proper women's causes (such as literacy or nursing). The political scholar Mary Anne Borrelli has noted that much of the work done on First Ladies emphasizes their individual biographies rather than the official nature of the office and that the degree to which the First Lady can take a direct role in political decision-making has been regularly debated.[43] The role invokes some degree of political influence, but the women who publicly relish such parts of the job are usually targeted with bad press.

The West Wing directly confronts this issue. Abbey Bartlet is a doctor who unwillingly gives up her career to be the First Lady. She often influences the president and is called in by the senior staff when they need someone to persuade him. She is supportive but also openly confronts him when she does not agree with him. In fact, she leaves the West Wing in protest at one point. In one episode, she challenges the president on his elitism, while in another, she provides important medical advice on an international matter.[44] She consistently stands her ground even when it means compromising the role of the First Lady.

However, she is also quite contained. She is regularly and significantly absent from the story lines on the show, and her interests in women's issues are consistently demeaned. She is not consulted on the president's decision to run for a second term, her issues are quickly forfeited in budget negotiations, and her commitment to building monuments to recognize prominent women forerunners is ridiculed by the president. In one episode, after relying on her medical advice in a foreign affairs matter, the president tells her to "go back to her sewing thing," which in reality is a women's caucus meeting, while in another, he tells her that she does not have to go to "silly" events such as a dedication of a memorial for an influential woman.[45] Though Abbey then gets him to apologize by dedicating a radio show to numerous women forerunners, she does so by withholding sex, a classic role for women that demeans the importance of the issue. Since he invalidates her feminist concerns, she is reduced to using her role as wife to make her point. Moreover, on numerous occasions, a personal discussion or argument between the president and the First Lady has to be set aside because of "more important" national concerns. Here, again, the First Lady is shown as the self-sacrificing wife being patriotic for the good of her man and her country, while the president's time with his predominantly male senior staff is rarely cut short.

Yet again, though, casting is key, as the show both upholds the limitations of the role while simultaneously troubling them. Stockard Channing is a formidable actress with a highly reputable career, and so her appearances carry with them a dignity and strength. There are times when she comments directly on the limitations of the role of the First Lady, such as when she notes that people care more about whether she changes her clothes before going to the postinaugural parties than they do about what she says in her speech.[46] Her ambivalence about the job becomes even more visible when she asks, "When did I stop being Dr. Bartlet?"[47] Political opponents unearth her malpractice suits and go after her career when they cannot unseat Josiah Bartlet for concealing his multiple sclerosis, so that ultimately she forfeits her medical license for the duration of their stay in the White House. When Abbey tells her husband of her decision, he looks remorseful but does not argue with her, and the look on Channing's face reveals the internal conflict she feels at giving up her career for the president's political protection.[48] In another episode, she is forced to tell a congresswoman to withdraw an amendment on child labor from a bill because the bill would not pass with it attached, and, while she does so reluctantly, the performance reveals the limitations of influence that smart women can hold in a system of old boys' school politics.[49] Her own personal and professional identity is put on hold in numerous ways during her husband's presidency. When Stockard Channing won the Emmy for her performance as Abigail Bartlet in 2002, she won it as Best Supporting Actress, not Best Actress, which says a great deal about the role of the First Lady, both on screen and off. The portrayal reveals that smart women in politics too often find that their primary role is to shore up the authority of the president. In fact, Abbey is also accused of being a liability to the president when politicians across the aisle go after her medical career when they cannot unseat the president for concealing his multiple sclerosis. In a meeting with Abbey, the White House counsel Oliver Babish (Oliver Platt) says that she will be the president's greatest liability. Even when brilliant women are themselves elected as congresswomen or senators, they usually have to balance their authority and political moves with constant assurances to the public that they are not deviating too far from their roles as proper wives and mothers.

Other smart women on *The West Wing* are rarely shown as regularly attached to a man (and never to a woman in a portrayal of a lesbian relationship), but instead are periodically shown involved with passing love interests, perhaps to reinforce the idea that they are still "proper" women. Their "lack of men" is portrayed as a sacrifice they are making to their country, such as when C. J. notes that she works so much that she has no time for a relationship. But just as commonly, their "spinster" state is subject to ridicule on the show, such as when Donna is repeatedly mocked for her poor taste in men or when C. J. falls off a treadmill while trying to make small talk with the handsome man next to her.[50] While Janney's ability to combine humor with strength is one of the many reasons she has won Emmys for her performance, the zany comedy often comes in regard to her inability to "catch" men. Once again, a woman's brilliance is contained by the need to conform to heteronormative expectations, while the show hints that the reason that they cannot hold men is precisely because they are too smart and too dedicated to their work. The notable exceptions, of course, are Congresswoman Wyatt, who refuses Toby's offer of marriage, and the First Lady, who has to prioritize marriage over career. Brilliant women seem to be allowed only so much room to push against the system before they are contained, and representation plays a role in shaping public opinion about the issue.

Smart Women, Feminized Positions

While many of the intelligent women characters I have discussed thus far are in prominent roles of power in Washington politics, the U. S. government relies on the labor of numerous other women in order to run itself. These intelligent women make up the support and administrative staff, and their portrayals on *The West Wing* highlight the marginalization they face despite their essential role in running a smooth system. The two most central support staff roles on the show belong to Charlie Young (Dulé Hill) and Donna Moss (Janel Maloney), who is an aide to Josh. Donna is regularly portrayed as a force in Josh's life, with all the romantic tension one would expect in a Hollywood show. She is also described as a naïve, innocent white girl from Wisconsin, despite the undeniable influence she wields over Josh. The prominence of Donna's role, and the role of Mrs. Landingham (Kathryn Joosten), the secretary to the president, is notable.[51] These representations illustrate the importance of support staff, usually filled by smart women in jobs that are feminized and undervalued. Donna regularly challenges Josh when he takes her for granted, and she becomes increasingly savvy and influential as the seasons progress. When the president snaps at Mrs. Landingham, she puts him in his place, and she is one of the few characters on the show called "Mrs." as a sign of respect. These roles reveal the influence that such positions can have on major political players and the essential nature of the work they do in helping to run the country.

However, they are, ultimately, still marginalized to supporting roles and regularly reminded of their lesser value in the hierarchy of Washington politics. Most of the other aides to Sam and Toby have regular but minor parts. While Donna is a central character, she is also regularly asked to check Josh's food, get him water, and meet with a foreign official because she is "unimportant." In addition, Margaret (NiCole Robinson), Leo McGarry's secretary, is an ongoing source of humor on the show. In one episode, she is accused of hacking the White House computers because of a spam e-mail she accidentally sent.[52] When she tries to explain to both Leo and Toby that she was simply informing other White House staffers that the calorie count in the muffins is wrong, both men demean her concern. Similar scenes abound. Leo (John Spencer) chastises her for assuming that she can sign the president's name on major documents, while Josh and others regularly suggest that she is a gossip.[53] *The West Wing* often uses humor to balance the intensity of the story lines, but the fact that it comes via ridiculing a smart woman whose job it is to run the office of the U. S. Chief of Staff demeans the importance of intelligent women in administrative positions. While some of the supporting roles reflect substance and depth, others belittle the importance of the support staff and the intelligent women who serve in them. Once again, *The West Wing* both problematizes stereotypes and upholds them.

The representations of the support staff underscore the pattern of portrayals of all the intelligent women on the show. Women who hold influential positions in systems of old boys' school politics inevitably find themselves facing the nexus of gendered and racialized ideologies that sexualize them, demean their abilities, or feminize them, so that success in those positions means striking a balance between playing according to the rules of the patriarchal game and challenging these rules enough to remain true to their own feminist politics. Such women need to be strong enough to advocate for their ideas in strident debates with men who hold equal or more power then they, while simultaneously retaining enough demure femininity to maintain their "womanhood" in the eyes of the system around them. Moreover, smart women are often positioned in complex racial dynamics with one another, so that white women hold race privilege that women of color do not, while both may be forced to uphold governmental policies that do violence to men and women of color. *The West Wing* reveals these contradictions facing smart women with a complexity rarely seen in prime-time television.

Given the power of representation, viewers can begin to think about these issues in different ways as the show troubles the constraints facing brilliant women in politics. The feminist theorist Susan Bordo argues that the public grabs hold of a good story and then reads any "facts" through the framework of that story.[54] If, as Foucault suggests, power produces meanings, the parallels between the portrayals on *The West Wing* television show and the actual executive branch have the potential for significant influence.[55] Both could reshape public opinion about brilliant women and their place in politics. Unfortunately, the contradictions on *The West Wing* mitigate that potential. Its representations of smart women highlight the forays women can make into shaping systems such as the government, but they also reveal the ways in which women are contained and regulated by the system.[56] The portrayals provide opportunities for the public to see brilliant women in influential positions and can therefore begin to alter public opinion about such women, though the representations simultaneously allay patriarchal insecurity by ensuring that they never challenge or transform the system too far.

Notes

1. *The West Wing*, first broadcast 22 September 1999 by NBC, http://www.nbc.com/The_West_Wing/

2. Terrance Smith, *The West Wing*, PBS Online News Hour, 4 October 2000, http://www.pbs.org/newshour/bb/media/july-dec00/westwing_10-4.html (accessed 21 November 2005).

3. "The West Wing," Wikipedia, 2005, http://en.wikipedia.org/wiki/The_West_Wing_ (television) (accessed 13 November 2005).

4. John Fiske, *Television Culture* (London: Methuen, 1987).

5. Tania Modleski, *Loving with a Vengeance: Mass Produced Fantasies for Women* (Hamden: Archon Books, 1982), 112.

6. The White House Project, "2005 EPIC Award recipients," http://www.whitehouseproject.org (accessed 10 November 2005).

7. Fiske, *Television Culture*; Tania Modelski and John Fiske, *Understanding Popular Culture* (Boston: Unwin Hyman, 1989); John Fiske, *Media Matters* (Minneapolis: University of Minnesota Press, 1994).

8. Donnalyn Pompper, "*The West Wing*: White House Narratives that Journalism Cannot Tell," in *The West Wing: The American Presidency as Television Drama*, ed. Peter C. Rollins and John E. O'Connor (Syracuse, NY: Syracuse University Press, 2003), 17–31.

9. Stephen J. Farnsworth and S. Robert Lichter, *The Mediated Presidency: Television News and Presidential Coverage* (New York: Rowman & Littlefield, 2006).

10. For an analysis of the power of representation to shape public perception, see John Fiske, *Power Play Power Work* (London: Verso, 1993).

11. Indeed, the former Clinton press secretary Dee Dee Myers has both consulted on the show and helped in writing the story for some of the episodes. She has also appeared on the documentary special, along with other prominent former staff members and presidents. "Documentary Special," *The West Wing*, season 3, episode no. 227223, first broadcast 24 April 2002 by NBC. Directed by William Couturie and interview material by William Couturie, Eli Attie, and Felicia Wilson, http://www.nbc.com/The_West_Wing/

12. The *West Wing* episodes, respectively, are: "The Short List," season 1, episode no. 225908, first broadcast 25 November 1999 by NBC, Directed by Bill D-Elia, written by Aaron Sorkin and Patrick Caddell, and story by Aaron Sorkin and DeeDee Myers; "Pilot," season 1, episode no. 475151, first broadcast 22 September 1999 by NBC, directed by Thomas Schlamme, and written by Aaron Sorkin; "Bartlett's Third State of the Union," season 2, episode no. 226213, first broadcast 07 February 2001 by NBC, directed by Christopher Misiano, written by Aaron Sorkin, and story by Allison Abner and DeeDee Myers; "Take Out the Trash Day," season 1, episode no. 225912, first broadcast 26 January 2000, directed by Ken Olin, and written by Aaron Sorkin. http://www.nbc.com/The_West_Wing/

13. "Documentary Special."

14. For an analysis of how women are portrayed in popular culture, see Marian Meyers, ed., *Mediated Women: Representations in Popular Culture* (Cresskill, NJ: Hampton Press, 1999); Rosemary Betterton, ed., *Looking On: Images of Femininity in the Visual Arts and Media* (London: Pandora, 1987); Janice A. Radway, *Reading the Romance: Women, Patriarchy, and Popular Literature* (Chapel Hill: University of North Carolina Press, 1984); June Sochen, *Enduring Values: Women in Popular Culture* (New York: Praeger, 1987); and Susan J. Douglas, *Where the Girls Are: Growing Up Female with the Mass Media* (New York: Random House, 1994).

15. Judith Williamson, *Consuming Passions: The Dynamics of Popular Culture* (New York: Marion Boyars, 1986), 179. Williamson is discussing the film *10* here, but the point is nevertheless relevant.

16. Sherrie A. Inness, *Tough Girls: Women Warriors and Wonder Women in Popular Culture* (Philadelphia: University of Pennsylvania Press, 1999); Susan Bordo, *Twilight Zones: The Hidden Life of Cultural Images from Plato to O.J.* (Berkeley: University of California Press, 1997).

17. "In This White House," *The West Wing*, season 2, episode no. 226204, first broadcast 25 October 2000 by NBC, directed by Ken Olin, written by Aaron Sorkin, and story by Peter Parnell and Allison Abner. http://www.nbc.com/The_West_Wing/

18. "Night Five," *The West Wing*, season 3, episode no. 227214, first broadcast 06 February 2002 by NBC, directed by Christopher Misiano and written by Aaron Sorkin. http://www.nbc.com/The_West_Wing/

19. "In This White House."

20. "Bartlet's Third State of the Union."

21. "Unofficial Continuity Guide," http://westwing.bewarne.com/third/57nightfive.html (accessed 21 November 2005).

22. Michel Foucault, *Discipline and Punish* (New York: Vintage, 1979); Sandra Lee Barky, "Foucault, Femininity, and the Modernization of Patriarchal Power," *Feminism and Foucault: Reflections on Resistance*, ed. Irene Diamond and Lee Quinby (Boston: Northeastern University Press, 1988), 129–154.

23. "In This White House."
24. Rosemary Hennessy, "Queer Visibility and Commodity Culture," *Cultural Critique* 29 (Winter 1994–1995): 31–76.
25. "The Short List."
26. "U.S. Poet Laureate," *The West Wing*, season 3, episode no. 227217, first broadcast 27 March 2002 by NBC, directed by Christopher Misiano, written by Aaron Sorkin, and story by Laura Glasser. http://www.nbc.com/The_West_Wing/
27. "And It's Surely to Their Credit," *The West Wing*, season 2, episode no. 226205, first broadcast 1 November 2000 by NBC, directed by Christopher Misiano, written by Aaron Sorkin, and story by Kevin Falls and Laura Glasser. http://www.nbc.com/The_West_Wing/
28. "Take Out the Trash Day."
29. "Women of Qumar," *The West Wing*, season 3, episode no. 227209, first broadcast 28 November 2001 by NBC, directed by Alex Graves, written by Aaron Sorkin, and story by Felicia Wilson, Laura Glasser, and Julia Dahl. http://www.nbc.com/The_West_Wing/
30. The White House Project, "2005 EPIC Award Recipients," http://www.whitehouseproject.org (accessed 10 November 2005).
31. "In This White House."
32. For a discussion of the gendered and racial complexities of women of color in patriarchal systems, see Linda Steiner, "*New York Times* Coverage of Anita Hill as a Female Cipher," in Meyers, *Mediated Women*, 225–252; and Toni Morrison, ed., *Race-ing Justice, En-Gendering Power: Essays on Anita Hill, Clarence Thomas, and the Construction of Social Reality* (New York: Pantheon, 1992).
33. For an analysis of the racialization of representation, particularly of black women, see Michelle Wallace, "Negative Images: Toward a Black Feminist Cultural Criticism," in *Cultural Studies*, ed. Laurence Grossberg, Carrie Nelson, and Patricia A. Treichler (New York: Routledge, 1992), 651–671; bell hooks, "The Oppositional Gaze: Black Female Spectators," in *Feminist Film Theory: A Reader*, ed. Sue Thornham (New York: New York University Press, 1999), 307–320; Jane Gaines, "White Privilege and Looking Relations: Race and Gender in Feminist Film Theory," in Thornham, *Feminist Film Theory*, 287–292; and Tania Modleski, "Cinema and the Dark Continent: Race and Gender in Popular Film," Thornham, *Feminist Film Theory*, 321–335.
34. I am not implying that Rice's politics are feminist; I am merely discussing the complex position that women of color in her role inherit.
35. "Enemies Foreign and Domestic," *The West Wing*, season 3, episode no. 227219, first broadcast 01 May 2002 by NBC, directed by Alex Graves and written by Aaron Sorkin and Paul Redford. http://www.nbc.com/The_West_Wing/
36. Gloria Anzaldúa, "Haciendo caras, una entrada: An Introduction," in *Haciendo Caras/Making Face, Making Soul: Creative and Critical Perspectives by Women of Color*, ed. Gloria Anzaldúa (San Francisco: Aunt Lute Books, 1990), xv–xxviii.
37. For a discussion of racial dynamics between white and black feminists in patriarchal systems, see Christine Stansell, "White Feminists and Black Realities: The Politics of Authenticity," in Morrison, *Race-ing Justice, En-Gendering Power*, 251–268.
38. "Women of Qumar."
39. "We Killed Yamamoto," *The West Wing*, season 3, episode no. 227221, first broadcast 15 May 2002 by NBC, directed by Thomas Schlamme and written by Aaron Sorkin. This story line continues in the next episode, "Posse Comitatus," season 3, episode no. 227222, first broadcast 22 May 2002 by NBC, directed by Alex Graves and written by Aaron Sorkin. http://www.nbc.com/The_West_Wing/

40. "California 47th," *The West Wing*, season 4, episode no. 175316, first broadcast 19 February 2003 by NBC, directed by Vincent Misiano, written by Aaron Sorkin, and story by Lauren Schmidt and Paula Yoo. http://www.nbc.com/The_West_Wing/

41. "Night Five."

42. "California 47th."

43. Mary Anne Borrelli, "The First Lady as Formal Advisor to the President: When East (Wing) Meets West (Wing)," *Women & Politics* 24.1 (2002), 25–45.

44. "War Crimes," *The West Wing*, season 3, episode no. 227205, first broadcast 07 November 2001 by NBC, directed by Alex Graves, written by Aaron Sorkin, and story by Allison Abner. http://www.nbc.com/The_West_Wing/

45. "And It's Surely to Their Credit."

46. "Bartlet's Third State of the Union."

47. "Gone Quiet," *The West Wing*, season 3, episode no. 227206, first broadcast 14 November 2001 by NBC, directed by John Hutman, written by Aaron Sorkin, and story by Julie Dahl and Laura Glasser. http://www.nbc.com/The_West_Wing/

48. "Dead Irish Writers," *The West Wing*, season 3, episode no. 227216, first broadcast 06 March 2992 on NBC, directed by Paul Redford and written by Aaron Sorkin. http://www.nbc.com/The_West_Wing/

49. "White House Pro-am," *The West Wing*, season 1, episode no. 225916, first broadcast 22 March 2000 by NBC, directed by Ken Olin and written by Lawrence O'Donnell, Jr., Paul Redford, and Aaron Sorkin. http://www.nbc.com/The_West_Wing/

50. "Pilot."

51. Christina Lane, "The White House Culture of Gender and Race in *The West Wing*: Insights from the Margins," in *The West Wing: The American Presidency as Television Drama*, ed. Peter C. Rollins and John E. O'Connor (Syracuse, NY: Syracuse University Press, 2003), 32–41.

52. "Let Bartlet be Bartlet," *The West Wing*, season 1, episode no. 225918, first broadcast 26 April 2000 by NBC, directed by Laura Inness, written by Aaron Sorkin, and story by Peter Parnell and Patrick Cadell. http://www.nbc.com/The_West_Wing/

53. "In The Shadow of Two Gunmen, parts I and II," *The West Wing*, season 2, episodes no. 226201 and 226202, first broadcast 4 October 2000 by NBC, directed by Thomas Schlamme and written by Aaron Sorkin. http://www.nbc.com/The_West_Wing/

54. Bordo, *Twilight Zones*.

55. Michel Foucault, *Power/Knowledge: Selected Interviews and Other Writings, 1972–1977*, trans. and ed. Colin Gordon (New York: Pantheon, 1980).

56. For a discussion of how media representations of women can be appropriated toward feminist ends, see Kimberlé Crenshaw, "Whose Story Is It Anyway? Feminist and Antiracist Appropriations of Anita Hill," in Morrison, *Race-ing Justice, En-gendering Power*, 402–440.

CHAPTER 10

Heckling Hillary: Jokes, Late-Night Television, and Hillary Rodham Clinton

Jeannie Banks Thomas

*G*raduate of Yale Law School. Successful Lawyer. Children's Advocate. Working Mother. First Lady of Arkansas. First Lady of the United States. Health-Care Expert. Senator. Member of the Senate Armed Forces Committee. "Most Admired Woman in the United States." Best-Selling Author. Recipient of the Military Coalition's Award of Merit. Presidential Contender.

Such is the stuff of Hillary Rodham Clinton's life; her achievements make it clear that she is a smart woman. This chapter examines what jokes make of her. They come primarily from late-night television shows, such as *The Tonight Show with Jay Leno*, and from the Internet.[1] Overwhelmingly, these jokes heckle and disparage Rodham Clinton. Her real life is quite different from the construction of her that emerges from the jokes: *Dumb Blonde. Witch. Bitch. Cheating Wife. Child Hater. Bill's Frigid Wife. Furniture Thief.*

The more visible a person is in the mass media, the more probable it is that she will show up in jokes. In other words, visibility is a key factor in influencing who is likely to appear as the butt of jokes. Hillary Rodham Clinton has chosen to live a public life, and her intelligence—in combination with her feminism—has made her enormously visible in the mass media. So Rodham Clinton's high profile as a smart feminist has also made her the target of jokes, and she is routinely skewered in the media. Given that many of the jokes on late-night television continually relocate her in more traditional gender roles than the ones she assumes in reality, the jokes indicate that there is still media discomfort with a smart feminist in such notable and powerful societal roles. Ironically, her intelligence draws media attention, but the jokes that circulate about her in popular culture disparage or ignore that same intellect.

More troubling than the fact that Rodham Clinton is lampooned—after all, male politicians are, too—is the basis on which she is mocked: her gender. Highlighting the gender-differentiated way the jokes construct Rodham Clinton is the manner in which jokes from late-night television and other popular culture sources construct male politicians. Unlike jokes about male politicians, the jokes about her generally ignore her policies and life experiences. Instead, they use her gender for their gibes, something that does not happen to her male counterparts.

This chapter includes brief views of Rodham Clinton's life—biographical aspects that popular culture, especially the jokes, ignores. These details from her life are meant to counter the stereotype of her as a humorless feminist by showing how laughter and humor are important to her in her personal life and public speeches. In a discussion of how the stereotype of the "humorless feminist" impacts Rodham Clinton, the chapter elucidates the factors that contribute to whether feminists and other listeners find political jokes funny or not.

Using the light-bulb joke, a perennial favorite, this chapter also shows how the same kind of joke treats a male politician differently than it does a female politician. Finally, the chapter delineates the common themes in Rodham Clinton jokes. The jokes fall into general patterns; they depict Rodham Clinton as a bitch and an unfit woman. While speculating about her sex life, the jokes also stereotypically place her in the domestic realm. The chapter concludes with a brief discussion of how a real-life intelligent woman deals with the heckling media constructions of her.

The media construction of Rodham Clinton ignores the actual complexity of her life, political views, and career. For example, the right often portrays her as the ultimate radical, feminist Democrat—even though some on the left find her too conservative. Rodham Clinton's roots and connections are more politically conservative and complex than the popular culture construction of her as a radical acknowledges. Her father was a "rock-ribbed, up-by-your-bootstraps, conservative Republican and proud of it."[2] During her youth, Clinton was a Goldwater girl, complete with cowgirl outfit and cowboy hat emblazoned with the slogan "AuH$_2$O."

She switched political parties during college.[3] In her early Wellesley days, she was president of the Young Republicans. However, she became disaffected with Republican stances on civil rights and Vietnam and turned to her mother's party, the Democrats.[4] Far-right media personalities, such as FOX television's Bill O'Reilly, paint her as the godless Lilith of the left, but she is more multidimensional and bipartisan than this construction acknowledges. For example, when she was First Lady, she belonged to a women's prayer group that included Republicans who regularly prayed for her.

Although she abandoned her father's politics, she kept something else she had inherited from him: a loud and distinctive laugh. Despite the stereotype of Rodham Clinton as perpetually serious and uptight, she actually possesses "a big rolling guffaw that can turn heads in a restaurant and send cats running from the room."[5] Also, contrary to the way popular culture typecasts her as a humorless Eastern elitist, she is a Midwesterner who writes about the importance of humor in her personal and political lives. The difficulties she experienced while she was First Lady caused her to develop coping strategies, and one of them was humor; she says, "Laughing at myself was an essential survival tool, and preferable to climbing back into the bunker."[6] She worked humor into her speeches, too. For instance, after college graduation, she took menial jobs in Alaska's fishing industry. In public speeches, she humorously connected these experiences to being First Lady. While in Alaska, she "slimed" salmon, which called for her to stand in bloody water and remove the fish's guts. She also worked on an assembly line, packing salmon into boxes. Once, when she reported to a supervisor that some of the salmon was bad, he fired her, telling her to collect her final paycheck the next day. When she returned to get her check, the entire operation had disappeared. Later, during a visit to Alaska as First Lady, she joked that this job experience was excellent preparation for life in Washington.[7]

In 1969 she entered Yale Law School as one of only 27 women in a class of 235. During this period, her style of personal presentation can best be described as hippie-geek. More interested in ideas and social justice than appearances, she wore thick glasses and paid so little attention to her clothes or hair that others, including her future mother-in-law, were sometimes taken aback. She moved away from this image when she lived in Arkansas, though she still wore big glasses. She abandoned the look entirely by the time she became First Lady. Certainly, mainstream, national politics would not embrace "hippie-geek" as a good look for the Beltway crowd. When she was First Lady, the media found her every hairstyle newsworthy. Such media scrutiny schooled her, sometimes harshly, in the cultural expectation that smart women in the public eye should be attractive and chic, which is exactly how she looks on the cover of her 2003 autobiography.[8]

The aspects of her political life that are most well known to the public came after her hippie period: successful career as a lawyer, First Lady of Arkansas, work with children and health care, and First Lady. Her Senate Web page reveals that, despite the facile portrait of her as the ultimate go-her-own-way-radical-liberal, the Military Coalition gave her its highest honor for her bipartisan work on military health care.[9] Even with the frequency of negative, simplistic depictions of her in jokes and in the right-leaning media, a Gallup poll found her to be "the most admired woman" in the United States, an honor for which she edged both Laura Bush and Oprah Winfrey.[10] However, despite the brilliance of her record and the public respect and attention she commands, her life experiences and career achievements are virtually ignored in the jokes about her that abound in popular culture. The main thing these jokes seem to "get" about Rodham Clinton is that her gender can be used to stereotype and denigrate her.

Getting the Gendered "Realities" of Hillary Jokes

To understand how the humor about this intelligent female politician works, it is important to understand a few basics about the workings of humor in general. The joke is a form that is synonymous with humor and laughter. Definitions of "joke" repeatedly use these two terms.[11] However, not all jokes are funny. This is an obvious statement, yet this aspect of the joke is rarely acknowledged. Why? One reason is the pressure for laughter that accompanies the form. Simply stated, a joke is a short narrative that contains mechanisms (or triggers) that can prompt laughter—or not. These triggers include depictions of incongruity, put-downs, the ambivalent, or the taboo.[12] The intent of a joke is usually seen as humorous, but it is also common that a joke will be found lacking in humor by those who hear it.

The fictional aspects of jokes are emphasized in scholarly definitions of the genre.[13] However, responses to jokes suggest that they are not always understood as fictions. In my earlier joke research, I found that well over half of a small joke audience reported that they liked jokes and found them funny when they understood them as "true."[14] This notion of jokes presenting some sort of "truth"—in tandem with the manner in which gender impacts the "truth" found in jokes—is illustrated in the two light-bulb jokes that follow. The first joke is about George W. Bush, and it provides a clear contrast to the subsequent light-bulb joke about Rodham Clinton. However, even though the light-bulb format is fictional, both jokes present what some see as "truths" about each politician:

> How many members of the Bush administration does it take to change a light bulb?
> 1. One to deny that a light bulb needs to be changed;
> 2. One to attack the patriotism of anyone who says the light bulb needs to be changed;
> 3. One to blame [Bill] Clinton for burning out the light bulb;
> 4. One to arrange the invasion of a country rumored to have a secret stockpile of light bulbs;
> 5. One to give a billion dollar no-bid contract to Halliburton for the new light bulb;
> 6. One to arrange a photograph of Bush, dressed as a janitor, standing on a step ladder under the banner: Light Bulb Change Accomplished.[15]

Note the joke's detailed engagement with George W. Bush's policies, behaviors, and media events. In this joke, the first two responses to the question posed by the joke critique the administration's approach to its critics, especially those opposed to the war in Iraq. Answer number 4 is also a direct reference to Iraq; the words "light bulbs" are a symbolic stand-in for "weapons of mass destruction." Number 5 points to the benefits that contracts in Iraq have held for Vice President Dick Cheney's former company, Halliburton. Number 6 skewers several possible "real-life" events— from the president declaring a premature victory in the early days of the Iraq war to his penchant for photo opportunities, ranging from his visit to Ground Zero after the terrorist attacks to a Habitat for Humanity construction site in the wake of Hurricane Katrina.

If someone who does not approve of the president's policies told this joke, the joke could be a figurative way to present a version of the "truth" about Bush and his policies. As I demonstrate later in this chapter, the put-downs of Rodham Clinton work in the same way by trading on people's perceptions of "realities" about her. Hillary jokes manifest a smaller range of "realities" than jokes about male politicians such as Bush. For instance, two of the most emphasized realities about Rodham Clinton are her gender and her husband. The George W. Bush jokes do not emphasize his gender or his spouse. Popular culture does not find gender an issue when the politician is male. In contrast to the Bush light-bulb joke, note the brevity, lack of attention to policy stances, and reliance on a gender-related stereotype found in a light-bulb joke about Rodham Clinton:

Q: How many Hillary Clintons does it take to change a light bulb?
A: One—she just holds the bulb and the world revolves around her.[16]

The joke is an implied critique of her arrogance and vanity; the latter is a trait that is stereotypically associated with women. It was also told as a dumb-blonde joke before it was a Hillary joke, so even though Rodham Clinton is an intelligent woman, stereotypes about "dumb" women are applied to her in joke formats. The jokes reduce this smart politician to a dumb blonde.

In previous research concerning political jokes, I found that political beliefs influenced the perception of humor in jokes. When asked whether they found a particular political joke funny, people commonly mentioned their political affiliation when discussing whether they liked or disliked a joke.[17] People also indicate that they "believe" the "facts" in some of the jokes they hear in the mass media. For example, in one study, 40 percent of the population under thirty years of age reported that they learned something about politics from the jokes in the monologues on late-night television shows.[18] This makes sense because so much of the humor in the monologues on late-night shows is tied to the day's news. Jokes are often written by drawing on current news stories. Increasingly aware of the connections between late-night television, politics, and what viewers think about politicians, politicians now visit such shows as part of their campaigns. For instance, Bill Clinton's saxophone-playing visit to *The Arsenio Hall Show* served him well in 1992. Unfortunately, the research about belief and jokes on late-night television also indicates that gender stereotypes embedded in the jokes still ring "true" for some of the audience.

Finally, finding a joke not funny does not necessarily mean that a person does *not* get the joke or lacks a sense of humor—a fact important to consider in relation to the media construction of the humorless feminist. Actually, the amount of emotional distance an individual has from a joke topic is a significant factor in how much a person buys into the humor of a joke. If a person is either too close to or too distant from a joke topic, she tends to find it *not* funny. For a person to find a joke funny, she has to have a reasonable amount of distance from the topic, but not so much distance that she has no interest in the topic at all.[19] For example, the space shuttle disaster in 1986, which claimed the life of schoolteacher Christa McAuliffe, produced jokes about the astronaut, which were largely told by people who did not know her. Her family and friends were not likely to tell these jokes because they were painfully close to McAuliffe's death. Laughter and "not getting it"—that is, not comprehending the humor in jokes—are not the only possible responses to jokes. Often those who hear jokes recognize the mechanisms that are supposed to produce laughter, but they still do not laugh. That is, they "get" the joke, but they do not find it funny.

This latter point is relevant to consider in relation to common stereotypes about feminists and humor: feminists do not lack a sense of humor because they do not laugh at some jokes. Like everyone else, feminists will laugh at the jokes they find funny: they will not laugh at jokes they "get" but do not find humorous. Some pundits characterize Rodham Clinton as a cold, humorless feminist, despite evidence to the contrary—such as the appreciation of irony and humor that is evident in her writing about her life and her assertion that having a good sense of humor is a key element in surviving as a politician and making her marriage work.[20] It is likely that some of these characterizations of her in the media are more influenced by the "humorless feminist" stereotype that circulates in popular culture rather than by a knowledge of her actual views and personality.

Some jokes about Rodham Clinton do not rely on gender or any other specifics about her, such as alleged personality traits. These jokes are so generic that, even though they refer to particular politicians, any politician's name could be substituted in the joke. These jokes rely on simple put-downs to express dislike of whichever politician is chosen as the butt of a joke. For example, the following joke is told about both George W. Bush and Hillary Rodham Clinton:

> One night, Hillary is awakened by George Washington's ghost in the White House. She asks: "George, what is the best thing I could do to help the country?"
> "Set an honest and honorable example, just as I did," Washington advises.
> The next night, the ghost of Thomas Jefferson moves through the dark bedroom. "Tom," Hillary asks, "what is the best thing I could do to help the country?"
> "Cut taxes and reduce the size of government," Jefferson advises. Hillary isn't sleeping well the next night, and sees another figure moving in the shadows. It's Abraham Lincoln's ghost. "Abe, what is the best thing I could do to help the country?" she asks.
> Abe answers: "Go see a play."[21]

This joke turns on the surprise punch line: the incongruity of Abraham Lincoln advising anyone to see a play, which works to disparage whichever politician shows up as the butt of the joke. Political jokes commonly rely on put-downs to generate laughs. The butt of these jokes is made to look stupid, so the audience laughs because it feels superior.

However, most Hillary jokes, especially those on late-night television, depart from such a generic mode and construct her as unintelligent, vain, arrogant, or unfit in some other fashion. Regardless of the fact that Rodham Clinton has a reputation as an intelligent woman, jokes routinely show her to be stupid:

> An airplane was about to crash, and there were 5 passengers left, but only 4 parachutes. The first passenger, Bill Clinton said, "I am president of the United States, and I have a great responsibility, being the leader of nearly 300 million people, and a superpower, etc." So he takes the first parachute, and jumps out of the plane.
> The second passenger said, "I'm Antoine Walker, one the best NBA Basketball players, and the Boston Celtics need me, so I can't afford to die." So he takes the second parachute, and leaves the plane.
> The third passenger, Hillary Clinton, said, "I am the wife of the President of the United States, a soon to be New York Senator, and I am the smartest woman in the world." So she takes the third parachute and exits the plane.
> The fourth passenger, Pope John Paul the second, says to the fifth passenger, a 10-year old boy scout, "I am old and frail and I don't have many years left, so as

a Christian gesture and good deed, I will sacrifice my life and let you take the last parachute."

The boy scout said, "It's okay! There's a parachute left for you. The 'world's smartest woman' took my BACKPACK."[22]

This joke portrays Rodham Clinton as both dumb and arrogant. While most of the male characters in this joke also have some of the same unsavory traits, such as arrogance, all of the men at least survive; Rodham Clinton does not. The joke presents her as arrogant enough to believe that she deserves to live as much as the men do. The joke constructs her as a heartlessly cruel and decidedly non-maternal woman who places her safety above that of a child. Not only is she depicted as not so smart after all, but she also receives the harshest punishment, death.

Like many politicians and public figures, Rodham Clinton is ridiculed in such jokes on television and the Internet. However, her gender (not her politics) is the "reality" that the majority of these jokes emphasize. The jokes ignore the complexity of her biography. She is the only First Lady to be elected to the Senate; this is unusual, not to mention historically significant, and a first for women. However, this defining feature of her life does not make it into the jokes about her. Instead, the jokes disparage her on the basis of stereotypical traits (such as vanity) that are generically associated with women. The jokes also portray her as self-centered and unintelligent. These turn out to be only the first of the defective characteristics that the jokes catalog. The jokes ultimately construct Rodham Clinton as the antithesis of everything that is essentially feminine.

The Witch, the Bitch, and the Unfit Woman

Arrogance and stupidity are the least of her sins; other jokes go on to cast her as evil and cruel. Among the most common of the jokes are those that construct Rodham Clinton as a witch, a bitch, and an unfit woman. Jokes that portray her as a witch appear in both the oral and media traditions. This joke circulated during the Clinton presidency:

Why doesn't Arkansas celebrate Halloween or Thanksgiving?
Because the witch took the turkey to Washington, D.C.[23]

Visual jokes with the witch theme also appear on the Internet; the following joke is accompanied by a photograph of a wrecked broomstick, the "aircraft," which the joke refers to:

The Associated Press reports that New York junior senator Hillary Clinton narrowly escaped injury in the aircraft that she was piloting when she was forced to make an emergency landing in Southern Texas because of bad weather. National Transportation Safety Board officials have issued a preliminary determination that pilot error contributed to the accident, and that the senator was flying in IFR conditions while only having obtained a VFR, single engine land rating. The absence of a post-crash fire was likely due to insufficient fuel on board. No one on the ground was injured. Pictures taken at the scene show the extent of damage to Senator Clinton's aircraft.[24]

Of course, statistically, in reality and in folklore, witches are women. Historically, women who did not fit into society's roles were branded as witches.[25] In contemporary times, critics demonized Rodham Clinton for not fitting into the traditional political role of a First Lady. The media did not know what to do with a First Lady who was also a health-care-policy wonk. Because she stepped out of her prescribed role, this intelligent woman became a witch in jokes circulating about her in popular culture.

Rodham Clinton recognizes that her willingness to transgress the traditional role of a politician's wife feeds into the desire to vilify her:

> Some of the attacks, whether demonizing me as a woman, mother and wife or distorting my words and positions on issues were politically motivated and designed to rein me in. Others may have reflected the extent to which our society was still adjusting to the changing roles of women. . . . While Bill talked about social change, I embodied it. I had my own opinions, interests and profession.[26]

Carol F. Karlsen argues that in colonial America, being a well-to-do single woman over the age of forty, with no male authority in her household, made a woman more likely to be accused of being a witch.[27] Contemporary society still finds these traits threatening. Like the women accused of witchcraft in colonial times, Rodham Clinton troubles some people because she makes it publicly clear that she is a powerful, mature woman who is not controlled by a man. While the punishment for a woman who steps out of her traditional gender role and amasses power fortunately has changed since colonial times, the word for her has not. She is still a "witch." It is striking that in modern times, Rodham Clinton represents social change perceived as threatening enough to put her literally into the witch role, even if "it is only a joke."

The key word in the punch line of one of the most common jokes about Rodham Clinton is one letter removed from a witch:

> The Clinton family goes to a baseball game. After they settle into their seats, Bill picks up Hillary and tosses her onto the field.
> His chief of staff shouts, "I said throw out the first PITCH!"[28]

In the world of jokelore about Rodham Clinton, supposed bitchiness trumps intelligence. The media construction of her as a bitch was furthered when Newt Gingrich's mother told network newswoman Connie Chung that her son frequently referred to Rodham Clinton as "bitch."[29] During the 1990s, Rodham Clinton's critics, such as Camilia Paglia, called her an ice queen, a drag queen, a snow queen, a man-woman, and a bitch goddess. Paglia also claimed somehow to know that Rodham Clinton "has difficulty integrating her intelligence with her sexuality."[30] In 2001, the right-wing pundit Michele Malkin echoed this theme with her descriptions of Rodham Clinton: "The cold, corrosive look in Hillary Clinton's eyes speaks for itself."[31] Other jokes and late-night television monologues widely employed the image of

Rodham Clinton as a bitch, someone so awful one would rather die than be around her, let alone married to her:

> Senator Hillary Clinton was attending a party, when she noticed Governor Arnold Schwarzenegger.
> She walked over to him, and in a quiet voice said; "If you were my husband, I would poison your drink."
> Schwarzenegger smiled, leaned forward, and whispered in her ear, "And if you were my wife, I would drink it."[32]

This joke focuses on her role as wife while indicating that she is horrifically unfit in executing a wife's duties. She is capable of coldly and cruelly dispatching her spouse, whose life with her must be so miserable that he would welcome death. Craig Kilborn, host (before Jon Stewart) of *The Daily Show*, also suggested the bitchlike qualities of Rodham Clinton. He referred to her autobiography, *Living History*, which was the subject of many jokes on late-night television, by saying that it allowed so much of her personality to come through that it would make any reader want to sleep with an intern.[33] Here, the implication is that she is so awful, such a witch, that she actually drove her husband to infidelity. The fault lies not with her husband but with her because of her awful personality.

Jay Leno told another joke on his late-night show that emerges from the publication of Rodham Clinton's book, and this joke points to the theme of her as the unfit woman. In this case her coldness extends to her sexuality. Leno said that Bill Clinton got more money for his book than his wife got for hers. The reason? His had some sex in it.[34] Here she is found lacking because she is not sexual enough. Other jokes with the unfit woman theme critique her body; she is just not sexy enough:

> Did you hear about the new Hillary lunch special at Kentucky Fried Chicken?
> It is two large thighs, no breasts, and a left wing.[35]

As this joke indicates, when it comes to dealing with a female politician, the modus operandi is that if you do not agree with her politics, make fun of her body. The process of mocking physical appearance is part of the put-downs of male politicians, too. For example, cartoons and Internet images of George W. Bush present him looking like a chimpanzee or Alfred E. Neuman. However, such parodic renderings do not sexualize Bush as much as they do Rodham Clinton. Typically, the humorous visual images of Bush focus on his face; the Hillary jokes focus on her body. The Bush jokes are not as based in sexualized anatomy as is the KFC Hillary joke; for example, Bush is not portrayed in jokes as having skinny thighs, no pectoral muscles, a small penis, and a right wing.

Finally, as demonstrated by this popular joke from the Internet, Rodham Clinton is an unfit woman not only because she is not good-looking enough but also because she is homicidally cruel to small children:

> Hillary Clinton goes to a primary school in New York to talk about the world. After her talk she offers question time.

One little boy puts up his hand. The Senator asks him what his name is. "Kenneth."

"And what is your question, Kenneth?"

"I have three questions: First—whatever happened to your medical health care plan? Second—why would you run for President after your husband shamed the office? And, Third—whatever happened to all those things you took when you left the White House?"

Just then the bell rings for recess. Hillary Clinton informs the kiddies that they will continue after recess. When they resume, Hillary says, "Okay where were we? Oh, that's right, question time. Who has a question?"

A different little boy puts his hand up; Hillary points him out and asks him what his name is.

"Larry."

"And what is your question, Larry?"

"I have five questions: First—whatever happened to your medical health care plan? Second—why would you run for President after your husband shamed the office? Third—whatever happened to all those things you took when you left the White House? Fourth—why did the recess bell go off twenty minutes early? And, Fifth—what happened to Kenneth?"[36]

Unlike some of the jokes about George W. Bush, which are based on his actual life events or policies, this joke twists Rodham Clinton's résumé. She has been a children's advocate all her life, perhaps beginning as early as when she babysat the children of migrant workers as a teenager and continuing through her adult service to the Children's Defense Fund—which included working in the 1970s to allow disabled children access to public education in the 1970s—and her pro bono legal work on behalf of children.[37] The Hillary joke cycle ignores these facts and instead favors the old stereotype that any high-powered, successful woman cannot possibly be maternal.

The joke image of Rodham Clinton as unfit draws on homophobia and related stereotypes: "What more unfit woman is there who does not like children and sex with her husband and also acts too masculine?" Some on the far right have attacked Rodham Clinton because, they assert, she has "lesbian tendencies."[38] This notion is sometimes evident in the jokes; for example, after the publication of her autobiography, Jay Leno noted that Hillary was everywhere—on Barbara Walters, on Diane Sawyer, and on Katie Couric. He concluded by saying that this is the first time she had been "on" more women than her husband.[39] The lesbian innuendo is yet another essentialist presentation of Rodham Clinton; in this case, she is unfit because she is not heterosexual enough. These jokes bespeak discomfort with visible, powerful, and politically influential women. They indicate that, culturally speaking, we have a long way to go before we do not demonize an intelligent female politician as a cultural outsider.

Bush jokes do not rely solely, or much at all, on his gender to put him down, as do many Hillary jokes. Since she is a woman, it is enough to denigrate her on the basis of her gender without bothering to take in the facts of her life. Generally, the jokes about male politicians allow for a more individualized rendering of their subject than do jokes about Rodham Clinton. For example, an Internet search for jokes about

George W. Bush turned up his unofficial resume, which turned out to be a lengthy (1,286 words!), biting, parodic—but "realistic"—account of his career.[40] I could find no comparable lengthy (if critical) resume for Rodham Clinton. To be sure, such jokes and parodies are meant to damn Bush, just as the Hillary jokes are meant to disparage her. However, Bush jokes turn to his life and policies; for Rodham Clinton, her resume is not needed, merely her gender.

Sex, Bill, and the Domestic Scene

Not only is her gender used as a basis for the put-downs in jokes but so is her husband's infamous "inappropriate encounter," as he refers to it, with Monica Lewinsky.[41] Early in the Clinton presidency, a recycled political joke circulated that used Rodham Clinton's sexual antics to belittle her husband. Other versions of this joke were told about previous First Ladies, such as Pat Nixon:

> Last winter, one of Clinton's aides came to him and said that someone had peed into the snow the words, "Clinton sucks." Clinton said if it happened again, to have it analyzed. Sure enough, it happened again, and the aides got it analyzed and told Clinton that it was [Vice President] Gore's urine and Hillary's handwriting.[42]

As the Clinton term in the White House progressed, the jokes quickly switched focus to the president's sex life and Rodham Clinton's alleged lack thereof. Rumors of Bill Clinton's infidelities, Paula Jones's accusations, and his relationship with Monica Lewinsky fueled the portrayal of an alienated First Couple in the jokes. Bill's sexual peccadilloes remained a significant theme in the joke cycle after he was out of the White House and Rodham Clinton was in the Senate. For example, in the fall of 2005, after California governor Arnold Schwarzenegger was met with political setbacks, Jay Leno joked that a politician had not heard "No!" so many times since Bill tried to get into Hillary's bed.[43] Even though the joke could mock Clinton's sexual excess more overtly, its focus is on Hillary as the ultimate naysayer. Instead of drawing a more sympathetic rendering of her as the wronged spouse, the joke creates a negative vision of Hillary on the basis of a depiction of her as hostile to sex. This construction works subtly to cast Bill Clinton as more sympathetic than his wife, who coldly and repeatedly rejects him. These political jokes routinely put Rodham Clinton's face on the stereotype of the frigid woman.

When she published her autobiography, which allows readers to discover how she constructs her own life, many of the jokes about the book on late-night television focused less on Rodham Clinton and more on her husband. The jokes perennially show more interest in her husband's libido than in her experiences, even though her life is unusual of its own accord. David Letterman said that 1,200 people attended one of Hillary's book signings—which meant that one in ten of those people must have slept with her husband.[44] In the world of jokes, Rodham Clinton's accomplishments, such as the publication of another book, provide just another excuse to talk about her husband's sexual escapades. When responding to the publication of Rodham Clinton's autobiography, Conan O'Brien, host of *Late Night with Conan O'Brien*, also honed in on her husband by saying that Bill read Hillary's book five times, which indicated that he spent more time in bed with the book than with her.[45] Not one of these jokes focuses on what Rodham Clinton actually said about herself. Instead the jokes posit that she is an unsatisfactory bedmate and, therefore, wife. The jokes about her autobiography ignore her intellect, career, and the revelations made in the book. They remain in the thrall of tired, old constructions, which posit that the intelligent feminist is, first and foremost, an unfit woman and wife.

Jay Leno told a joke that initially seems to recognize her political career—the joke speculated that Rodham Clinton would run for president in 2008. However, the punch line of the joke was that the reason she wanted the office was so she could see what it was like to sleep in the presidential bed.[46] The joke's punch line does not emphasize Rodham Clinton the politician; instead it points to her as the sexually unfit wife. Political jokes frequently rely on the presentation of taboo matters, such as sexuality, as a trigger for laughter.[47] Sex figures in jokes about both male and female political figures. However, the Rodham Clinton jokes demonstrate both a greater fascination and discomfort with the female gender and sexuality than do many jokes about male politicians, which do not focus on their sexuality.

Some Hillary jokes manage to get past sex; for example, after the Clintons left the White House, Jay Leno joked that when Hillary hosted her first party in her new home, her guests said that it was just like all her parties in the White House—even the furniture was the same.[48] When she is not linked to her husband or sex, she is still stuck in the domestic realm. The allegation that the Clintons stole furniture from the White House and vandalized it along with Air Force One was widely reported in the media and was the subject of many jokes on late-night television. However, in response to a request for an investigation into the "vandal scandal" from a Republican senator, the General Services Administration (GSA) found that the charges were false. The Clintons did take some furniture, which they said had been given to them personally and not to the residence. The GSA said that nothing out of the ordinary occurred when the Clintons moved out of the White House.[49] Unlike the gossip about the "vandalism," the GSA report that cleared the Clintons was *not* a popular topic of the jokes on late-night television.

One personal, real-life detail about Rodham Clinton that some jokes address is her insistence on keeping her maiden name. As a lawyer in Arkansas, she was known as Hillary Rodham; she added "Clinton" later. During her husband's time as governor of Arkansas, some people were "upset" when they received invitations to the Governor's Mansion from "Governor Bill Clinton and Hillary Rodham."[50] Her husband said that her name was her business and that he did not think his political future depended on it. However, others thought differently and told her so, including adviser Vernon Jordan. Ultimately, Rodham Clinton decided that it was more important for her husband to be governor again than for her to use her maiden name. She has consistently referred to herself as Hillary Rodham Clinton since then—just like her own grandmother, Hannah Jones Rodham, who also insisted on using all three of her names throughout her lifetime.[51]

Even after adding "Clinton" to her name, she still had to fight to keep "Rodham." When her husband was campaigning for president, she ordered new stationery that said "Hillary Rodham Clinton." When she received the stationery, her name was changed to "Hillary Clinton." Someone on her husband's staff thought that it was politically expedient to drop "Rodham," but she did not agree. She refused to compromise her feminist values and her own identity, so she returned the stationery and ordered a new batch.[52] Jokes, like the defective box of stationery, continually drop "Rodham" from her name. She is either "Hillary" or "Hillary Clinton." Some view her own name and her separate identity from her husband as a liability. For example, Jay Leno joked that Rodham Clinton's name caused a personal crisis. He said Hillary could not decide whether to drop "Clinton" or "Rodham" because she could not figure out which was the most embarrassing.[53] This joke again links her to her "embarrassing" husband and indicates that a woman having an identity of her own is an "embarrassment," too.

Finally, I did find a scant few jokes that focused specifically on Rodham Clinton's policy stances. The irony of her legal work for a congressional committee on Nixon's impeachment was not a presence in the Hillary joke cycle—even though her own husband underwent impeachment proceedings for lying about his relationship with Monica Lewinsky. Since she was well known for her work on health during her husband's administration and afterward, I expected to find more jokes about Rodham Clinton and health care than I did. One humorous list surfaced during the Clinton years in the White House, "Hillary Clinton's Definitions of Health Terms," which includes the following "terms":

Vein—conceited
Caesarean Section—a neighborhood in Rome
D&C—where Washington is
Impotent—distinguished, well-known
Labor Pain—getting hurt at work
Pap Smear—fatherhood test
Pelvis—a cousin to Elvis.[54]

This list portrays Rodham Clinton as someone who does not understand basic medical procedures—several of them associated with women's reproductive health and some of them procedures, such as Pap smears and C-sections, with which she has had personal experience. Again, before this list was attributed to her, it was a dumb-blonde joke. In this popular culture construction of her, she is interchangeable with a dumb blonde. At least the joke's topic is a major policy issue of hers. The joke is an implied critique of her health-care initiative, but unlike the Bush light-bulb joke, it does not go into her health-care policy in any detail. The joke indicates discomfort with her as policy maker. Its use of gender as a means to accomplish its criticism once again reveals the cultural uneasiness generated by a smart, politically powerful feminist who was both First Lady and a policy wonk.

These Rodham Clinton jokes obsess about sex and domesticity. Even when a joke ostensibly is about her, its focus often veers to her husband. If a joke finally turns to her, it constructs her as a woman whose sexuality is nonexistent or defective. In her professional life, she has always used the name "Rodham," yet the jokes never employ this name. They do not grant her that measure of autonomy. They create an image of her that emphasizes the "Clinton" part of her life—especially her marriage to a philandering president. Typically, jokes in popular media divest Rodham Clinton of her own specific, political identity.

A Smart Woman, Late-Night Television, and the Last Laugh

One fascinating result of popular culture's "joking" construction of Rodham Clinton as a dumb blonde, a witch, a child hater, and a humorless feminist is that this image takes on a life of its own. It has some impact in real life. For instance, Rodham Clinton's comments reveal that she is aware of the mocking media image of her and has sought out models to inform her responses to it. When in the White House, Rodham Clinton looked to history for examples of ways in which others handled negative media constructions. She found, of course, that when Eleanor Roosevelt was First Lady, she also drew media attention because of her intelligence and activism. Like Rodham Clinton, Roosevelt insisted on being her own woman, and the press described her as icy, sexually unappealing, and seeking too much power. She was the butt of jokes and ridicule.[55] Not surprisingly, Rodham Clinton found much of interest in the life of this other intelligent, maverick First Lady; she even jokes that she had imaginary conversations with Roosevelt to solicit her advice.[56] She also employed Roosevelt as a model, inspired by the fact that Roosevelt never let the mocking laughter of her critics slow her down.

Because the mass media is ubiquitous today, Rodham Clinton faces more ridicule than Roosevelt did. For decades, Rodham Clinton and her family have been disparaged in the joke monologues on late-night television. However, she has internalized the Roosevelt indomitableness when it comes to facing heckling laughter in the media.[57] Given late-night television's negative construction of her through joke monologues, one could understand it if Rodham Clinton chose to turn her back on the media entirely or "climb back into the bunker," as she put it. However, being a smart politician, she did just the opposite.

She has deliberately used the medium of late-night television for her ends. For example, in January 2000, amid speculation that she might run for a New York senate seat, she appeared on *The Late Show with David Letterman*. Letterman had been calling her communications director regularly asking that she appear on the show, and he turned this into a running gag in his monologue. Rodham Clinton finally decided to visit the show, remarking,

> I hoped it would be fun, but I also knew that late-night comics sometimes skewer their guests, so I was a little nervous. Letterman, who lives near Chappaqua, asked me about our new house and warned me that "every idiot in the area is going to drive by honking now."
>
> "Oh, was that you?" I said. Letterman and the audience roared, and, after that, I relaxed and had a great time.[58]

Following this appearance on *Letterman* and the joke she made at his expense, Rodham Clinton received a surge of public support. This spike was due in large part to her use of humor on a late-night TV show—a nice reversal from the norm of late-night television using her as the butt of the joke. Her joke changed the normal order; this time she was on late-night television issuing jokes about the male host. Her ability to joke in this setting and use it to further her political ends gave her the proverbial last and best laugh vis-à-vis late-night television.

Despite advances in the rendering of fictional women on television, actual women in the public eye still face plenty of gender hurdles and media stereotypes. Real-life intelligent women have to be tough to negotiate the treacherous terrain of popular culture. Rodham Clinton provides an example of such a woman. Even though the mass media routinely confronts her with negative portraits of herself, she has maintained her equilibrium and advanced her political career. Her strategy for dealing with hostile media constructions draws on her intellect, sense of humor, and emotional fortitude. She has cleverly used the very medium that heckles her against itself. She deftly demonstrates how a smart woman can hold her own with the boys of late-night television or, for that matter, the good old boys of DC.

Notes

1. Many of the jokes cited in this chapter are from Internet joke archives. All the jokes from late-night television come from http://politicalhumor.about.com. This site maintains a more extensive joke archive than the television shows' Web sites. The jokes are referenced with the site's permission. I typically refer to Senator Hillary Rodham Clinton as "Rodham Clinton." However, the jokes about her are known as "Hillary jokes," and I often use only her first name when talking about these kinds of jokes.
2. Hillary Rodham Clinton, *Living History* (New York: Simon & Schuster, 2003), 11.
3. Rodham Clinton, 22, 27, 31.
4. Rodham Clinton, 25.
5. Rodham Clinton, 21, 168; see also Gail Sheehy, *Hillary's Choice* (New York: Random House, 1999), 25.
6. Rodham Clinton, 266.
7. Rodham Clinton, 43.
8. Bill Clinton, *My Life* (New York: Alfred A. Knopf, 2004), 182–183; see also Sheehy, 88, and Clinton 44, 50.
9. "New York Senator Hillary Rodham Clinton: Biography," http:clinton.senate.gov/about/biography/index.cfm (accessed 26 November 2005).
10. "Poll: Bush, Hillary Clinton Most Admired by Americans," http:www.cnn.com/2003/US/12/30/most.admired.ap/ (accessed 26 November 2005).
11. See Alison Jones, *Larousse Dictionary of World Folklore* (New York: Larousse, 1995), 250–251; and Henry Bosely Woolf, ed., *Webster's New Collegiate Dictionary* (Springfield, MA: G. C. Merriam Company, 1981), 619.
12. Jeannie B. Thomas, *Featherless Chickens, Laughing Women, and Serious Stories* (Charlottesville: University Press of Virginia, 1997), 43.
13. Elliott Oring, *Jokes and Their Relations* (Lexington: University Press of Kentucky, 1992), ix.
14. Jeannie B. Thomas, "Dumb Blondes, Dan Quayle, and Hillary Clinton: Gender, Sexuality, and Stupidity in Jokes," *Journal of American Folklore* 110.437 (1997): 307.
15. "How the Bush Administration Changes a Light Bulb," http:// politicalhumor.about.com/library/jokes/bljokebushlightbulb.htm (accessed 26 November 2005).
16. "Question and Answer Clinton Jokes," http://www.ahajokes.com/cqanda.html (accessed 14 December 2005).
17. See Thomas, "Dumb Blondes," 292.

18. James Bennet, "Did You Hear the One About the '96 Campaign?" *New York Times*, 9 July 1996, A17.
19. See Oring, 13.
20. Rodham Clinton, 266.
21. "Hillary Where Are You?" http:/www.maineiac.com/Clinton/hillary_where_are_you. html (accessed 14 December 2005).
22. "Joke of the Day, April 06, 2005," http://www.poorandstupid.com/2005_04_01_ jotdArchive.asp (accessed 14 December 2005).
23. Thomas, "Dumb Blondes," 301.
24. "Senator Narrowly Escapes Wreck," http://www.emmitsburg.net/humor/archives/ political/political 9.htm (accessed 14 December 2005).
25. Brian P. Levak, *The Witch-Hunt in Early Modern Europe* (London: Longman, 1987), 124.
26. Rodham Clinton, 140.
27. Carol F. Karlsen, *The Devil in the Shape of a Woman: Witchcraft in Colonial New England* (New York: Vintage, 1987), 71, 115.
28. "Clinton Jokes," http://joecasaletto.com/jokes/clinton.htm (accessed 14 December 2005).
29. Rodham Clinton responded by inviting Gingrich and his family on a personally guided tour of the White House. See Rodham Clinton, 263.
30. Camille Paglia, "Ice Queen, Drag Queen," *New Republic*, 4 March 1996, 24–26.
31. Michelle Malkin, "Hillary Clinton in Crisis," 6 September 2001, http:// www. townhall. com/opinion/columns/michellemalkin/2001/09/26/167751.html (accessed 14 December 2005).
32. "Hillary and Arnold," http://urbanlegends.about.com/library/bl_hillary_arnold.htm (accessed 14 December 2005). This is another recycled joke; earlier versions have Winston Churchill and Lady Nancy Astor engaging in the exchange.
33. "Hillary Clinton Jokes," http://politicalhumor.about.com/library/blhillaryquotes.htm (accessed 14 December 2005).
34. "Hillary Clinton Jokes."
35. Thomas, "Dumb Blondes," 302.
36. "Hillary Clinton Visits School Children," http://politicalhumor.about.com/library/ jokes/bljokehillaryschool.htm (accessed 14 December 2005).
37. Rodham Clinton, 81.
38. See Edward Klein, *The Truth about Hillary: What She Knew, When She Knew It, How Far She'll Go to Become President* (New York: Sentinel, 2005).
39. "Hillary Clinton Jokes."
40. "George W. Bush's Resume," http://politicalhumor.about.com/library/blbushresume.htm (accessed 14 December 2005).
41. Clinton, 773.
42. Thomas, "Dumb Blondes," 298.
43. "Late-Night Political Jokes," http://politicalhumor.about.com/library/bldailyfeed3.htm (accessed 14 December 2005).
44. "Hillary Clinton Jokes."
45. "Hillary Clinton Jokes."
46. "Hillary Clinton Jokes."
47. For more about the mechanisms of laughter and how they can work together, see Thomas, *Featherless Chickens*, 43–48.
48. "Hillary Clinton Jokes."
49. David Goldstein, "No Truth in Clinton White House Vandal Scandal, GSA Reports," *Kansas City Star*, 18 May 2001, http://www.commondreams.org/headlines01/0518-04.htm (accessed 14 December 2005).

50. Rodham Clinton, 92.
51. Rodham Clinton, 93.
52. Rodham Clinton, 111–112, 265.
53. "What Quote," http://www.whatquote.com/quotes/Jay-Leno/20931-Senator-Hillary-Rodh.htm (accessed 14 December 2005).
54. Thomas, "Dumb Blondes," 305–306.
55. Blanche Wiesen Cook, *Eleanor Roosevelt*, vol. 1 (New York: Viking, 1992), 4–5, 1–2, 12–13.
56. Following a somewhat sensationalized account by Bob Woodward, this event got twisted into stories that the White House was hosting séances with Rodham Clinton channeling Roosevelt. This was untrue, but enough for fringe sites on the Internet to assert that this was just more "proof" that both Clintons were indeed witches. See Bob Woodward, *The Choice: How Clinton Won* (New York: Simon & Schuster, 1997), 129–134. After the Woodward "exposé," audiences found the way Hillary joked about it in her speeches funny, according to Sheehy, 262.
57. Rodham Clinton, 259.
58. Rodham Clinton, 512.

Contributors

Linda Baughman is assistant professor of English at Christopher Newport University in Newport News, Virginia. Her specialties are cultural studies and critical theory, especially in regard to media production of gender and sexuality. Her article "When They Were Cursed: Examining the Media's Production of the Red Sox" (cowritten with Allison Burr-Miller) was published in the *North Carolina Annual 2005*. She is working on a book on *Bewitched*.

Beth Berila is assistant professor and director of the Women's Studies Program at St. Cloud State University. Her research analyzes the feminist praxis of community-based arts and the representations of gender, race, class, and sexuality in U.S. popular culture. Her work includes "Reading National Identities: The Radical Disruptions of Gloria Anzaldúa's *Borderlands/La Frontera*," in *EntreMundos/AmongWorlds: New Perspectives on Gloria Anzaldúa*, ed. AnaLousie Keating (Palgrave Macmillan, 2005); "Metrosexuality the Middle-Class Way: Exploring Race, Class, and Gender in *Queer Eye for the Straight Guy*," *Genders*, no. 42 (2005); and "The Links Between Environmental Justice and Feminist Pedagogy: An Introduction and Conclusion," *Feminist Teacher* 16.2 (2005).

Allison Burr-Miller is a PhD student at Colorado State University in the Speech Communication department. Her specialties are media and cultural studies. Her article "When They Were Cursed: Examining the Media's Production of the Red Sox" (cowritten with Linda Baughman) was published in the *North Carolina Annual 2005*.

Cindy Conaway is a PhD candidate in the American Culture Studies department at Bowling Green State University, Ohio. She is currently completing her dissertation "Girls Who (Don't) Wear Glasses: The Performativity of Smart Teen Girls on Television Dramas." Her specialties include television studies, girls' studies, and popular culture. She published "Cinderella in the High School Hallways: The Place for Smart Girls on Teen TV" in the *Mid-Atlantic Almanac* (2004).

Leigh H. Edwards is assistant professor of English at Florida State University. Her work on U.S. literature and popular culture has appeared in journals such as *Narrative* and the *Journal of Popular Culture*. Her recent publications include "'What a Girl Wants': Gender Norming on Reality Game Shows," *Feminist Media Studies* 4.2 (2004) and "Chasing the Real: Reality Television and Documentary Forms," in *Docufictions: Essays on the Intersection of Documentary and Fictional Filmmaking*, ed. Gary D. Rhodes and John Parris Springer (McFarland, 2005). She has a forthcoming work on Johnny Cash and popular music from Indiana University Press and is completing a book-length study on the family and reality TV.

Rebecca C. Hains is assistant professor of Communications at Salem State College. Her publications include "Power(puff) Feminism: *The Powerpuff Girls* as a Site of Strength and Collective Action in the Third Wave" (*Women in Popular Culture: Representation and Meaning*, forthcoming, Hampton Press), and "The Problematics of Reclaiming the Girlish: *The Powerpuff Girls* and Girl Power," *Femspec* 5.2 (2004).

Sherrie A. Inness is professor of English at Miami University. Her research interests include gender and cooking culture, girls' literature and culture, and women in popular culture. She has published over a dozen books, including *Intimate Communities: Representation and Social Transformation in Women's College Fiction, 1895–1910* (Bowling Green, 1995); *The Lesbian Menace: Ideology, Identity, and the Representation of Lesbian Life* (University of Massachusetts Press, 1997); *Tough Girls: Women Warriors and Wonder Women in Popular Culture* (University of Pennsylvania Press, 1999); *Dinner Roles: American Women and Culinary Culture* (University of Iowa Press, 2001); *Delinquents and Debutantes: Twentieth-Century American Girls' Cultures* (editor, New York University Press, 1998); *Kitchen Culture in America: Popular Representations of Food, Gender, and Race* (editor, University of Pennsylvania Press, 2001); *Pilaf, Pozole, and Pad Thai: American Women and Ethnic Food* (editor, University of Massachusetts Press, 2001); and *Disco Divas: Women, Gender, and Popular Culture in the 1970s* (editor, University of Pennsylvania Press, 2003).

Lorna Jowett is senior lecturer in American Studies at the University of Northampton, UK. Her main research interest is the representation of gender in popular culture, and her current work examines gender and genre in science fiction and horror texts. She has published on Anne Rice's *Vampire Chronicles*, utopia and dystopia, and the television shows *Buffy the Vampire Slayer*, *Angel*, and *Dark Angel*, as well as on science-fiction film. She is the author of *Sex and the Slayer: A Gender Studies Primer for the Buffy Fan* (Wesleyan University Press, 2005).

Linda Manning is assistant professor at Christopher Newport University in Newport News, Virginia. Her specialties are the study of family and adoption. Her essay on the production of family identity, "Presenting Opportunities: Communicatively Constructing a Shared-family Identity," was published in the *International and Intercultural Communication Annual*. Her work has also appeared in *Communication Teacher*. She is writing a book about the television show *Bewitched*.

Michele Paule is senior lecturer in Media and Culture at Oxford Brookes University. She is a PhD candidate at Oxford Brookes and researching gifted girls' identities in and engagement with popular culture texts. Her work involves exploring conditions and cultures, both real and electronic, surrounding giftedness for adolescents and their teachers. Her publications include "Superheroes and Super Learning: *Buffy the Vampire Slayer* in the Gifted Classroom," *MEJ: The Media Education Journal* (2004); "Issues in Gifted Education in England," in *Diversity in Gifted Education; Global Issues*, ed. B. Wallace (Routledge, 2005); and

"Gifted Identities in Popular Culture: What Clark Kent Could Learn from TV," *NATE: English, Drama, Media* (2006).

Sharon Sutherland is clinical instructor in dispute resolution at the University of British Columbia Faculty of Law and practices as a child protection mediator. Sutherland's research interests include the intersections of law and theater, especially legislative theater. Her recent publications include "Piercing the Corporate Veil—With a Stake? Vampire Imagery in American Caselaw," in *Vampires: Myths and Metaphors of Enduring Evil*, ed. Peter Day (Rodopi, 2006); "Tell Me Where the Bomb Is or I Will Kill Your Son: Situational Morality on *24*," in *Reading 24: TV against the Clock*, ed. Steven Peacock (I. B. Tauris, 2006) (coauthored with Sharon Sutherland); and "The Rule of Prophecy: Source of Law in the City of *Angel*," in *Reading Angel: The TV Spin-Off with a Soul*, ed. Stacey Abbott (I. B. Tauris, 2005).

Sarah Swan is a lawyer practicing in Vancouver, British Columbia. She writes on law and popular culture, with a particular focus on the portrayal of law in television. Her recent publications include "The Rule of Prophecy: Source of Law in the City of *Angel*," in *Reading Angel: The TV Spin-Off with a Soul*, ed. Stacey Abbott (I. B. Tauris, 2005) (coauthored with Sharon Sutherland), and "Tell Me Where the Bomb Is or I Will Kill Your Son: Situational Morality on *24*," in *Reading 24: TV against the Clock*, ed. Steven Peacock (I. B. Tauris, 2006).

Jeannie Banks Thomas is professor of English and Folklore and director of the Folklore Program at Utah State University. Her work focuses on gender, legend, and material culture. Her publications include *Naked Barbies, Warrior Joes, and Other Forms of Visible Gender* (University of Illinois Press, 2003); *Featherless Chickens, Laughing Women, and Serious Stories* (University of Virginia Press, 1997), winner of the Elli Köngäs-Maranda Prize; and *Haunting Experiences: Ghosts in Contemporary Folklore* (Utah State University Press, 2007) (coauthored with Diane Goldstein and Sylvia Grider).

Karin E. Westman is associate professor of English at Kansas State University. Her specialties are modern British literature and women's literature. She published *Pat Barker's Regeneration: A Reader's Guide* (Continuum, 2001), as well as essays on Virginia Woolf, Georgette Heyer, A. S. Byatt, Pat Barker, and J. K. Rowling. Her recent publications include "Generation, Not Regeneration: Screening Out Class, Gender, and Cultural Change in the Film of *Regeneration*," in *Critical Perspectives on Pat Barker*, ed. Margaretta Jolly, Sharon Monteith, Ron Paul, and Nahem Yousaf (University of South Carolina Press, 2005); and "'For her generation the newspaper was a book': Media, Mediation, and Oscillation in Virginia Woolf's *Between the Acts*," *Journal of Modern Literature* (2006). She is completing a book on realism in contemporary British women's fiction.

Index